PROFITABLE CHILD CARE

How to Start and Run
A Successful Business

. . . .

PROFITABLE CHILD CARE

How to Start and Run
A Successful Business

· ·

Nan Lee Howkins
with
Heldi Kane Rosenholtz

☑®
Facts On File, Inc.

Profitable Child Care
Copyright © 1993 by Nan Lee Howkins

Facts On File, Inc.
11 Penn Plaza
New York, NY 10001

Library of Congress Cataloging-in-Publication Data
Howkins, Nan Lee.
    Profitable child care: how to start and run a successful business /
Nan Lee Howkins, Heidi Kane Rosenholtz.
        p. cm.
    Includes index.
    ISBN 0-8160-2236-4 (alk. paper)
    1. Day care centers —United States—Handbooks, manuals, etc.
    2. Child care services—United States—Handbooks, manuals, etc.
    I. Rosenholtz, Heidi Kane. II. Title.
    HV854.H69   1993
    362.7'12'068—dc20   92-42537

Facts On File books are available at special discounts when purchased in bulk quantities for businesses, associations, institutions or sales promotions. Please call our Special Sales Department in New York at 212/967-8800 or 800/322-8755.

You can find Facts On File on the World Wide Web at http://www.factsonfile.com

Text design by Robert Yaffe

Printed in the United States of America

MP VB 10 9 8 7 6 5 4 3

This book is printed on acid-free paper.

To our understanding husbands,
Stuart and Harry,
and wonderful children,
Heidi and Julie,
and Sam and Joshua.

ACKNOWLEDGMENTS

. . . .

Many colleagues and professionals have contributed gener-
ously of their time and intelligence to the completion of
this book but perhaps none have done so as freely and without
reservation as Jean Rustici and David Pierson. Jean, as a trusted
mentor and friend, has always been there to share thoughts and
insights and to give a gentle push in the right direction; David
thankfully wrote the original concept into a new format in *Child
Care Review* and was very supportive for many years in promoting the concept that child care systems must be cost-effective in
order to provide quality services for children. Both have been a
constant source of encouragement and inspiration over the years.

Many other professionals have shared experiences and materials, added their professional expertise to the manuscript and
brought renewed insight. Special thanks go to Victoria Schonfeld
and Tom Gotimer for their legal review, to Frank Ballatore for
his accounting and business expertise, to Tom Biracree for his
publishing acumen, to Rich Scofield of *School-Age Notes* for his
review of the school-age care section and to Mary Arnold, Pat
Dotson and Marge and Joe Heffel for sharing their materials with
the readers. And the ever present support and help of the staff
has always been appreciated, especially that of Evelyn Joyce,
Barbara Comerford, Emily Buzzeo, Paige Hamilton, Lynn Brand-
ner and Chris Wallace who have all contributed in ways large
and small.

Every book has its team of editors and supportive publishing
staff. We are especially grateful to Karen Van Westering for her
perceptive and intelligent editing of the manuscript. Our special
thanks as well to the helpful, insightful and patient editorial team

at Facts On File, Susan Schwartz, Michelle Fellner, Joe Reilly and Gloria McDarrah.

Most of all we would like to acknowledge the hundreds of children, parents, teachers and directors who have all unknowingly contributed to the message of this book: that children are a valuable resource and the future of our country and we must provide the very best child care services possible in order to promote each child's health, emotional and physical security, happiness and individual development and thus further insure the stable growth of our society.

CONTENTS

. . . .

INTRODUCTION
CHILD CARE: NEEDS AND OPPORTUNITIES TODAY

• •

The need for child care in this country today is a vital, pressing issue. Although there are presently 90,000 licensed child care centers and 500,000 to 800,000 family day care homes in the United States, the number of infants and toddlers and preschool and school-age children requiring care vastly exceeds the number of openings in most communities. Nearly 60% of women with children under the age of six are in the work force, including half of the women with a baby under age one. And not surprisingly, 65% to 70% of mothers of school-age children are working outside the home. Studies have shown that even more women would be in the work force if affordable, high-quality child care were available.

Why haven't more child care centers been established to meet this need? One important reason is that there are few trained managers available to staff new centers. From a management standpoint, this young industry is still in chaos. Only three colleges in the entire country offer management degree programs in child care, and their curricula do not include a comprehensive program on how to establish and operate a profitable center. Most materials that have been published focus on the how-tos rather than on the business of child care. The result is there are many entrepreneurs, legislators, government officials, corporate executives, early childhood educators and individuals looking for information about this exciting new field.

But perhaps the overriding reason is that traditionally child care has not been thought of as a business that could or should be profitable—a misconception this book is devoted to dispelling.

Fortunately, there is a child care system that addresses these issues: namely, how to provide the best possible care, meet the requirements of the many people who need it, and do so profitably. This *flexible* child care plan is based on the premise that a center should be designed to meet the needs, requirements and changing lifestyles of the parent.

For years, child care operators have assumed that they should provide only full-time, full-week care, and they have discouraged clients who want to use their center on a part-time or occasional basis.

The flexible child care center allows children to attend according to the needs of the parent; the center that is truly flexible encourages part-time, hourly students and strongly recognizes the *parent* as the primary child care provider. This philosophy encourages the child to be at the center a minimum amount of time.

Right now there are not many truly flexible programs in most areas, and parents will add many miles to their commute in order to obtain flexibility at a high-quality child care center. Traditional marketing studies have not considered flexibility, because it has not been perceived as a major issue for parents. However, as information systems and cottage industries help parents work part-time at home, or in professions like nursing with non-traditional hours, the flexibility factor is becoming increasingly important. Owners who have made their centers' hours more accommodating have found that parents will go out of their way to reach the program AND pay higher fees for the privilege!

Experience has shown that even centers operating at full licensed capacity—i.e., centers that have the maximum number of full-time students registered—are usually utilizing less than 60% of the total available child hours. By implementing the kind of flexible program detailed throughout this book, a new center can reach its break-even point sooner than otherwise might be expected, and an existing center's gross income can be increased dramatically in a short period of time. How is this possible? The flexible center encourages part-time students who pay on an hourly basis that is higher than the rate for full-time students. As a result, the unused 40% of the available hours are booked at that higher rate, and the center makes more money.

Many individual owners have had financial success using such a flexible program. The story of one new center in the Northwest demonstrates the program's potential. The proposed center was to have a rather small licensed capacity of 40 children at any given time, but it was in a very good location. The market analysis revealed that there was a particular need in the community for care for younger children and that the area had no programs that offered flexibility. Problems with the licensing agency unfortunately delayed the opening, which had been scheduled for March, until May—traditionally a time of year when enrollments are at their lowest. However, the flexible scheduling sold the program to many prospective clients, and the business reached its break-even point in less than six weeks. Within a year, the owner was planning to open two more centers and then an additional center a year for the next five years.

In another instance, the owners of a Southern center approached us with their bleak situation. They, in fact, had had difficulty paying their bills for the past three years. To institute a flexible program, they needed to change their room use and arrangements, rewrite the parent policies and agreements, create new brochures and advertising materials and set up a new bookkeeping system. In eight weeks' time they had turned the business around. Annual gross revenues increased $150,000 on rates of only $40 to $50 per week for full-time care and $2 to $3 hourly fees for part-time children. Aside from their own hard work, the necessary changes cost less than $5,000!

A flexible program is not difficult to implement or run and is actually not new to the child care industry. In fact, family day care home providers have been offering flexibility for years with the resulting financial gains. However, it is a relatively new and "strange" concept to child care center owners, especially as they worry about how to manage various children coming and going throughout the day. The management and organizational techniques (discussed in full in Chapter 11) are not difficult and well worth learning because flexible programs can bring success and profits to a child care business—whether new or on-going.

If you are considering starting a new child care business, this book will help you:

> **Determine** if the child care business is right for you, and if there is a need for a new center in your community; and if so, how to plan, finance and equip a new child care business. (Part One)
> **Implement** age-specific flexible programs, set up efficient

administration of your center and build excellent relationships between you, your staff and clients. (Parts Two
and Three)

Maximize your center's success through creative marketing
and awareness of potential problem areas (Part Four)

*If you already own and operate a child care center, this book
will help you:*

Re-evaluate the basic components of your child care operation to pinpoint any existing weaknesses and help you
correct them. This evaluation includes surveying your
physical setup and equipment, seeing how to expand and
still be within regulations and up to code, obtaining financing for improvements and deciding when and how
to hire outside experts to help you with specific problems. (Part One)

Implement a more flexible program—a proven way to maximize the use and profits of your center. Age-specific
program recommendations; guidelines for administration, personnel and parent relations; and summer programs are provided in Parts Two and Three.

Market your center effectively and creatively to maximize
your success. Keep in mind the most common pitfalls
and worries and learn how to avoid them. (Part Four)

Our goal is to explain how a child care center's profitability is
maximized by the implementation of a flexible program. *Profitable Child Care* will show you how to build this type of program
into every aspect of a new center from the outset or how it can
be gradually and easily integrated into an ongoing operation.

The other vital ingredient is you. Why are you here? If you're
thinking about entering the field, now's the time to consider if
you are truly suited to it. If you are already involved in child care,
a re-evaluation of the various skills required to be successful can
help you pinpoint your greatest strengths as well as weaker areas
where you may need some help.

Initially, you need to evaluate your aptitude for business and
decide if you have the natural instincts and ability to be an entrepreneur. And you need to know if you possess the skills neces-

sary to direct a child care center. Ideally you will be combining an interest in children with business skills to build a profitable and enjoyable career in child care.

Some of the following characteristics probably describe you:

From your early teenage years of baby-sitting, you have always enjoyed children and felt that you had a natural rapport with little ones. Or you truly enjoy older preschoolers and know that this is the age group where you'd like to concentrate your efforts. Perhaps you've even worked in a child care center or at a camp during the summer.

Or maybe you're bored with your job in the corporate world and have always enjoyed children. You are hesitant to enter the child care field with little formal education in early childhood, but you do not feel you have the time or energy to go back to school right now. You've found very little information on the business of child care in either the bookstores or library. However, you know that your corporate experience and business training have given you considerable management skills.

You may have heard that child care is in great demand and that it is even a business that can give you a decent income! And so you catch the "business bug." But . . .

> How do you decide whether you have the ability to run your own child care business and the knowledge and skills to succeed?
>
> Can your business experience or perhaps your experience as a teacher and your love for children be combined?
>
> Can you manage staff, purchase equipment wisely, negotiate leases, hire consultants, market your programs, handle difficult referrals, set up efficient bookkeeping systems, develop new programs, etc.?
>
> Has your business experience sufficiently prepared you to deal with the clients in this service business?
>
> Will you know what constitutes a creative and innovative program?
>
> Do you know what equipment and materials will be appropriate for each age level? Will your design of the space really work in practice?

The first two questions are addressed below; the rest are covered in the remaining chapters of the book.

As you begin the difficult task of deciding whether you are truly suited to operating a child care center, you need an honest self-evaluation of your strengths and weaknesses. First, consider how well you identify with these 12 traits that often characterize entrepreneurs:

Adventuresome—is willing and able to accept a challenge.
Self-directed—needs little outside help to stay motivated.
Opportunistic—seizes on the first chance to expand or improve in business.
Flexible—able to adapt to changes in the business community and the needs of the customers.
Knowledgeable—values any information about the business and keeps current.
Determined—follows through even when the times are tough.
Innovative—sees new trends and applies them creatively.
Courageous—dares to take risks and is not afraid of a new path.
Competitive—has a sense of striving for excellence.
Secure—is willing to admit when a mistake has been made or when someone else's idea is better.
Dedicated—can truly feel a sense of purpose.
Positive—always keeps a positive attitude and turns even adverse situations into a learning experience!

While you evaluate your natural abilities as an entrepreneur, you also should define what your role in the business will be, and determine whether you have the necessary skills. If you don't, you must decide whether to hire someone to supplement your skills or obtain the necessary training yourself. To direct a child care center you need to be able to:

- hire and fire staff
- market your program
- oversee curriculum
- manage staff
- interview parents
- handle problems
- make referrals
- organize bookwork
- manage finances
- promote public relations
- control purchasing
- coordinate scheduling

These are the specific skills but, generally speaking, to be truly successful you need most of all to be able to deal with people and problems in a skillful and efficient manner.

As you consider your role in the proposed business, you may decide to act as the administrator only. In this case you will need to hire a director, and then your responsibilities will depend upon the amount of control you want to retain and/or the skills of the person you're hiring. This arrangement can be very effective, especially if you continue to work elsewhere on a part-time basis.

To gain insight into the child care business before making a decision to get involved, visit as many centers as possible and speak to the owners and managers. If you are using a local consultant, ask which centers are best to visit; if not, get a list from the licensing agency or turn to your Yellow Pages. When you are visiting a center at this preliminary stage, you should ask the owners and managers quesions such as:

- How did you get into this work?
- What do you like most about it?
- What do you like least about it?
- Where else would you suggest I visit?

Another obvious goal of your visit is to try to determine whether the center is a financially profitable venture. A word of caution—few child care center owners will admit that their business is profitable, partially because they fear the competition in a local area and partially because they are hesitant to admit that they are "making money off children."

This brings up another important issue; for years some early childhood professionals have been very self-effacing, actually ashamed that there is money involved in educating and caring for young children. This is nonsense—you will be providing a valued service to the children and parents in the community and should expect to be monetarily rewarded for your work! We certainly do not see the toy stores, children's clothing stores or pediatricians acting embarrassed about the amount they charge.

The viability of the proposed business is the final consideration. This of course means that in any given locality you will need to do a careful market analysis (see Chapter 1). The child care industry is among the fastest-growing industries in the country; even in times of economic decline, this business is still a dependable profit-maker if you are flexible and can shift with the needs of the work force.

Remember the statistics mentioned at the beginning of this Introduction—the number of women working in this country has increased drastically in the past 20 years. And current trends indicate that the need for child care services will continue to increase during the next decade. According to Department of Labor statistics, "By 2000, 61.5% of all women will be at work and three out of five new workers will be women." Furthermore, as cottage industry grows in the United States, there will be a larger demand for new child care delivery systems with more flexibility.

It is estimated that only 30% of the child care need is being met in regulated centers and homes. The remainder is being met by unlicensed care or care by a relative. However, the number of relatives available to assist with child care is diminishing as workers stay in the work force longer, lifestyles change and the former extended family life disintegrates. And with the increase in abuse charges, parents are becoming more concerned about their children's safety and cautious about leaving their children in unregulated care.

The need for quality services for children will continue to grow, making child care a very good business prospect in most communities. Throughout the country there are still communities that are very restrictive regarding child care regulations. But the restraints are gradually being lifted, growth is being encouraged, and with the acceptance of the child care industry as a necessary entity in the American business scene, new possibilities are opening every day. If you have the necessary skills and motivation to create a quality, flexible child care facility, financially you can be a successful part of this exciting industry.

PART ONE
THE BASICS OF A CHILD CARE BUSINESS

• •

Whether you are interested in starting a new child care venture or improving your current operation, a solid working knowledge of the basic components of a child care business is the foundation on which to build. This phase involves careful planning, accurate estimating and thoughtful analysis of a number of factors. These important activities often occur simultaneously—you'll be checking out the competition, evaluating potential sites and studying zoning regulations while you prepare a business plan and look for financing. To help you address these essential issues, this section details:

1. How to analyze the existing and potential market for child care in a community.
2. How to select a site, with particular emphasis on zoning, building and fire regulations, and then plan the physical facility itself.
3. How to determine the structure your business should have, write a solid business plan and obtain financing.
4. How to obtain expert advice from a variety of outside professionals, including lawyers, accountants, child care consultants, bankers and computer specialists.
5. How to purchase equipment and supplies during both the start-up phase and on-going operation while avoiding the most common pitfalls and getting the most out of your purchasing dollar.

1
ANALYZING THE MARKET
. . . .

Whether you take over an existing center, convert a building for child care use or start with a new site from the ground up, you first need to assess the local child care market. The entrepreneur must not only know what the present needs for child care are in the community, but also must be able to make a fairly accurate projection about future child care needs both short term and long range. You'll also need some market forecasts and a thorough understanding of the demographics of the area.

NEEDS ASSESSMENT

The first step in ascertaining the current need for child care in a given community is an in-depth study of the existing child care services. Whether you pay a consultant to provide you with this information or conduct your own assessment, there are seven essential components of each existing center to examine:

1. Location: the exact location.
2. Size: the number of children cared for at any given time.
3. Enrollment: the total number of children using the center.
4. Type: the form of care provided and the ages cared for.
5. Potential: the growth potential of each center.
6. Fee Structure: the rates charged on an hourly, daily, weekly or monthly basis.
7. Reputation: the community's perception of each child care center.

What Facilities Are Currently Providing Child Care in This Area?

To begin your study, obtain from the local or state regulatory agency a list of the licensed or registered facilities that are currently providing child care. In some areas this information will be available at the state level; in others it is better to contact the local Board of Health or other appropriate governing body. The lists from the licensing agencies usually give an accurate assessment of the quantity of *licensed* child care, including child care centers in corporate settings. (See Appendix A for a list of state licensing agencies.) In some states, part-day preschool programs must be regulated, while programs of three hours or less are unregulated. In others, the number of hours that the center is open determines its status for licensing. In other words, you must understand how the governing body for your area determines what child care services will be regulated.

In the past 10 years, coordinating agencies for child care have developed throughout the country. These services are referred to as Resource and Referral Agencies and should have accurate and current information about the services available in a local area. When you contact the agency for information, be sure to ask when the last updates on the data were made and also what are the most frequent requests from parents in the area.

Where Are These Facilities Located?

Once you have the list, get an accurate map of the area and indicate every center clearly with colored pins, each color denoting a type of care or age group. It will also come in handy to know whether each center is located on the "morning" or "evening" side of the street—in other words, is the center on the right-hand side of the street for the majority of the parents dropping off their children in the morning. (In an area of great need and/or when the program is top quality, this may not greatly affect the success of the program, because parents will often go out of their way to reach an excellent facility.)

For future reference, also label on the map the elementary and private schools in the area, as well as the major employers or office centers.

What Is the Licensed Capacity of Each Center?

Use the lists available from the licensing agency to determine the *licensed* capacity of each child care center. Also, include the capacity in the regulated family day care homes. Make a list of these capacities, breaking them down into the age levels served wherever possible. You may want to arrange them in a format like that of Table 1-1 or Table 1-2. If you have difficulty determining the number of children allowed in each age group, call the centers and ask, or stop by your local child care resource and referral service. If you cannot obtain information on capacity by age level, the total capacity of the center will be adequate for making your earliest decisions.

How Many Children Are Actually Using Each Child Care Facility?

The number of children actually using the center in the course of the week is the *enrollment.* This number can vary drastically from the licensed capacity of the center. For example, a center licensed for 75 may be used by over 300 different children if the

TABLE 1-1   CHILD CARE IN BURLINGTON

Full-Time Centers	Ages	Capacity	Price/week	
Creative Child Care Center	4 weeks–12 years	104	0–2.9 years	$162.50
			3 years	$135.50
			4 years	$129.00
			K	$90.00
			Bef/Aft school	3.25/hr
Wee Ones	4 weeks–12 years	48	0–2.9 years	$135
			3 + years	$115
The Child's Place	4 weeks–4 years	41	0–2.9 years	$165
			3 + years	$140
Licensed Family Day Care Homes	0–School age	44 <2 years 88 2–5 years 66 School age	Varies but generally more expensive than full-time centers	
Total Full-Time Capacity		391		

Part-Time Centers	Ages	Hours	Price/week	
Kids Korner	18 months–K	8—5 School year	0–2.9 years	$130
			3–4 years	$115
			K	$70

TABLE 1-2   LICENSED CHILD CARE IN NORFOLK

The following figures are collated from information received from the departments that license family day care homes, group day care homes, child care centers and nursery schools for the state.

	Child Care Centers All-Day Children	Child Care Centers Part-Day Children	Family Day Care Homes	Totals
Total Licensed Facilities	12	12	29	53
Licensed Capacity	517	315	118	950
Programs accepting before/after school	5	2	29*	36*
Programs accepting children under 3 years	1	2	29*	32*
Potential openings for children under 3 years	4	12	58*	74*

*estimated

center has part-time and hourly children or before- and after-school children. The best way to estimate the enrollment of a center is to study its philosophy and attendance requirements, and then visit and see if there are spaces in particular programs. As a last resort, take a tally by observing the number of children entering and leaving.

What Types of Child Care Are Being Provided by the Various Centers?

The type of child care is defined by the center's hours of operation, its philosophy, the age groups served and the degree of flexibility.

First, note the hours of operation and see if they meet the community's needs. For example, are the majority of centers in the area open from 7:30 A.M. until 5:30 P.M., although the area commuters and shift workers need child care between 6:30 A.M. and 6:30 P.M.? Are these centers open for evening, overnight or weekend hours where there is a need?

Next, categorize each program according to its philosophy, i.e., Montessori, "open," structured, religious, etc. You may find that parents are searching for a type of program that is not being provided.

See if there is any flexibility in the hours and days that the centers may be used. Time and again, we have found that not a single child care center in a given community allows attendance on a *flexible*, part-time basis; most are actually afraid to do so! This will probably be your most important marketing advantage.

Finally, note the ages served—this is a crucial step and often brings surprising results. For example, the analysis of one community showed that there was a critical need for infant and toddler, and before- and after-school care, but there were over 60 spaces available in existing facilities for three- and four-year-olds! Unless a new center could find a critical need for three- and four-year-olds not being met by the existing centers, it would be foolish to try to establish a three- and four-year-old child care program in this particular community.

How Much Is Each Center Likely to Expand?

Try to establish each existing center's potential for expansion. This means examining two very different factors: the physical expansion possibilities of the facility AND the extent to which the current operators are likely to make improvements. As you can imagine, these factors can be very difficult to measure exactly, but they often can be estimated by determining:

  the age of the center
  how long it has been under the present owner
  the community's building, fire and zoning laws

If the center has been in existence for a long time and is successful, it is likely to stay as it is. On the other hand, the owner may be ready to sell and/or retire, in which case there may be drastic changes in the offing. A new owner will usually make renovations and/or program revisions in the first few months and then wait for another six months to a year before trying anything else new.

Local and state fire, building and zoning laws can restrict, severely limit or even prohibit expansion. In many communities, these codes have restricted child care centers so much that future competition is unlikely. Naturally, this has kept the supply of child care constant while the demand continues to grow. This can be a blessing for the entrepreneur who can buy or renovate an existing facility.

What Fee Structures Are the Centers Using?

Knowing what type of fee structure each center uses is a critical piece of information in analyzing the current market. This knowledge will also help you with certain aspects of your business plan. Carefully study the various methods used. For example, does a center charge on a monthly, weekly or hourly basis? Are the parents happy with this approach and are the accounts receivable easy to collect?

Experience has shown that with the demand for child care increasing rapidly and the financial stability of many communities wavering, it is best to charge on a weekly basis. This policy helps parents by making the payments regular and smaller; also, any necessary increases in fees appear lower. When hourly fees are used in a flexible program, a "pay as you use" policy works best and improves cash flow.

For marketing purposes, you need to determine whether the competition's policies are popular with the parents and actually encourage them to choose one center over another. Also, note enrollment fees, registration charges and absentee policies, although these will not affect the actual operating budget or fee structure decisions.

What Is the Community's Perception of Each Center?

The community's perception of each child care center is very important in the market analysis process. If the parents and educators in the area think that a center is safe and well run, then marketing its openings will be relatively easy. Naturally, a center that is relatively unknown will have to convince the community that the center is safe, with a high-quality program.

Ironically, a center may even have a somewhat tarnished reputation but still be very popular. For example, a facility may be thought of as "dirty," but if it is conveniently located or has low fees or a great teacher in one area, it may still be filled to capacity. In this instance, it would be important for you to know that this perception exists and then to proceed to fill the gap in the market with a center that has low fees, an excellent location, top employees and is clean too!

The only way to gather this information is to talk to parents and professionals in the community. Realtors are often very knowledgeable about local centers' reputations as well as the needs of residents in the area. The local child care resource and referral service may be able to provide this information also. In some communities, you can hire a child care consultant if you are unfamiliar with the area.

However, the young parents in the community are always the best source of information if you survey a good cross section of them. A visit to a popular local park with a preschooler in tow can bring a wealth of information. Other resources are the newcomers' clubs, welcome wagons, barbershops and beauty parlors, newsstands and senior centers. Other helpful people might be children's librarians, social workers, employees and patrons of coffee shops or any popular local spot. Not all of these sources will pan out and the ones that do may be of the "hearsay" variety, but they can provide a quick overview of the child care community.

Family Day Care: How Much of a Threat Do These Homes Pose to Your Child Care Operation?

One last area to study is the family day care homes in the area—both regulated and unregulated. The regulated homes should be listed with the regulatory agency, which can usually be contacted through the local health department. Obtain a copy of the regulations and try to determine if the homes have the number of children allowed and whether they are inspected on a regular basis. Throughout the United States, there is a large system of underground, unmonitored family day care homes unknown to the state regulatory agencies. It is estimated nationally that the proportion of family day care homes that operate underground is from 70% to 94%. You must obtain at least a sense of the strength of this underground competition. The unregulated homes are usually advertised in the classified sections of the newspapers, on bulletin boards in stores and by word of mouth.

Be sure to gather information on the fees charged by the homes. And finally you will want to know the number of children in the regulated homes and an estimate of the number in the unregulated homes. To do the unregulated estimate, you can divide the number of regulated homes by .06 to .30 (using the national figures above). This will give you a rough idea. Recently it has become obvious that the unregulated market becomes stronger during an economic decline as working parents who lose jobs care for a few children in their home as an "easy" way to fill the income gap. This has been disastrous in some areas of the country. However, as parents become better educated about the potential for abuse and unsafe conditions in these unregulated homes, their competitive threat diminishes.

MARKET FORECAST AND DEMOGRAPHICS

Once you've studied the existing child care services, examine the demographics of the area. Usually the local school district and state board of education will have annual preschool projections for the community as well as accurate school-age figures. These can be coordinated with Census Bureau statistics (see Appendix B for Census Bureau regional numbers and addresses) for the area and with projections of the number of working mothers and single-parent families for the current year and several years into the future. These figures will give a fairly accurate estimation of the number of children in each age group in the community who will need child care. Compare these figures with the number of spaces physically available in the existing child care facilities to ascertain the specific number of slots needed for each age group.

Although complicating your analysis, it is useful, particularly in suburban areas, to include surrounding commuter communities in your survey. Usually it is sufficient to survey preschool ages only because the school-age children most likely will remain in their school district. However, if it is possible to provide or obtain transportation for school-age children and the prospect seems even remotely cost-effective, include them in this initial analysis. If you have difficulty determining which routes local commuters use or the towns that area employees come from, you may want to ask the larger employers in the area to provide you with this information. If they perceive that there is something in it for them, i.e., an additional employee benefit provided at no expense to them, they are more likely to be helpful. The best person to contact is the director of personnel.

The next dimension in the demographic study is income range and percentage of homes in which two parents work and therefore need child care. To obtain these statistics, contact the U.S. Census Bureau—Labor Statistics and Income Statistics.

Also, your local library will usually have articles on child care needs in the recent issues of area papers. Use these with caution, since the accuracy and interpretation is only as good as the reporter and his or her sources. However, the articles will give you some indication of the situation in your community, and often the reporter may have further statistics to share that were not printed. The library will also have recent articles and statistics on child care from various national sources that may be of interpretative value.

At this stage, it is valuable to analyze the population growth and to try to gauge what is happening to the birth rate and how it will affect the area. In doing this, the traditional statistical methods may prove misleading. For example, in the late 1970s and early 1980s many state officials were predicting a drastic decrease in the number of children in elementary schools and recommending that communities close their schools wherever possible. However, many child care professionals were at the same time seeing the opposite trend: The preschool population was increasing, particularly in upwardly mobile areas. They predicted a "double boom" as older parents in their late thirties and early forties began to think of having a child or two while young people in their twenties were starting their families. In the mid to late '80s this came to pass, and the school-age population began to increase. As the turn of the century approaches, there may indeed be a reverse trend with a decrease in the preschool population and a consequent leveling off. The moral is to use the existing statistics and predictions carefully and gear your decisions toward fulfilling the needs of a portion of the market not currently being met, rather than planning on an absolute increase in the need for child care.

Finally, you should assess the strength of the local business community and its future growth. An obvious question would be whether any new corporations plan to settle in the area in the near future and, if so, what the child care needs of the employees will be. At the same time, try to determine if existing businesses are stable or if they are planning new hiring, cutbacks or moves.

The first place to look is the local newspapers; however, impending corporate moves may not be publicized for obvious reasons. Usually the easiest and most reliable source is the local business community itself. For a sense of its general health, the local Chamber of Commerce and local business associations can be invaluable. The Board of Realtors can be most helpful and can also provide you with the names of realtors who deal in commercial properties. Local accountants and financial planners who work with small and medium-sized businesses will often have a good handle on the health of the business community, because this knowledge is necessary and available to them. Even informal breakfast get-togethers of local business people can be very informative.

Corporate-Sponsored Child Care Centers

A corporation may be willing to assist you by gathering information from employees on their child care needs; this information could in turn help you provide a service to their employees. As part of your initial contact, be sure to emphasize that there is no cost to the employer; in general, corporations are inundated by child care providers looking to work "with" the corporation at the corporation's expense. If you are considering locating your center at a corporate building, your market analysis must include an accurate needs assessment of families within the corporation, as well as careful community projections for the first five years. Without continual corporate sponsorship, an employee base must be very large for you to cover the expenses and space usage of a child care center in such a location. It may be advisable at the outset to include a percentage of community enrollments, which can also enhance the community image of the corporation. Consortiums with other area companies may also be attractive as a way to broaden the financial base.

However, if a corporation perceives that its employees need the child care benefit quickly and wants to provide it at a minimum expense to itself, or if the corporation does not want to be directly involved in the delivery of child care, their best alternative could be to contract with you—a private child care professional—to provide either on-site or off-site care using a voucher or vendor system.

In the voucher system, the center agrees to accept from the parent a "voucher" or coupon that is guaranteed by the corporation. Usually the employee has purchased the voucher from the employer with pretax dollars, and in some cases, the corporation may decide to pay a percentage of the child care cost. In rare instances, the corporation will pay the total cost of care.

With the vendor system, a center agrees to give preferred placement to the children of employees of a corporation. In this case, a center usually agrees to reserve a small percentage of slots in return for start-up assistance or a monthly cash payment. When making a vendor arrangement, you must state clearly the exact terms of the preferential treatment and the fact that advance payment is expected. In either case, the needs assessment and market analysis will still be critical for accurate projections of the business.

FINAL ANALYSIS

Finally, you must decide if the shortfall in child care services is large enough to justify your venture. As a general rule, you can plan on readily attracting 10% to 20% of the market shortfall. For example, if there is an estimated infant/toddler population of 2,500 and you know that, according to the latest statistics, 40% of all mothers of children under three are entering the work force, then the community will need a child care supply for this age group of 1,000 infant/toddler slots. If your market analysis shows slots for only 550 infants/toddlers, then you have a shortfall of 450 and could expect to attract 45 to 90 children under the age of three. Using this method, you can calculate your potential number of clients and feel more certain of your success from the very beginning.

2
SELECTING A SITE AND PLANNING A FACILITY

· ·

Once you have decided that there is a definite need in the community for a new child care center, you can begin looking for a location. In the ideal situation, you'll find a building in the prime area targeted by your market analysis and one in compliance with local building codes. As an added attraction, the facility is available at a reasonable price tag per square foot, and has definite expansion potential. Unfortunately, this scenario rarely happens in the real world, but there are methods to use and precautions to take that can make your search easier.

Keep in mind that simultaneously you will be searching for a site; estimating what size center a potential site can accommodate; and familiarizing yourself with local building, health and zoning codes. Your search will vary depending on whether you're looking for a lot on which to build, an existing building or space to convert to a child care center or an operating center to take over. But no matter what type of site you are looking for, your understanding of the local codes is of vital importance in evaluating potential sites and facilities and later in obtaining necessary board approvals more easily.

Once you've chosen a site, you will need to consider the design and layout of your center. The ultimate success of your business will depend significantly on the quality of the physical facility and the amount of thought you put into its planning, preparation and decoration.

SITE SELECTION

Site selection is critical in making your center into a long-term, profitable business. The wise entrepreneur gives plenty of time and effort to this process and studies all avenues with an open mind.

Location, Location, Location . . . and Flexibility

Various studies about the factors that determine parents' selection of a child care facility have shown location and cost to be the top priorities. The major child care chains in the country try to locate their centers on the morning side of the street (the side of the street most commuters use on their way to work), as near as possible to major traffic interchanges and in upscale suburban areas. Remember that the "morning" side of the street means the right-hand side, so the commuting parent will not have to cross traffic and risk being late for work. The theory is that parents are more tolerant of this inconvenience at the end of the day. While the theory is debatable, it does provide a good rule of thumb in looking at locations. However, in several instances where the center is not on the morning side of the street, the owners have circumvented the problem by hiring an off-duty or retired policeman to direct traffic and assist the parents in and out. A center at a major intersection or near an exit ramp of a highway can be more convenient for the commuting parent; however, the disadvantage for the owner is that the cost of land or rental space may be disproportionately higher there.

The premise behind an upscale location is that parents will theoretically be able to pay higher fees. However, there is a need for child care at every income level, and your market analysis may show that the potential volume and immediate need in a middle- or low-income area may far outweigh the premium price possible in a higher-income neighborhood. Your selection of a location will be much less restricted if your program is based on the highly cost-effective, *flexible* form of child care described in this book. The reason for this is that your center, because of its flexible program, will be more popular with parents, and the location of the center will be less of a factor.

Be creative in your search for an appropriate site. As a child care operator looking for a new site, you can sometimes use to your advantage quirks in local ordinances. For example, child care is often prohibited in heavy industrial zones but may be allowed in light industrial zones. Thus, the astute site shopper might look for space on the border between the two that has been difficult to rent or sell for any number of reasons.

As a result of an interesting trend in the larger business community, still another possibility is a site in a corporation's building or in an office park.

Sites at Office Parks and Corporate Structures

The availability of on-site child care can greatly enhance the desirability of space in office parks and multiple corporate structures. Some communities have even required that new office structures include child care space in order to increase the amount of child care available in the community. For these two reasons as well as for the perceived potential profit in the child care industry, many developers, investors and venture capitalists are approaching child care professionals to help them establish centers in newly built or planned office space.

Some of your costs to secure the necessary approvals, or set-up or renovation costs, may be picked up by the owner or developer for the "privilege" of having a quality program in their structure to attract other business clients and rentals. This factor may also give you an advantage when negotiating contracts and special considerations for some necessary services. Developers will often throw in some minor services such as lawn or parking lot maintenance to attract a quality child care operator and may even make other concessions.

More recently, there has been gathering interest from some building owners and developers to have a silent, small share in the child care business itself, and this investment could reduce your start-up and/or renovation expenses as well. It is usually advisable for the child care operator to own all equipment and materials necessary to run the business and to maintain a controlling interest at all times. You should have expert legal advice before entering such an agreement.

In any negotiations with an investor or a developer, remember that the center cannot be established without expertise and that this expertise is not in abundant supply. Thus you, as the child care professional, should be able to insist on certain advantageous conditions. At the same time, the whole package must be attractive to the investor and, for example, truly provide the type of care that will attract rental clients to the site. For all concerned, this type of arrangement can be an excellent alternative as long as objectives and ownership lines are clearly drawn.

A corporation may also be willing to lease you space that you would in turn use to provide vital child care service to their employees. As part of your initial contact with a corporation, explain that your system of child care delivery will be different, that is, flexible, to better meet the needs of their employees and their spouses. Having the flexibility "angle" may just be the edge you need to get your foot in the door.

Getting a Site That's the Right Size

At this stage in the site selection process, you should have a general idea of what size center any potential site could accommodate. The site you select does not have to be exceptionally large. A square footage capacity of 35 square feet per child is generally the minimum requirement, although this varies from state to state. (Check with your local regulatory agency.) If you find an existing building of 4,500 to 5,000 square feet or a site that can accommodate a building that size, you probably have room for 90 children.

For outdoor play space, an area of 6,750 square feet (75 square feet/child) will be adequate for 90 children; if the maximum number of children outside at any one time will only be 20, an outdoor space as small as 1,500 square feet may be sufficient. Although it is desirable to have your own space for the children to run and play, you may be able to use a nearby park instead. Interior atriums also are becoming popular as alternative playgrounds and may be advantageous when structures are proposed in areas subject to high crime, vandalism or air pollution.

See Facility Planning and Design for more information on both interior and exterior space allocation and design.

Getting Approvals . . . with the Right Advice

The regulations and approvals vary considerably throughout the country as well as the interpretation of the various codes. Check your local requirements thoroughly, since this factor can drastically affect the purchase or rental price, increase the start-up costs or even negate a possible site.

When purchasing or renting a building or taking over an existing child care operation, it is possible to protect yourself against the various interpretations of codes and regulations. However, you must do it carefully. First, obtain a list of regulations pertaining to child care facilities from the local authorities—include fire, zoning, building and health. Then study them thoroughly and make a list of your questions. However, do NOT directly approach the local officials with these questions. Although asking local officials (or board members, if that's the same thing) might appear to be the least expensive way to get answers, you may instead further complicate your situation. The risk is that you will prematurely raise doubts in their minds, making the process more expensive for you in the long run or even foolishly negating a perfect facility.

Local officials, who often worry about the rapid growth of the child care industry, may not themselves understand the local codes pertaining to child care or the interpretation of them. In some cases, the codes are outdated and do not even make provisions for full-day child care facilities but only concern themselves with part-time preschools. You will need to hire the right lawyer— meaning someone who understands the various idiosyncrasies of the governing authorities, and who is also familiar with both local laws and child care legal issues. This may mean using two attorneys: one to cover the local issues and another attorney, perhaps from outside the local area, who specializes in the interpretations of codes for child care centers. This is also the time when a child care consultant familiar with legal issues and other similar cases can be an invaluable resource. Leave the list of questions you compiled to these legal and child care experts. (See Chapter 4 for further details.)

At this stage, you may also be able to enlist the help of an advocacy group. Check the various early childhood agencies and state and local child care organizations; many have referral services and, at the very least, the officers may have resources to tap or knowledge of similar issues in other communities for you to investigate. At the same time, you will need to persist in attempting to master an understanding of the issues no matter how complicated they may be.

If you find an existing building that is attractive according to your market analysis, thoroughly study the zoning, building and fire approvals that the current operators have already obtained. Also, if the existing structure is in a residential zone, you should be especially vigilant for restrictive, hidden conditions that could affect the continued operation of the business. You need to be aware of any zoning laws that may restrict the size of the business, making future expansion extremely difficult. Or, for a long-standing business, there may be a "pre-existing condition" clause in the regulations that only applies if changes have not been made to the structure. Or, there may have been an addition to the original structure which negates the exception.

Consider building and fire codes. State fire codes may have been revised, and with a change in ownership, you, as the new owner, may, for example, be required to install a sprinkler system. Such an installation is expensive under any conditions, but can be prohibitive if the water source for the facility is a well system. Building codes can be significantly different for a child care center and may require, for example, that only the ground floor of a "non-combustible" building be used; this makes any space on the upper floor unusable.

If you are taking over an existing center, a list of special precautions to take is included later in this chapter under the heading "Special Considerations." Just one potential issue for you would be that space requirements per child may have changed on the state or local level, OR the space may have been incorrectly measured and regulated for more children than will be allowed with new owners. The square footage of older facilities was often based on *outside* measurements instead of the interior ones, which would significantly alter the amount of usable child space. As in previous considerations, the agency determining the square footage requirements will have "grandfathered" the approvals, but these will be dropped once the facility changes hands. Obviously this would affect your income and may require an adjustment on the purchase price or even reconsideration of the actual purchase or rental. Or the original space may have had special considerations because of the nonprofit status of the previous center, which will be dropped once a private entrepreneur takes over.

In any negotiations with the current owner of an existing child care business or landlord of a building you are going to convert, there should be conditional clauses written into your contract whereby implementing the business commitment is contingent upon your obtaining approvals from the local building, fire, zoning and health departments and the state regulatory agency. One additional note of caution: be sure not to make costly renovations for the fire marshal or building inspector before you have had a feasibility check by the state agency.

Obtaining approvals can be a costly and frustrating experience, particularly in small communities. The following example is about a center that was started from the ground up, but the lessons it provides are germane for anyone faced with getting necessary approvals.

A new facility was being considered in a small midwestern community. It was clear that the community elders on the local zoning commission felt that the children in the community should not be cared for in child care centers, and they had successfully blocked 17 previous applications for new sites. The individual seeking approval hired a lawyer who understood local politics and an experienced child care consultant to help gather background information and to speak at the zoning meeting. The owner and consultant thoroughly researched the previous applications and accounts of the board's refusals in the local papers. The research provided a profile of the zoning board members and helped them determine the proper approach to take. It quickly became evident that the local building inspector was the primary obstacle in previous meetings and that he had a great deal of influence over the other members of the commission. The local lawyer added further valuable insight during strategy conferences preceding the zoning meeting. The team decided to deliver a low-key, nonthreatening but professional presentation with the consultant acting as a friendly, knowledgeable resource for the commission, answering their questions and allaying their fears about child care.

On a hot summer's day after two full hours of discussion, the zoning commission approved the first child care center in the community. The building inspector was not happy, but parents were thrilled that 30 children would have a small, quality, licensed facility. The owner continued with the preparations having previously obtained the other required local approvals; the final licensing approval was contingent upon the zoning board's approval as well as the building and fire inspectors' approvals.

Approximately one month later, when the owner was finalizing state approvals and had the facility "informally" but fully booked (registration could not be done until the final license came through), the unhappy building inspector said that he had reviewed the state building codes and realized that all public facilities had to have a bathroom and entry equipped for the disabled. This would require replacing a standard toilet with one appropriate for wheelchair use and building a five-foot ramp to one of the exits. The owner immediately realized these extra expenses could not be absorbed in her original budget, and worse yet, the state required one toilet for each 15 children. The accessible toilet would be too high for preschoolers to use so there would probably have to be another standard toilet for which there was absolutely no room. The owner was not against having disabled children in the program and, in fact, had children with minor disabilities enrolled. However, she knew that she would be unable to afford a staff member who could handle a child with multiple handicaps and that the need for wheelchair access for a preschooler in the community was negligible. Her careful research had shown that the two preschool disabled children in the area were already being bused to an excellent facility in a neighboring community with a highly trained, professional staff.

Her lawyer told her that she could challenge the building inspector in court and had a good chance of winning. But this would take years, during which time she could not operate the center because final state approval required that all local approvals be in place, including that of the building department. Fortunately, the state agency was lenient about the true use of one toilet by the preschoolers, and the owner decided to install the accessible toilet and access ramp. The center opened successfully but with a considerable increase in start-up costs.

The owner had legal recourse but decided that peace was a better alternative in the small community. An interesting side note is that a year after this fiasco, the son of a local unlicensed home provider (who was caring for 18 children) was found guilty of eight counts of risk of injury to a minor. As in many areas, there were numerous large, unlicensed homes that were ignored by the town officials.

This example illustrates why you, as a new business operator, must be diligent in pursuing approvals, and although some of your efforts may be thwarted, a thorough understanding of the codes and politics will help a great deal. Before giving up entirely on a difficult approval, remember that unfair restraint of trade is illegal; investigate the dispute thoroughly and discuss your options with legal counsel.

FACILITY PLANNING AND DESIGN

Once you've chosen a site, there are certain factors to keep in mind as you examine the existing structure or plan construction of a new building. Attractiveness should be a major consideration with emphasis on space and light. However, your primary concerns will be the allotment and design of the areas the children will use. Your state's individual regulations regarding interior and exterior square footage requirements will, of course, influence your design plans; but your personal tastes and the philosophy of the program will also affect the center's spatial concept. For example, a true "open classroom" program requires plenty of open space to accommodate the rotation of the children through the various areas. On the other hand, a traditional Montessori program will require less open space and more square footage allotted to tables and storage units for classroom materials.

Usable Child Space and Unit Size

First, you will need to determine how many feet of usable space per child is required by the regulatory agency. Although state regulations vary in their square footage requirements, the following figures should be close to the minimum in most areas: 35 square feet of usable interior space per child and 75 exterior square feet per child. The key word here is *usable,* as this is often open to various interpretations. The agencies usually mean any space that is used exclusively by children or that contains furniture for classroom use by the children *only.* Thus, in many instances, the area occupied by cubbies for children's belongings, by the teacher's desk or by arts and crafts storage units cannot be included.

The entire facility should be used to its feasible maximum in order to have as large a licensed capacity as possible. Depending on the local cost of child care, each "extra" 35 square feet of usable child space that you find can represent an increase in the center's gross income of $2,600 to $10,000 per year. There are ways to modify existing space to make more of it usable. For example, by using the lower shelves of the arts and crafts storage unit to hold children's puzzles and manipulatives, the space may become usable child space. Additional examples follow throughout this chapter.

Second, determine the size of each unit or group of children that best works for your anticipated operation. The unit sizes and classroom numbers used here are those that work best for flexible child care and that maximize the quality of care. We'll use eight children per unit or multiples of eight for the children under four, and 10 children per unit or multiples of 10 for children four and up. This will satisfy many staff ratios and is easy to adjust for smaller and larger groups. The number of units of eight or 10 that are in each room will be determined by the age group of the children and the maximum group size allowed by your regulatory agency. Here are some guidelines:

> Infants: One unit of eight for each room or divided space.
> Toddlers: Two units of eight for each classroom or divided space.
> Three-year-olds: Two units of eight per classroom.
> Four-year-olds and above: Two units of 10 per classroom.

The staff-to-child ratios required by the regulatory agencies (particularly for children above the age of three) will probably be considerably higher than eight or 10, but we will be using these figures only for planning the physical space. Please note that regulations may strictly limit the maximum class size allowed in each classroom; make sure you know the state requirements. For example, it would be unwise to plan a four-year-old classroom of three units of eight for a total of 24 children in the classroom, when the total class size allowed for this age by a regulatory agency might be only 20 children per room.

Space Allotment

There is often a question as to how much space should be allotted for the office, toilets, sinks, entrance areas, kitchen and staff areas and storage closets. As explained previously, this will depend somewhat on the philosophy and the licensed capacity of the center. Table 2-1 gives estimates of the square footage ranges for the space other than that actually used for the children:

Specific suggestions for planning each of these areas follow:

Storage The general rule for an attractive, quality child care setting is that the only materials visible should be materials the children are allowed to use. Also, the number of toys and manipulatives available to the children at any given time should be limited to those that the children can easily store themselves. Extra materials should be stored so that they can easily be rotated into the classrooms on a regular basis to maintain the interest of the children.

Efficient storage design is essential to a quality program because lack of storage can throw even a quality program into chaos. If storage space is well planned from the beginning, any increase in size or change to a more flexible program will be easy to accommodate. Your staff will also be more organized and relaxed

TABLE 2-1 LICENSED CAPACITY BY SQUARE FOOTAGE

Licensed Capacity- Number of Children	Storage/Closets (10 sq. ft./ 10 lic. cap.)	Toilets/Sinks (1 toilet/15 children)	Kitchen (If meals are served)	Office	Staff Area (Optional)	Entrance Areas	Totals
1–50 children	10–50 square feet	50–150 square feet	100–300 square feet	50–100 square feet	125 square feet	50–100 square feet	385–825 square feet
51–100 children	50–100 square feet	150–300 square feet	250–500 square feet	100–300 square feet	200 square feet	100–200 square feet	850–1600 square feet
101–300 children	100–300 square feet	300–950* square feet	250–500 square feet	300–600 square feet	200 square feet	200–350 square feet	1350–2900 square feet

* non-disabled.

as a result. Naturally, the storage requirements will vary depending on the size and type of program.

Keep in mind that storage units can be very dangerous if objects can topple off the shelves. A heavy toy stored on a high shelf can fall and seriously injure a child. Cubbies, particularly if used as dividers, must be anchored to the floor; if not, they can easily tip over. Most models are top heavy and some have been known to crush, even kill, children. Shelves for wooden blocks must be firmly anchored to the floor or a wall or to another cabinet, since children empty blocks from the bottom up, making the cabinet more unstable and top heavy.

Storage areas for the teachers, with shelving, should be placed well out of the children's reach. Allow for a minimum of two square feet of "teacher" storage space per licensed child capacity. This means that for each unit of eight children you'll need 16 square feet of storage space. The interior of this storage space should not be visible when entering the room; otherwise you create a disorganized impression.

To save administrative aggravation and avoid a cluttered appearance in the rooms, there should be a door or curtain to conceal any storage area. Teachers' belongings, such as pocketbooks that may have dangerous medications, must be kept well out of the children's reach. Also, cleaning supplies must be securely locked up and stored well away from play areas or meal preparation surfaces.

Toileting and Bathing   Another parameter that will greatly influence your planning is toileting and bathing requirements. If, for example, regulations require running water in the infant and toddler rooms, this must be feasible in the given space. You may not need toilets in the infant room, but a smaller training toilet or two may be needed in a hygienic area in or near to the toddler room. Note that portable potty chairs are not a viable alternative, because they cannot be properly sanitized and create a high risk of infection for both children and staff.

For preschoolers, toilets are a necessity, and this raises two important issues; privacy for the children and supervision to insure that there is no chance for sexual abuse. Some schools use mirrors to maintain discreet supervision. Another alternative is to have Plexiglass walls starting three feet above the floor in one side of the children's toileting area. This will allow adult supervisors to check easily on activities in the toileting area. For school-age children, you would need to provide separate male and female areas with definite privacy while still protecting against any possibility of abuse. A very simple, small room containing one toilet with the sink outside the room offers the best protection for your center and the maximum privacy for the older child. For the center's protection, you should be very leery of, or even refuse to use, toilet space in a rental facility that is shared with other tenants.

Management Areas: Kitchens, Offices and Entrances   If you have decided to offer meals to the children, then you will need a kitchen that meets all state and local health codes. This can be an expensive proposition; however, it may be seen as an advantage by a potential client, and it may be a necessity for you to keep up with the competition. And there are ways to cut costs. For example, you could eliminate an expensive range hood by using a steam table and microwave for cooking instead of a range top. To save additional overhead, you might have the meals catered by an outside service. The extra expense can be passed on to the parents, if necessary.

Each center will need an office area, but its size will vary depending on the size of the center—the larger the center, the more staff it requires. The size of the office staff is usually determined by the licensed capacity. A good rule of thumb is that centers with a licensed capacity greater than 50 need two office staff—one director and one office staff worker—and each 50 children thereafter will require an additional half-time office position. For a flexible program to work well, there will have to be at least one person on duty in the office during all operating hours. Some centers use time clocks or bar code cards linked to a computer system to track the clients' hours and automatically do the billing. Of course, you may need less office staff if you use a computer and one of the new, readily available software programs for child care administration.

The entrance area should not only be attractive but also functional, allowing each client to be welcomed in an orderly manner. With a large flow of hourly students, you may also need a sign-in, sign-out area for the parents. For security reasons, you may want to ensure that outsiders cannot enter the center by having entrances opened only by a magnetic card (which can later be connected to a computer system and automatically record each child's hours). It is usually best to locate the reception area adjacent to the office space to facilitate administrative tasks such as recording available openings, scheduling staff, billing, handling accounts payable and ordering supplies and equipment.

Space Considerations in an Existing Child Care Center If you are considering the purchase of an existing child care center, the facility's design will have been determined to a great extent by the current owner. However, there may be room to improve the structure or make more efficient use of the space. Perhaps you feel the center is ideal but does not seem to have as large a capacity as it could. The procedures outlined below could also help you if you are considering converting a space for child care.

1. Measure the square footage very carefully and make an accurate floor plan.
2. Think of innovative ways to make more square footage usable. For example, use hooks and a shelf in the hall for belongings, rather than cubbies. (Cubbies for children's personal belongings are not considered usable child space.) Or take the door off a closet and put a mirror inside to make a lovely dress-up area. Perhaps the area under the stairs can be made into a play house. Or the kitchen area (when meals are not being served) can be made into a cooking and science area for use with the children. Maybe the office space can be moved to a smaller area or even into a part of the entrance partitioned off with dividers; then the current office can be converted to classroom space. Maybe a fireplace can be carpeted for a cozy book area. If outdoor equipment is stored in an interior closet, consider adding an outdoor storage shed to free up more interior space.
3. Consider whether it will be possible to expand the facility in the near future. Will the property, the local codes and your finances make expansion feasible? Is any adjacent property available? When considering expansion, remember that the zoning ordinances may have parking requirements for the additional staff; this is particularly a factor with labor-intensive infant and toddler care.

Outside Areas

An attractive exterior is a terrific advertisement to area employees and passersby who need child care or are considering a change in their current care arrangements. Playgrounds especially should be as visible as possible with brightly colored, attractive equipment. At the same time, for safety's sake, make sure this area is also well fenced. Additional suggestions for designing and equipping outside areas can be found in Chapter 5 and in the individual program chapters in Part Two.

Outside there should be flowers wherever possible, even flower boxes at the windows or large tubs with nonpoisonous plants. (See Appendix C: Safety–for a list of poisonous plants to avoid.)

To make a good first impression, access to the center should be clearly marked, and the center's sign should be clearly visible from *both* traffic directions. Be very careful about access ways to the center, and make the exits and entrances onto the main thoroughfare as easy and safe as possible. Try to provide adequate parking for staff AND parents, even though local planning laws will probably dictate the amount of parking spaces.

Atmosphere

A common challenge in child care center design is creating a warm atmosphere that alleviates the institutional feeling. Begin by using soft, indirect light wherever possible. Install soft, curving surfaces and noninstitutional equipment and decorations. For example, one area might be divided by a curved wall covered with burlap on one side to create a bulletin board and with carpeting on the other, which can double as a large flannel board surface. Hang curtains with bright patterns wherever possible to add a "homey" touch. Find unexpected small places to put interesting textures and colors. One center uses a yard of bright, patterned material to cover various surfaces, particularly those that get dirty easily, such as the wall behind the wastebasket. You can use theme-oriented materials and change them throughout the year. Then simply wash and store for next year! A pretty scalloped paper border such as those found in the teacher-parent stores adds a nice touch as well. Remember, using fabric or carpeting anywhere in a room will help the acoustics by absorbing noise.

A good general rule is to keep the setting informal without sacrificing a professional, organized atmosphere.

SPECIAL CONSIDERATIONS

Taking Over an Existing Child Care Center

Initially, the most important concern in purchasing an existing center has little to do with the physical plant itself: why is the present owner selling? Is there a problem with the market in this area? Has there been a serious charge against the existing facility that will adversely affect the business's reputation, even under new management?

As far as the physical plant is concerned, issues to investigate are:

1. Does the building have a serious fault that you will have to repair at great cost in order to bring it up to code?
2. Is the facility structurally sound? Is the septic system failing?
3. Do new fire codes require a sprinkler system? If the water system is dependent on a well, a sprinkler system can be installed only after placing a large holding tank in the ground to supplement the well, with an installation cost of as much as $100,000.
4. Might the current approvals be subject to change if a new owner takes over? For example, one owner purchased a facility licensed for 25 children, but three days after they moved in the state ruled that the facility was large enough for only 16 children! The previous measurements had been made on the *exterior* of the building and included hallways, bathrooms, a stairwell and other unusable space; the new regulations considered only the interior, usable child space. Also the previous regulations had allowed 30 square feet per child, whereas the new regulations required 35 square feet per child.
5. What is the status of zoning regulations in the community? The center you are considering may have been approved in a certain area but only with stringent zoning restrictions. In one case, a buyer found that a new approval was required to have children below the age of three or to operate outside of the hours of 7:30 A.M. to 5:30 P.M. This new owner had intended to have primarily infants and toddlers and to extend the hours of operation of the center. In this case, the owner took legal recourse, which required professional representation and considerable anguish and ex-

pense. Eventually, the zoning was changed and the center prospered. However, it is much easier and less costly to look for possible restrictions before the purchase is agreed upon. Even with restrictions, an existing center may still be an attractive prospect, but remember that you can use these restrictions as bargaining points to lower the purchase or rental price.

Converting an Existing Structure

If your market analysis and site selection research point to an existing building or space, the most difficult task will be making the facility comfortable for child care and renovating it at a reasonable cost. Rarely is an existing structure ideal for a child care center, and the degree of renovation required to create a quality setting will vary greatly. Of course, the precautions regarding renovations, local approvals and professional advice discussed above apply here as well.

As with the takeover of an existing center, you'll need to make a floor plan designating spaces for the children's use, for storage, the office, etc. Pay particular attention to the location of the sinks and toilets and the kitchen, if any, as converting these areas to meet requirements can be very costly. You will have to determine how the space will be divided and who will pay for the renovation costs. If you are leasing the space, the owner should pay for any permanent renovations to the facility. Technically, the same should be true for the fencing of the outdoor space and upgrading of the playground area; however, experience has shown that the cost of creating and securing the playground area generally falls to the child care operator.

New Construction

If one of your options is to build on a new site, choose the prime areas targeted by your market analysis and try to make projections about it in terms of the factors discussed in Chapter 1: location, size, enrollment, type, potential, fee structure and reputation. Use the square footage guidelines discussed earlier or those required by your regulating agency to plan for an average size child care center.

When you are considering construction of a new facility, you will undoubtedly need to hire design professionals. Even if the architects have had experience with child care centers, they need to be open to your ideas in order to make your center compatible with your child care philosophy. When designers don't have experience with child care facilities, frivolous and costly features that all too often are useless to the children can appear in the plans. For example, designers will often plan a large, spacious entrance area, which, though attractive, can increase the square footage rental fees by as much as $1,000 a month. This is excessive for space that you cannot use for the children.

Quality design should be simple and make the use of space as flexible as possible; in other words, the operator should be able to change the purpose of the space readily if the initial use proves impractical. For example, a new center was designed for 90 children with two infant rooms of eight children each, two toddler rooms of 12 children each, two preschool rooms of 20 each and a private kindergarten room of 10 children. Within the first six weeks the infant and toddler rooms were full with a large waiting list, but there was only one child for the kindergarten program and the preschool programs were only half full. The layout was such that one small infant room could become a preschool room, and the vacated preschool room could be divided into two additional infant areas; the same thing was done for the toddler area. The private kindergarten became a "transition" classroom for older four-year-olds. The center filled up quickly and is considering expansion.

Another large, new center had an 1,800-square-foot indoor gym that was intended as an area for children to run and play in during the winter months. However, the center filled its large licensed capacity within six months of opening and decided to renovate the gym area for additional classrooms.

A relatively recent concept in new child care center construction is that of the modular structure. A modular structure uses a form of construction in which the structure can be designed in smaller units and built complete at a factory. The "modules" are then transported to the construction site and joined together. This form of construction is gaining in popularity for several reasons. First, several companies have already done extensive research into the best basic designs that will accommodate child care. Second, the operator can start with a small- to medium-sized center and expand as financial conditions and management experience allow. Third, the cost is usually much lower overall. Fourth, the contractor generally agrees to obtain all local building and fire permits and may assist with zoning approvals as well. Finally, the construction is "turnkey"—the interior comes complete with carpeting, fixtures, heating, air conditioning, plumbing, etc.,—everything except the furniture, equipment and materials for the program. As designs improve, this construction may well become the predominant type in the child care industry, particularly where the number of existing buildings that could be converted to child care facilities is limited and/or where construction costs for new structures are high.

In new construction, you have the opportunity to plan an innovative playground as an integral component of the building's design. Several new centers have designed atriums and courtyard playgrounds as alternative outdoor play areas, and these are gaining in popularity in many areas of the country. In congested, industrial areas these may be the only feasible playground alternatives and may greatly ease the security burden for the staff. Indoor areas are also weatherproof and, particularly in urban areas, can enhance security for infant playgrounds.

To insure the success of a well-located center, keep these considerations in mind as you make your final site selections and plan the design of your facility.

- Review all aspects, including the business plan, with the appropriate professionals. (See Chapters 3 and 4.)
- Be sure to obtain several estimates for any renovations (or new construction) and then add on a minimum of 25% to cover cost overruns.
- Insist on contingencies being written into all contracts concerning building, zoning, fire and local and state health approvals to further protect yourself.
- Make sure that you are able to cancel the lease in the event that state or local government approvals are not obtained.

3
WRITING A BUSINESS PLAN AND OBTAINING FINANCING

• •

One of the first decisions you must make as you set up your child care center is which type of business structure will best fulfill the legal and accounting needs of your business. Then comes the crucial process of writing a business plan, which you will need to obtain your initial financing. Financing your business can be difficult and tedious; in order to reduce the amount of wasted time and to avoid rejection, you must clarify your objectives, determine the amount of control that you are willing to give up and have the right resources at your fingertips. An effective business plan will also be your short- and long-term guide to business success. Needless to say, this type of planning requires professional legal and accounting services.

BUSINESS STRUCTURES

There are four basic ways to structure a business, and your choice will be governed by the short- and long-term goals of the business, an evaluation of your risk exposure and tax considerations. The four structures are:

Sole Proprietorship
Partnership
S Corporation
Corporation

The number of investors or people involved may dictate the format to some extent. For example, in a sole proprietorship, "sole" means only one owner, but that owner can have several employees. This is the easiest and least costly way to set up a business. The sole proprietor is entitled to all profits, but must also take full and personal responsibility for all business risks, losses and liabilities.

A partnership is an association of two or more persons for the purpose of conducting a business-for-profit as co-owners. A partnership can be created by either a formal agreement or an oral understanding and in certain cases can be implied by the conduct and acts of the persons involved. It is always advisable to have formal written agreements wherever possible when entering into a partnership, and any contracts with key employees should be written clearly so as not to imply partnership, i.e., ownership, if this is not intended.

There are two types of partnerships, general and limited. In a general partnership the partners have unlimited liability. Partners also share in all profits and losses equally or at some agreed percentage. The losses can flow through to the personal assets of the partners, and to this extent, the liability is also unlimited. General partnerships can be risky in that each partner is legally liable for the other's actions, and any individual assets contributed to the partnership become the property of the business.

In a limited partnership, the liability of the partners is limited to the extent of their capital contributions. Each limited partnership must have a managing partner, which can be a person or a corporate entity. Limited partnerships are primarily used for investment purposes and should not be used for on-going participation on a day-to-day basis.

A corporate structure is the most secure foundation for a business, because the corporation exists as an entity separate from the individual. In effect, the owner becomes an employee of the corporation, and the corporation alone is responsible for its liabilities. Initially, this may not seem necessary, but as a child care business grows and becomes successful, the shield from potential liability becomes increasingly important.

The corporate structure can be a financial disadvantage, as there may be double taxation: the corporation pays taxes on its net income, and the individual pays taxes on any profits received from the corporation as well as income. Also, in the early stages it may be better to have any losses flow through directly to the individual's tax return. However, business owners generally increase their own salaries in order to decrease the net profit of the corporation and avoid double taxation.

The double taxation issue is eliminated in some states with the use of an S Corporation. Subchapter S allows the losses or profits to flow through directly to the individual shareholders. Thus the problem of losing the initial business loss as a deduction on an individual tax return is eliminated. However, any profits also flow through as part of the individual shareholders' gross income but are taxed at an individual (as opposed to a corporate) tax rate, which is usually lower. Some states and cities that recognize S status may tax these businesses at that level. But partnerships are also often subject to local unincorporated business tax. As with a regular corporation, the S Corporation acts as a liability shield for the assets of the individual shareholders.

No matter what type of structure you decide on, it is vital that it be set up by professionals. Agreement among the investors is also critical—especially in dealing with issues such as death, disability or an investor leaving.

WRITING A BUSINESS PLAN

Once you've determined the structure your business will take, the next step is to prepare your business plan. The process of creating a business plan will force you to take a realistic and unemotional look at how feasible your proposed business is. The plan will also be the primary tool for obtaining financing, and you must thoroughly understand it in order to be able to "sell" a prospective investor. This is one project where a professional consultant may add the finishing touches but you must lay the foundation. A sample of a complete business plan is provided later in this chapter.

The basic outline for a business plan is as follows:

Executive Summary
Business History
The Market
Delivery of Service
Financial Projections
Management

Executive Summary

The executive summary should provide a clear, concise overview of your business's objectives without addressing financial issues. The purpose of this section is to give the financial institution enough of an introduction so that they know whether to even consider your proposal. For example, for what type of community do you intend to provide child care? Are you reaching out to a larger community with your long-term goals? Is this center the first in a chain? Is the center going to remain the same size, or do you have expansion plans for the same site? In the introductory section, be clear about exactly what you want to do with your business. Include a description of the legal structure of the operation. Then explicitly state the amount and purpose of the loan being requested (you may have to leave this blank until you have completed the entire business plan), the repayment schedule and the collateral, if any, that you are going to offer. You may want to list estimated costs for any equipment or property that you plan to purchase.

Business History

Here you will explain the previous background of the business. If you are purchasing an existing child care center, you will need to give the number of years of operation, an analysis of its reputation, licensed capacity, a description of the community served, details of any additions to the physical structure or major renovations and the number of clients served. On the other hand, if you are starting a new business, you should give any relevant personal business history, such as whether you began as a home family day care business or a baby-sitting service, or whether your center is an outgrowth of a parent cooperative preschool. Give whatever information is necessary to convince the lending institution that this business—even if it was conducted on an informal basis—has a good track record.

Provide an accurate description of the location of the proposed child care center, with maps and floor plans where appropriate; all drawings and maps should be clear and look professional.

The Market

Next, summarize the findings of your market analysis, including a synopsis of the competition. Stress the price range, total capacity for each age group and occupancy rate of each competing center. Relate the totals in each age group with the projected needs for child care in the community. Include what segment of the market you are targeting and explain your plan for getting the edge over your competition. You will certainly want to mention the relative strength of your competition and suggest where new centers may locate in the area. Be sure to emphasize the potential for growth. For example, if you are purchasing an existing center that is licensed for 35 children, explain how it may be enlarged to accommodate another 35.

Be sure to include the demographics of the community and a brief description of the working population and their needs. Refer to outside sources often. For example, lending institutions are often impressed by the use of demographics and by analysis of the preschool population in the area.

In the conclusion of this section, show how your competition is not currently able to meet the community's needs and how your program will fill the gap.

Delivery of Service

Next, show how you will deliver child care service better than anyone else. This is the appropriate place to mention that your program will be top quality, but the main emphasis should be on pricing and location. Many surveys have shown that parents are most concerned with whether the price is reasonable and whether the location is convenient. The quality of the program is usually a lower priority.

However, emphasize whatever factors you have found to be important to the community. If, for example, your analysis has shown that many parents are eager for a private kindergarten, then this would be an important factor to mention. In some communities, the hours of operation are a major issue, especially where there are companies with several shifts, and if relevant to your plans, this should also be stressed in the section.

You do not need to elaborate on your plans for the curriculum. Remember, a business plan is for a financially, not educationally, oriented audience. To the extent, however, that this is an overview of your business and how it will operate, mention what ages will be served and that the program will be new and innovative.

Consider inserting the financial statements from the current owner here, or include them later with the financial documentation. In addition, if there is reason to believe that the business has been poorly run, say so without demeaning the current owner; the business community, particularly in smaller towns, is usually very tight.

You must convince your reader that your center will outshine all others and serve a segment of the market currently not being served.

Financial Projections

Financial projections should consist of projected profit-and-loss statements for the first three years—that is, a summary of your center's projected income and expenses. Explain that in a properly run center, the break-even point is often reached within two to three months. This will justify your preparing monthly profit-and-loss statements for the first year and quarterly statements for the next two years. A projected profit-and-loss statement is only your best guess as to the course your business will take; it is in no way a guarantee. To convince the financial community, you must make plausible predictions; lenders want to have a clear idea of how valid your projections are before they decide on a loan.

Simply put, a profit-and-loss statement, Table 3-1, shows what your gross revenue will be over the course of a given period, less your expenses. The lending institution will want to see the repayment on the money that they are lending you as part of the expenses.

There are several ways to estimate your gross. For the purpose of preparing the financial statement, use the direct calculation method described below assuming a 90% occupancy. The easiest way to estimate annual gross income is to multiply the number of children you can have at any given time by the number of hours per week by your hourly rate (if you are charging hourly), or the number of days in the week by your daily rate (if you are charging daily) or by the amount per week (if you are charging weekly), and then multiply the result by the 52 weeks in the year.

Since you will rarely exceed 90% of the estimated gross income due to absenteeism and turnover, you should use only 90% of the full annual total in your projections. In Chapter 8 there is a thorough discussion of how to estimate your gross income based on a flexible program—the quickest way to make money in child care.

Next, calculate your start-up costs. First, decide how much financing you will require to cover start-up costs and expenses

TABLE 3-1 STATEMENT OF REVENUES AND EXPENSES
(Sample P and L)

	Actual 1991	Forecast 1992	1993
Revenues			
Fees	$434,000	$520,000	$690,000
Expenses			
Rent	18,000	19,260	20,610
Heat & Electric	1,200	1,350	1,500
Supplies/Consumables	13,500	14,300	15,700
Maintenance	4,700	5,000	5,500
Advertising	2,500	2,700	2,200
Training	2,800	3,500	4,800
Snacks	12,200	12,900	13,700
Field Trips	750	1,200	2,100
Telephone	3,000	3,800	4,200
Office Supplies	2,500	2,750	3,000
Legal/Accounting	2,500	3,000	3,500
Insurance	3,800	4,200	4,600
Workman's Compensation	2,600	3,500	4,200
Payroll	202,000	260,000	335,000
Benefits (with taxes)	40,400	52,000	67,000
Contingency Fund	5,000	6,000	7,000
Total Expenses	317,450	395,460	494,610
NET INCOME	116,550	124,540	195,390

during the initial phase of the operation. The start-up expenses should be determined fairly accurately. Table 3-2 illustrates the ranges that you can expect on the various costs. These ranges have been calculated assuming a center of licensed capacity ranging from 30 to 90 children. The amounts are only guidelines to be used in your estimates.

Most businesses have a longer start-up period (six months to three years). However, the demand for child care services generally is so great that you can expect to reach break-even in a shorter period of time, and a flexible program will decrease the time needed even further. As a precaution, your accountant may advise you to have a six-month payout or cushion.

Then determine your operating costs. Divide the operating expenses into two categories: *Fixed Expenses*—those that are inevitable and are always essential to the program; and *Variable Expenses*—those that depend on the type of program that you are

TABLE 3-2   START-UP COSTS FOR TWO DIFFERENT SIZED CHILD CARE CENTERS

Capacity	30	90
Deposits on utilities/phone	$ 150	$ 450
Initial payments on mortgages, loans for renovation or rent (3 months)	1,000	5,000
Equipment	12,000	25,000+
Initial supplies	100	500
Attorney/accountant/consultant fees	500	5,000
Advertising, signs, brochures	250	1,000
Payroll (3 months)	10,000	20,000+
Owner/operator salary (3 months)	5,000	15,000
Insurance	900	3,000
TOTAL	$29,900	$74,950

TABLE 3-3   SAMPLE START-UP BUDGET

The sample is for the infant/toddler portion of a center (48 Infant/toddler slots). Assumed that it takes six weeks to reach the break-even point.

Salaries (6 weeks @ $3,840)	$23,040
Benefits @ 20%	4,608
Administration	5,600
Insurance	320
Legal	1,300
Diapers/Wipes	900
Snacks	840
Computer (portion of)	1,400
Advertising (one time)	1,500
Equipment/Renovation	14,400
TOTAL	$53,908

running or the ages that you are serving. For example, diapers, where supplied, are not a fixed expense; they vary with the number of infants and young toddlers enrolled.

Table 3-4 is a list of the line items to include on a schedule of fixed and variable expenses:

TABLE 3-4   OPERATING COSTS FOR A CHILD CARE CENTER

Fixed Expenses

Salaries and Benefits*
Mortgage/Rent
Taxes
Insurance
Loan Repayments
Utilities
Telephone
Maintenance

Variable Expenses

Advertising
Classroom Supplies
Snacks/Food
Diapers
Games
Transportation
Field Trips
Subscriptions
Workshops

*These may be variable, depending on arrangements with your employees.

Although many organizations are trying to compile cost estimates for generic child care centers on a regional basis, particularly for the fixed expenses, these figures are not yet available. Costs will also vary in different geographic areas; for example, some centers need more air conditioning in the summer and others more heat in the winter, which would vary the utility cost estimates. You need to carefully estimate the costs for your particular circumstances.

Insurance rates have varied greatly in recent years but appear to be stabilizing again. In the late 1980s, a child care center serving 30 children could expect to pay $5,000 per year for liability insurance; however, that figure has come down as of 1992 to between $1,200 and $1,500 a year. It seems the insurance industry is being more realistic in its risk assessment of the child care business. This is an area where it pays to shop around and make sure the quoted prices are in line with current rates.

In many cases, your lending institution will not be looking for a detailed profit-and-loss statement. Instead they will want a very concise overview of the projections. Of course, you should be prepared to answer questions on specific expenses when you meet with them. You need to know when you expect your business to reach the break-even point, i.e., when your income covers your operating expenses so that any additional income brings a profit. For your own assessment, you may find it helpful to know the cost of each classroom and at what point the individual classroom will turn a profit.

In presenting your projections, you should be aware of what is considered a realistic profit margin or bottom line for the child care industry. The estimates for the traditional full-day, minimal flexibility child care programs are 8% to 10% of gross after the first two to three years. With a highly flexible child care center utilizing 90% of the operating hours at 90% capacity, you can expect between 28% and 35% of the gross during the first year! It is not unusual with the latter to reach break-even in as little as six weeks.

When you calculate your projections, you will soon recognize that with a flexible program you need minimal cash reserves. However, to be safe it is best to have sufficient cash in your start-up budget to cover the first three month's expenses.

Finally, if you are applying for a loan, you will need a financial document that describes the collateral you are going to offer. This probably will be a statement of the financial viability of both partners or the individual owners. In a tight economy, the lending institution will usually request a personal asset such as stock or a home or a personal guarantee as collateral if the borrower is a corporation. The statement should include the profit-and-loss statement of any existing business and individual and business tax information for the previous one to three years. Different lending institutions have different requirements, however, so at the very least, have your accountant prepare a balance sheet.

Management

This section should provide background information on any owners, key employees or consultants who will be involved in managing the business. Some people provide both personal and business summaries while others give business information only. In your summaries, emphasize why you (as an individual or as a group) would be a good risk to any lending institution and what expertise each partner, director or consultant can contribute.

In a partnership, particularly, demonstrating that your joining of forces is compatible and complementary can lend more credibility to the business plan when you present it to a lending institution. At this point it may be helpful to sit down with your partner(s) (and managers as well) to really assess each other's strengths and weaknesses. In order to avoid a major confrontation later that could even cause the business to fail, establish an honest, realistic view of your partnership right from the planning stages. Chapter 17 contains an exercise on making a partnership work in the "A Potential Parting of a Partnership" section.

If you plan to hire a director to run the center, be sure to include an accurate description of his or her education and experience.

And who are you going to hire for those areas in which you collectively have less experience? Ask the consultants you plan to use for permission to include a description of their backgrounds and the services they will be providing.

Most lending institutions are aware that child care industry entrepreneurs are often strong in the teaching and interpersonal relations areas but weaker in management and business skills. For this reason, be sure to point out that there is a competent management team or consultant on board.

Final Preparation

Once your complete plan is drafted, have your advisors review it and provide their input, especially concerning any portions that should be deleted.

Make the final printed version very professional. Get a dark cover, preferably black, from a stationery store and put your logo, business address and phone number on it. Include a list of the principals who own the business on the cover and on the cover page inside. After the title page, start with your Executive Summary followed by a Table of Contents, the Business History, the Market, Delivery of Service, Financial Projections and finally the section on Management. Bank loan officers receive many, many business plans each month and are more likely to look favorably at the ones that are well prepared, highly professional and brief.

Remember that the plan is also a tool that you will use from time to time to gauge your business's success and find ways to strengthen and improve your operation.

Here's an example of a plan for a center.

PROPOSED CHILD CARE CENTER
UNITED METHODIST CHURCH
65 MAIN STREET
BURLINGTON, IDAHO

Executive Summary

The business plan has been developed to present a profile of the proposed child care center at the United Methodist Church to possible investors and to seek immediate funding for such. The principals involved are highly qualified and bring a desirable mix of child care knowledge and business expertise to the venture.

The purpose of establishing the facility is to create high-quality child care services for the children of the community while still operating a profitable business. The goal is to have the lower portion of the facility operational and licensed by the first of September with the completion of the upper portion by October first. The facility is conveniently located. With affordable pricing and flexible hours available, the center will quickly reach capacity and should break even in the first three months even with the projected construction delay on the upper level.

The long-term goals for the facility include remodeling additional space and building a small addition for the infant and toddler section. It is projected that the country setting and ideal location will make this a model child care facility that will be profitable and meet the needs of the community's young families.

History

The proposed child care center would be located in space owned by the United Methodist Church at 65 Main Street. The facility consists of just under 2,000 square feet of classroom space with extra space for office areas, kitchen and storage.

The church restored the proposed area in the early 1950s. Beginning in 1961, a portion of the space was used for a nursery school operated directly by the members of the church.

However, by the early 1980s the enrollment of the nursery school was not sufficient to augment the church's income. Driven by both this need and the desire to assist in providing a needed service to the community, the Board of Trustees of the church contacted Jane Smith with regard to finding an entity to establish a child care center at the church. Ms. Smith contributed her consulting services and explained the pros and cons of shared space, outlining what the church's guidelines should be in establishing a center and selecting the owner for the business. In the process she suggested five possible tenants and the church decided to rent to the Nest.

Thus the Nest began in 1981 and has operated until today. In its initial years, the center was highly successful and had, at one point, over 100 children a week using the facility. However, over the course of the years, there have been financial problems and management difficulties at the center. In 1989, the facility was sold to a parent using the services; however, this past January the previous owner was forced to take it back because of financial difficulties. The owner has just given the parents notice that the facility will close on April 30th of this year.

The Facility

The physical facility is located in southern Burlington at the intersection of major commuters' routes to business to the south in Burlington and to the northern areas from the greater Burlington area. The location is only two miles from General Feed and Grain, IBM and the expanding west side of Burlington. And the Spud City Mall is located 1.5 miles from the facility, which is convenient for seasonal employees and shoppers.

Aside from the commuter and business clients, there are also many young families located in the area who are in need of supplementary care for their children. Also, as the center will have a flexible schedule, there are at least 15 clients from Little Leprechauns Nursery School (owned by Jane Smith) who will be using the facility on a regular basis and will be taken by van to the facility before and after the preschool sessions.

The buildings and grounds are lovely and have easy access from all directions. In the past many parents have chosen to use the facility not only because of the price and location (the two major factors at present in selecting a child care center) but also due to the beautiful country setting.

Although the building is in disrepair and needs work, the setting is exceptional for children and very convenient for a large number of parents. It should be noted that the repairs are primarily cosmetic in nature, and it should be possible to complete these repairs and the redecorating in a relatively short period of time. The plan would be to complete the lower portion of the facility by September 1st and use this space for the existing children, with the upper area completed in the following two weeks.

The Market

On a national basis, the increasing number of women in the work force, the high divorce rate and the disappearance of the extended family are trends that have created a high demand for child care.

Several studies, including *Child Care in Idaho* and the United Way's Needs assessment, have determined that these trends are mirrored in the Burlington area and that the demand for high-quality, affordable child care greatly exceeds the available supply.

There are approximately 2,200 children under the age of 10 in Burlington for whom child care is needed. (Sources: Idaho State Department of Education, United Way Needs Assessment and *Child Care in Idaho*.) Currently, there are only four full-time day care centers with a total capacity of 193 children. Also, there are 22 licensed family day care homes with a maximum total capacity of 198. The difference, approximately 1,800 children, are cared for either in unlicensed homes, in their home by a nanny/au pair, in another town or they take care of themselves (latchkey children). Several part-time programs, such as nursery schools, are available, but they do not meet the needs of the vast majority of working mothers. **We have taken the conservative estimate that we only need to capture 8% of the available demand to generate the economics presented in this business plan.** We have also not included the certain customer potential from nearby Red Eye County. The following chart provides information on the existing child care options in Burlington [Refer to Table 1-1 in Chapter 1.].

Principals

The partners who will own and operate the business are Jane Smith and Kitty Haas. For practical purposes, Ms. Smith will be administrator and Ms. Haas will be the site director.

Jane Smith is known locally for providing fine preschool programs in the community for the past 18 years. During this time she has owned and operated two nursery schools and has been instrumental through her consulting in establishing several other child care centers. During the past 10 years, she has been an active advocate for children and has served in many state offices in professional early childhood organizations. Most recently she has been writing management articles for a child care magazine and has begun to lecture on management of child care centers. Ms. Smith's resume is enclosed.

Kitty Haas has been actively involved in child care services for the past 12 years. She has several years of direct management experience and during one full year successfully installed a flexible program in the center she was directing, increasing the center's annual bottom line by $125,000. For the past year she has been assisting at Child Care Management Systems and consulting for existing services that are in financial trouble and are adding a flexible program.

Financials

The initial proposal for licensure is for a facility for 52 children ages one month through five years. The financial projections will be based on these ages and numbers. However, it should be noted that within the first year we plan to add space for an additional 30 children and plan to expand the infant capacity by another 40 spaces within the first three years.

The income calculations for the center based on the licensed capacity of 52 are:

Fees:

Age Group	Weekly	10–33 Hrs	≤10 Hrs
Infant/Toddler	$150	4.50	5.50
Preschool	125	3.75	4.25

Revenues:
Infant/Toddler:

28 slots @ $150/week x 60%	= $2,520
28 slots × 30% × 11 hrs × $4.50 × 5 days	= 2,079
28 slots × 10% × 11 hrs × $5.50 × 5 days	= 847
	$5,446

Preschool:

24 slots @ $125/week × 60%	= $1,800
24 slots × 30% × 11 hrs × $3.75 × 5 days	= 1,485
24 slots × 10% × 11 hrs × $4.25 × 5 days	= 561
	$3,846

TOTAL ESTIMATED REVENUE PER WEEK:	$9,292
Assume 90% occupancy:	8,360
ESTIMATED ANNUAL REVENUES:	$434,720

The center should reach break-even by the eighth week of operation and will aim to realize a profit margin of no less than 20% (we usually see a 28% to 35% margin). In the projections we would expect the following based on the above calculations:

Year One	$434,720
Year Two	685,520
Year Three	1,019,920

Expenses:
The primary expense in a child care center is the staff as this is a very labor-intensive business. Thus, the staff salaries are calculated as follows:

	Weekly
9 Staff @ $8/hr average	$2,880
2 Head Teachers @ $10/hr	800
1 Director @ $25,000/yr	480
Bookkeeper/Secretary (part time)	160
Weekly Total	$4,320

Item	Yearly
Salaries	$224,640
Benefits @ 20%	44,298
Rent	16,750
Heat and Electricity	1,200
Insurance	2,400
Maintenance	4,780
Legal/Accounting	2,500
Supplies/Consumables	13,520
Loan @ 3 years	19,932
Meals/Snacks (lunch provided)	12,200
Diapers/Wipes	6,240
Training/Development	1,500
Telephone	3,000
Office Supplies	2,500
Advertising	4,200
ANNUAL TOTAL	$359,660
NET	75,060

The above figures are based on a capacity of 51 children; however, the projected license will now be for 60, thus increasing the financial projections. It should be noted that the salaries and benefits are above the industry average of 45% and that extra has been added in several areas as a cushion.

Conclusion

The expertise required is available to run a child care facility at the location on a cost-effective basis. The profit margins in child care go up exponentially with the increase in licensed capacity. Thus, an initial goal would be to establish the existing center and expand and promote the program as rapidly as possible.

Past experience indicates that the center should reach breakeven within six to eight weeks. The marketing strategy will be aggressive and there is already, without formal notice being given, a considerable waiting list.

OBTAINING FINANCING

Once you have a completed business plan and have lined up the needed experts, it is time to find financing for your child care center. This step is critical for your business's success both during start-up and for long-term planning. With an accurate assessment of your financial requirements in the business plan, you are ready to approach potential funding sources. The business plan should reflect a certain amount of equity invested, as well as money borrowed along with assumed interest payments. You may be pleasantly surprised to find that financing is readily available since child care is becoming a major industry and an attractive investment.

What are the methods used to raise capital, that is, to get the money you need to start your business and keep it going? There are two types of financing—equity or debt—and usually a combination of the two is the best option. Equity is an ownership interest subject to the risks of the business and is generally not repaid. Debt must be repaid.

Simply put, you can attempt to find others to raise the capital for you or you can try to raise it yourself. Depending on which course you take, there are certain rules that come into play. If you obtain the majority of your capital from one large investor, you probably will end up with a much smaller interest in your company. On the other hand, if you attempt to raise the money yourself from your own acquaintances or your own resources, you will usually be able to retain a much larger portion of your business.

To raise money you must carefully assess the proposed value of your business, determine how much capital you are going to need, in what increments and over what period. Then you have to decide if your source should be a small investor, private resources (including your own), private placement of securities with friends or relatives, private placement through a securities firm or a public offering for a larger center either through a firm or self-issuer. This last option is least likely since a minimum of $2 million is required.

For any of these you must first have a business plan, and once you have chosen a course of action according to your particular financial needs, you must follow it tenaciously. If your plan has merit, you must be willing to back it to the fullest.

Personal Resources

Your own money is the very best source of financing when starting your own business. It is, of course, the most readily available form of capital to acquire. There is no interest to pay back unless you take out a personal loan, and you don't have to surrender any of the equity in your business. However, you may find that the total investment required is beyond your own personal finances. If this is the case, there are several other methods you can use to raise capital.

Debt Financing

Friends and relatives Next to your own money, friends' and relatives' finances may be the next best sources. However, you must treat these as true loans and have proper agreements drawn up professionally. Signing loan papers actually protects both parties; it obligates you to pay back the money, and it prevents their obtaining an equity interest in your business unless that is part of the written agreement.

Banks Banks are the most obvious source of debt financing. Establishing a good relationship with a banker is detailed in Chapter 4. Although banks may appear to be the best source, they are notoriously conservative, so to satisfy them you have to present an excellent business plan and demonstrate that you are going to be successful in a viable business.

Almost all banks will require some sort of collateral as security for the loan. Collateral may range from real property or assets on a long-term, larger loan, to a savings account or a life insurance policy on a smaller, short-term loan.

A bank may also require a signature, or personal, guarantee; if your credit is very good, you can usually borrow several thousand dollars with no collateral. These loans are usually short term with high interest rates. There are also commercial loans, which offer lower interest rates, but are relatively difficult to get if the economy is tight, because most banks are unwilling to take the risk of investing in a new venture. However, child care is one of the least risky business ventures and banks do recognize this.

If you demonstrate your expertise, banks will generally approve a loan. If you own real estate, you can usually use it as collateral to secure a loan of up to 75% of your property's value. Again, in a poor economy this percentage may be less, but the loan may be extended to either 20 or 30 years.

If you have an existing business, you may be able to get a loan using your equipment, your accounts receivable or your inventory as collateral. The bank will usually give you 40% to 50% of the total value of the inventory and equipment. Loans can be secured for up to 80% on the accounts receivable, depending on the business climate and the bank's assessment of your ability to collect the monies.

Small Business Administration Loans The United States government's Small Business Administration finances small businesses. This financing is very difficult, but not impossible, to get. The SBA is allowed to make or guarantee a loan to a small business only if the business is unable to obtain financing from two other conventional sources, such as banks. Proof of your inability must be provided to the SBA with your application for SBA financing. You must also show that you are seeking financing for an independently owned and operated business. Your venture cannot be part of another firm or financial enterprise. SBA loans are for small businesses only. Another important part of your application is a demonstration that your business has the ability to compete and succeed in the child care field.

The maximum you can borrow from the SBA is $550,000. The interest rate on the loan will be based on the cost of the money to the government at the time, and this varies. The term of the loan is usually between two and 25 years, but the majority run 10 years. Collateral for an SBA loan is required, and you can use land or buildings, machinery, equipment or the personal guarantee of a third party. The guarantor must be a friend or relative who is willing to repay the loan if you default.

Credit Cards An innovative way to obtain start-up capital without having to deal with loan applications is to use your credit cards. Although you will probably be charged a very high interest rate, you can obtain several thousand dollars immediately (much more quickly than you would if you went to a bank and had to wait several weeks for a reply) as long as you don't go above your specified credit limits. For example, one child care center operator had two credit cards each with a credit line of $5,000. Having already obtained a rental location, she needed approximately $10,000 for equipment. Because her business had no track record upon which a bank could judge her viability, she used her credit cards to get the full amount and buy the equipment she needed. She felt certain she would be able to reach break-even very quickly, and she had another source of funding for her other start-up expenses—payroll, utilities, etc. Setting up the business and reaching break-even after six weeks, she applied for and received a loan for a three-year period for about 10% interest from the bank. With the $10,000 from the bank, she paid off the credit card balances, which were carried at a very high annual percentage rate. After another six months she was able to pay off the bank loan.

Finance/Mortgage Companies   Finance/mortgage companies will accept more risk on a loan than do banks, but they also charge a higher interest rate. They are generally more interested in your track record in business, no matter what your field of expertise. Although they will be very concerned with the potential of your new business, they do not look quite as intently at the strength of your credit. Keep in mind that there are severe consequences if you miss your payments; they have been known to repossess businesses relatively quickly.

Equity Financing

Sometimes in order to get capital you have to give up a portion of your business to investors who may or may not participate in the operation of the business itself. There are no loans involved. Equity investors become partners in a partnership or shareholders in a corporation. In this case the investor gets a percentage of the business with the associated profits and losses. Friends and relatives are the most likely source for this type of financing.

In some cases this seems like the best route to raise capital, but there can be drawbacks. First, you give up a portion of your business (including its future growth) and probably a certain amount of control. Also, you are going to have to share your profits with your partners until such time, if ever, as you can buy them out. Legal advice is essential when obtaining this type of funding for your business. The amount of equity that you must relinquish is negotiable, depending on the amount of money sought, your leverage and your relationship with the investor. The equity is negotiable particularly in the child care field right now, because so many people want to get in on this rapidly growing industry.

Venture Capital   If your company is not going to reach the $10-, $20- or $30-million range in a relatively short period of time, you may not be able to attract the interest of venture capitalists, because they don't generally invest in small businesses. There are some small venture firms that may be interested in financing new child care centers even if the gross prospects are not that high, provided they feel such centers could be a model to develop further. If you are willing to give the venture capitalist a substantial piece of the action and you are prepared to accept this person as a partner, you might be a candidate for venture capitalist financing.

Obtaining start-up money from venture capitalists is probably the most risky avenue to take and possibly the most detrimental to your business; however, it may be the only avenue open to you. Not only are venture capitalists beginning to see that child care is a viable industry, but they also are more likely to invest in a relatively new field that, although risky, has a successful track record and the potential for a relatively high profit and growth. To protect yourself when entering into venture capital negotiations, of course, you must have a reliable, competent lawyer. Also, be aware of how venture capitalists work; they expect two things from the companies they finance—high returns and an easy way out that could leave you holding everything. Only a small percentage of the companies that they back will succeed, so they have to make sure that each deal they make has potential for a five- to tenfold return on their initial investment. This could mean they will want to own anywhere from 40% to 70% of your company. Each situation varies, and the amount of equity the venture capitalist holds will depend on your business's stage of development. It will also depend on the risk that the venture capitalist perceives, and the amount of capital required.

Suppliers

When you are first starting a business, suppliers usually won't extend credit and will generally work only on a COD basis. However, you may be able to get on a credit basis with your equipment suppliers by showing them a proper business plan or by making and paying for one large initial purchase. Your child care consultant may also have a relationship with a supplier that could work to your advantage. It depends in large part on how the distributors and manufacturers are faring at the time of the year in which you approach them. Their sales will generally be high just before school starts or just after the beginning of the school year and then drop off; they tend to increase again in April and May, when customers are ordering for new summer programs and reordering for the next year. During the slow months you can sometimes purchase your equipment and supplies on favorable terms. In time you can even defer payment for 30, 60 or 90 days, and interest and shipping costs may be dropped.

4

SELECTING THE EXPERTS

I f you are starting, expanding or improving a center, or if you are adapting your current program to a more flexible one, chances are that there will be times when you will need the advice of outside experts. Even if you've been operating a center for years without having worked with outside consultants, you may find the need for doing so now.

You may need a lawyer familiar with local zoning issues or an accountant who is experienced in dealing with child care to help you with bookkeeping procedures or a business plan. A marketing expert can analyze the state of local child care business and help you plot strategies to promote your center.

Except for consultations with a banker, you will have to pay a fee, and if you are charged on an hourly basis, the fee may seem high. However, if you've defined the problem to be solved beforehand and carefully chosen the expert, the advice will usually be well worth the cost.

DEFINING THE PROBLEM

Before looking for a particular expert, you need to define the problem(s) facing you. If there is more than one problem, you will also have to decide which one to attack first. Defining your problem areas is one of the most important, yet often overlooked, planning steps; without it, you can waste expensive hours on the wrong problem with the wrong professional help.

For example, if your two issues of concern are establishing (or improving in the case of an on-going operation) enrollment and staff salaries, enrollment has to be the priority before you can consider offering higher salaries. If marketing your new or improved program is one difficulty, but you have not yet been able to obtain local approvals, obtaining the necessary approvals is the priority.

To analyze your specific needs, make a list summarizing the main problems that confront you. Write down everything you can think of; your litany of ideas will even help you identify your business's long-term potential pitfalls. (This is an exercise you should repeat whenever you feel your business is slipping.)

Once the initial list is done, organize it according to which problems will have the most impact on the business. Set priorities. Is the problem confined to the immediate operation of your business or will it continue to affect it over a long period? This evaluation will help you determine whether you need short-term or long-term advice. If you find that a certain type of expertise will be needed on a long-term basis, consider making an employee responsible for that area or hiring an expert on a retainer or monthly fee basis. When more hours are involved, many professionals will negotiate their fees.

Your scheme will probably look something like the list in Table 4-1.

You may feel reluctant to hire experts because of the expense involved, but this can be penny-wise and pound-foolish. All too often entrepreneurs are bombarded with well-meaning advice from friends and relatives. As a business owner, you will do better if you get the best professional advice you can. One way to establish or increase your own professional status and win the respect of the community is to have the support of other professionals—even ones you have to pay for their advice.

FINDING AND HIRING CONSULTANTS

With your requirements defined, it is time to find the right expert. It pays to move carefully at this stage, or you can waste a great deal of time and money. For example, if your problem is refining a business plan and obtaining financing, you don't need a consultant with early childhood training who has neither experience nor training in budgeting and finance. On the other hand, this same person may be just right for planning or revamping a preschool program or checking curriculum goals.

TABLE 4-1   PROBLEM-SOLVING SCHEME

Problems (in order of priority)	Affects Start-up	Affects On-going	Short Term	Long Term	Solution	Expert Needed
Low income/enrollment	X	X	X	X	Improve marketing	Child care or marketing specialist
Poor salaries		X	X		Increase income	Same as above
Low capacity		X	X		Expand capacity	Lawyer, architect, child care consultant
Equipment	X	X	X	X	Determine needs; plan purchasing	Child care consultant, accountant

Likewise if you are building a center, remodeling or assembling a modular structure, be sure to obtain accurate advice on licensing requirements and quality program development. The most common mistakes with the physical facility involve obtaining approvals or planning a center from a practical point of view. In design, for example, lack of storage and poor traffic flow within the center are the type of problems from which the right expert can protect you.

Whether you are looking for a banker, lawyer, child care consultant, accountant or any other expert, your best method of finding a good advisor is often networking. Ask the officers of early childhood associations for referrals. Get to know other small business owners in the community and the other child care center owners; if they seem fearful of competition, visit some in a nearby community. But generally, child care operators are very open and willing to share information.

In every community successful realtors know experts in many areas. They are also an excellent source of financing referrals (with inside information on lending institution trends in the area) and contacts with potential investors or new developers. Remember that local business organizations, such as the Chamber of Commerce, are always ready to assist new businesses—especially child care operations, which will be an asset to the business community's contingent of working parents.

In some circumstances it may be necessary to use a long-distance consultant. The headquarters of some national organizations provide lists of experts. Although these organizations do not grant accreditation, their directories offer a starting point. (See Appendix D for names and addresses of professional organizations.) Of course, local or state-based consultants should be less expensive because travel expenses will be lower. If the issues at hand warrant a specific expertise, you can often handle the discussions effectively by phone and by fax. Also, consultants in other states may be able to refer you to appropriate experts near you.

In your search, remember that some of these experts will be licensed while others will be in professions that have no formal accreditation systems in place. Moreover, a license does not guarantee quality service. To protect yourself, ask for references and check them carefully. Contact other professionals in the area to see if they have heard of or used the individual. Call relevant state associations and ask if they have any information about this expert. If you are in doubt, follow your instincts and keep searching. It is very important to remember that the expert is giving advice; the ultimate decisions are yours. Thus, if you do not have absolute confidence in this person from the beginning, you are not going to respect the advice that is given.

Once you have located possible consultants in the specific area of expertise needed, thoroughly explain your situation to them and ask for a brief proposal. In some cases you may need both long- and short-term proposals, with several different consultants working concurrently. Ask what resources she or he has available, request both time and cost estimates and try to ascertain what other current commitments the consultant has. This aspect is very important, because you don't want to wait for a long time until they get around to dealing with your problems. Explain that you are speaking with other consultants and truly appreciate the input from each.

In selecting one consultant over another, do not base your decision on cost alone. If the proposal that you prefer exceeds your present budget, speak to the consultant; usually there is room for negotiation. Your money will be well spent on the right consultant. Be sure to reply to all proposals, and leave the door open for future consultations.

If you are asked to sign a contract, make sure that your interests are protected. It is advisable, particularly if there are large sums involved, to have your attorney examine the agreement.

The following brief descriptions will give you an idea of what types of experts you'll be most likely to use and what qualities to look for in them as you establish your working relationships.

Lawyer

Having the right lawyer is critical for every stage of your business. The three key qualities your lawyer must have are honesty, availability and an interest in your venture. If you trust your lawyer and are honest and explicit about the issues involved, he should be able to tell you whether he can handle your business or refer you to a colleague if the issues are outside his area of expertise. Once you have hired a lawyer, you should be able to reach him within a reasonable length of time. If you keep calling only to be told repeatedly that he's in conference or will call you later, you have to question whether he is really interested in having your business. The lawyer may have an excellent reputation, but that's useless if he is not available when you need him.

You need a lawyer who understands business as well as personal issues and who has had experience in real estate, business and child care regulatory matters. Try your best to find a lawyer who has worked successfully with other child care centers. This experience may not be terribly important for matters such as incorporation, but can mean the difference between success and failure in disputed zoning or liability issues. As mentioned before, you may find it necessary at certain times to work with two attorneys with different areas of expertise.

Banker

From the beginning, a good banker can be your best friend and advisor. Cultivate a key person at your business bank whether you are starting or expanding your business. If your business is already in operation, describe your success to the banker informally, perhaps over lunch, or invite her to visit the center. Share your knowledge of and enthusiasm for your profession, presenting yourself as a local expert. In both informal and formal meetings be sure to dress and act professionally—you want to establish yourself as an excellent financial risk for financing and business referrals. You will often find that a banker will be a good resource for referrals and a highly trained business consultant who does not charge for her services.

Accountant

Probably your most important long-term expert will be your accountant. Find someone who can communicate with you on your level of financial expertise. If you can't understand what your accountant says to you, there may be a disaster brewing. If you do not know what he is doing or how you are supposed to complete a task, say so immediately. Also, make sure the transfer of information between your offices is timely and efficient. When filing your taxes, for example, a lack of communication can cost thousands of dollars in time, unnecessary IRS penalties and interest.

When you are starting a business, your accountant can assist you in setting up your bookkeeping system, help you understand your federal and state obligations and explain the best way to deal with accounts payable and receivable. You may eventually decide to use a computer to help you with much of this, so it would be wise to also have an understanding of the computer process from the start—or an accountant familiar with computer capabilities. Remember, you do not have to be an expert in accounting principles; you just have to understand enough to apply them to your business.

If you find you are having difficulty with the accountant you've been using, get a new one! One new center owner had five different accountants in less than three years and finally found the right one, who has been doing the accounts successfully now for 14 years.

Computer Specialist

Computer programs can help you with accounts receivable and payable, tracking hours and availability, organizing payroll and taxes and scheduling staff. However, without the proper advice and continuing support, you might not utilize your computer equipment fully or, worse, at all.

It can be expedient to hire a knowledgeable computer specialist to help you select the right hardware and software and to train you or someone on your staff to use it. This is one expert who will probably come to you through a business acquaintance. Once she is hired, make sure you understand all her explanations and instructions. Even if you have no previous experience with computers, a good trainer will alleviate your fears. You only need to understand what the computer does, not *how* it does it. Also, be sure that she will be available for questions and further training, should you need it. As with any consultant you hire, if you can't understand her within a short time, cut your losses and find someone else.

Child Care Consultants

In the ever-growing field of child care, you will find that there are many people claiming to be experts, so you should be especially careful when hiring consultants in this area. First, decide what age groups you need help with (infant/toddler, preschool or school-age care). If you are looking for an educational consultant, it is not difficult to find someone who is academically qualified in all three age groups; however, most people have had hands-on experience in only one. If you are going to provide sick child care, you will definitely need someone who has special expertise in this area. If your program is going to be a private for-profit program, make very sure that the prospective consultant has worked in profit-oriented child care. If the consultant tries to convince you that you cannot make money in this industry, you should reexamine your goals and perhaps get a second opinion.

If you decide that you will provide child care for the employees of a specific company, you need an expert who can assist you with the various options, such as a vendor/voucher program, an on-site child care center in cooperation with the employer or a consortium venture with several area employers. The method of establishing each of these is quite different, and you will need an expert who has had experience in analyzing which approach is best for the market, approaching the key people in the company or companies and implementing the proper program. In your consideration of employer-supported child care, remember that each employer has probably already been approached by several child care experts and will seriously consider only a plan that is very professional and is cost-effective for the company. The employer must also have total confidence that you and/or your consultant can be successful with the project and that the employees will be happy with the results.

If your primary field is not early childhood or child development and especially if you have no practical experience, you will be more likely to need help with choosing and/or training staff. You need to be very sure that the teachers and head teachers you hire are qualified to run the particular type of program you have in mind. This type of consultant should also be able to help you plan a high-quality program that will be more marketable.

As outlined in Chapter 1, child care market analysis is quite different from other business analysis, and you may need expert advice to analyze your market initially and then to plan your marketing strategies. Be sure to check references for this consultant, as you need someone who has an established track record for accuracy.

There is a new organization, the Association of Child Care Consultants International, set up for consultants in the United States. (For more information on ACCCI, see Appendix D.)

There is currently no accreditation system for child care consultants, so again, you must ask specific questions, check references and make sure that you can work with whoever you hire. Remember that the consultant is only an advisor and should be able to train you to manage all aspects of your business with confidence.

Architect

When you are planning the space for your child care center you may need an architect for original construction or renovations. Some architects have experience in designing child care facilities, but usually this is not the case. Above all, make sure your architect understands children, or failing that, that she is willing to listen to your input and that you have a very good idea of what the space should be like. You may later find that you need a design consultant for interior work. To find out whether an architect is accredited, check with The National Architectural Board located in Washington, D.C.

Visit as many centers as possible and ask critical questions about various facets of the design. For example, does the design encourage the children's interaction? Can the children easily enter the classroom with a minimum of disruption? Is the noise level comfortable or overpowering? Could the infants be easily evacuated in case of fire? Often you will find that the owner or director will be glad to share information and ideas. If you listen carefully, you can often save hours of design work and avoid major mistakes in the planning stages. Be sure to speak to the teachers as well and see if the space is working for or against the staff. When you attend conferences, try to fit in time for one or two visits to local child care centers. This will help to orient your thinking about the design of your center.

If you decide to go with modular construction, you may find that much of the designing is basically done and that there are very few changes that will be needed for your center. Using the designs provided by modular companies may save you a very expensive step in your start-up phase.

With any consultation, the expert is there to offer ideas and advice, but the business is ultimately yours and you will have to make the final decisions. At the same time, remember that you are paying for the advice, and if you respect the consultant, listen to the advice with an open mind. A true professional will give sound advice that speaks from experience and/or education and will ultimately train you to make independent decisions and solve management problems rationally and cost-effectively.

5
PURCHASING EQUIPMENT AND SUPPLIES

Purchasing equipment and supplies is a major undertaking for a child care center. Unlike many businesses, child care centers do not have purchasing departments or even a specific person in charge of researching best buys and finding the newest equipment in the marketplace. This chapter will help you avoid the common pitfalls as you initially buy equipment and supplies to set up a center and then keep it going. There are two basic types of purchases: one is capital equipment, which depreciates over a period of time, and the other is consumable supplies, which will be used and reordered on a very regular basis. The methods involved in purchasing each of these two types vary slightly.

START-UP

During the 1980s the child care field expanded tremendously, and many manufacturers and distributors began to focus on the child care market. As a result, every child care center is bombarded by sales pitches for equipment, supplies and commodities, making it hard to know exactly what is essential and when and how to get the best deal once you decide to buy.

If you are purchasing a large amount of equipment, you should be able to negotiate a discount on the price or the shipping or both. Many manufacturers do not sell directly so you will be buying through a distributor. Try to find a distributor that services the products they sell, as service is typically not included for child care products. You don't want to purchase a piece of expensive equipment only to discover that it does not work in the classroom or is of poor quality. Distributors themselves now offer consulting services for centers that are starting up; however, you want to be careful that their philosophy matches your own. You should also ask for references.

If you are in a start-up phase, it is best to hire a child care consultant who has worked in purchasing equipment and supplies. She may indeed be able to save you a great deal of money and time by having a comprehensive list of distributors and manufacturers with whom she has previously worked. She also should be current on equipment in a field that changes frequently and dramatically.

The equipment you need to start up your center will vary, of course, according to the type of program you plan to run. What follows is a guide to purchasing basic equipment for a general program. We do not cover, for example, Montessori equipment or specific learning materials that may be particular to your philosophy.

When planning a child care center, use the layouts of the physical plant to help you plan placement of equipment. Generally, children work much better in smaller spaces than in larger ones, which tend to make a room look chaotic. Also, the more you divide a room, the larger and more interesting it will appear, particularly for the children who are there on a full-day basis.

Make sure that you have plenty of storage space available so that your center appears organized. If the space you are using has plenty of built-in storage, you will not have to add many storage units in the classroom space. The attractiveness of each play and storage area establishes your image and also can make the children's and staff's attitudes more positive.

Many new operators ask, "How do I decide what equipment I need and where I need it?" If you have not run or worked in a center before, hire an early childhood specialist or a good consultant to help you. You also need—and this cannot be emphasized enough—to get out and look at other centers. Ask your state licensing agent or consultant for a list of centers and check out both the good and the bad. You need to look at the competition in your community and in other areas to give you ideas on what type of equipment you want. Pick one center as a prototype, and improve on it to gain a marketing edge.

Take along a pad to make notes as soon as you leave, while everything is fresh in your mind. For example, list what you liked and disliked and what new ideas you gleaned from this center. Are there attractive handcrafted pieces of equipment or materials? If there is a custom-made piece that you really like, is it worthwhile to have it copied, or is there something comparable that you can buy on the market? Also look at the different storage options for ideas.

Next we are going to look at what is typical in each classroom and what would be needed for basic supplies in each age group. Supplies are defined as those products used in the center that cost less than $100 and/or have a life of less than one year; these are considered consumable items. Equipment, on the other hand, is considered a fixed asset and thus can depreciate over time.

I N F A N T S

E Q U I P M E N T

Cribs
Changing table
Rocking chairs
Playpens
Storage cabinets
Carpeting or rug for crawling space
Walkers
Baby seats
High chairs
Infant swing
Microwave for heating food
Sink
Storage for belongings
Mirror

S U P P L I E S

Diapers, if provided
Paper for changing table
Plastic gloves
Sheets
Linens
Bumper pads
Mobiles
Baby toys

Wipes
Books

OUTDOOR EQUIPMENT

Stroller for four or six infants
Enclosure or "playpen"
Small covered sand box
Low climber
Small house
Low slide
Water play table
Small riding vehicles

OUTDOOR SUPPLIES

Balls
Sand box toys
Water play toys

TODDLERS

EQUIPMENT

Storage units
Tables
Chairs
Carpet
Cots, cot storage unit
Changing area
Sink
Coat storage area
Storage for belongings
Indoor climbing apparatus
Easel

SUPPLIES

Paints and brushes
Paper
Paste and glue
Changing paper
Cups
Diapers, if provided
Wipes
Toddler toys

Manipulatives
Books
Blocks

O U T D O O R   E Q U I P M E N T

See Infant list.

O U T D O O R   S U P P L I E S

See Infant list.

P   R   E   S   C   H   O   O   L   E   R   S

E Q U I P M E N T

Storage units
Carpet
Dramatic play units like puppet theater, toy kitchens or work-
    bench, etc.
Easel
Tables
Chairs
Coat storage
Storage for belongings
Manipulative storage
Cots, cot storage unit

S U P P L I E S

Paints and brushes
Smocks
Crayons and markers
Paper
Paste and glue
Manipulatives
Clay and dough
Books
Blocks

O U T D O O R   E Q U I P M E N T

Balance beam
Climbing apparatus
Sand box
Swing set
Low teeter-totter

Bouncing toy
Big wheels/tricycles
Slides
Water table

OUTDOOR SUPPLIES

Balls, bats
Hoops, jump ropes
Parachute
Sand box toys
Water table toys

SCHOOL-AGE CHILDREN

EQUIPMENT

Storage for games
Tables
Chairs
Homework area
Couch
Coat storage
Storage for belongings

SUPPLIES

Games
Paint, paper, art materials
Cooking supplies
Books

OUTDOOR EQUIPMENT

Goal and net for soccer, football, etc.
Swings
Climbing apparatus

OUTDOOR SUPPLIES

Cones
Bases
Outdoor games
Jump ropes

Balls, bats
Nature study materials

The cost of equipment and supplies will vary according to your philosophy, as mentioned before. However, currently the cost per room for set-up is running between $5,000 and $9,000, depending on the amount of equipment used. Alternatively, you may decide to estimate your equipment costs on a "per child" basis. Most equipment manufacturers and distributors agree that the cost per child is $300 for indoor equipment and material and $100 for outdoor. So a center for 50 children would cost approximately $20,000 to set up. One word of caution: do not place too much equipment in any room initially, because the room will look much better if it is not too crowded. Also, you may find that your needs and desires change.

ON-GOING PURCHASING

As in any other business, the key to effective, budget-wise purchasing is planning. Avoid impulsive buying at all costs. Also, remember that your center will have predictable needs such as paint, glue and construction paper. For example, consumable supplies will need to be ordered at least twice a year. Try to make purchases when there are sales; obviously sales are less likely just before September, although some of the distributors and manufacturers are trying to be competitive even then. The following steps will help you set up a good on-going purchasing plan.

Creating a Purchasing Plan

Take inventory
    Assess what you currently have on hand. Make a list for each age group's inside area, using list A below as a guide. Also make one general list for the outside area using list B.

A.   Indoor Program Areas (for each age group):
      Number of children
      Large equipment
      Arts and crafts supplies
      Educational materials
      Manipulatives
      Decorative materials

B. Outside Play Area (if playgrounds are divided by age group, list separately):
Riding vehicles
Swings
Sandbox and toys
Climbing apparatus
Balls, bats, jump ropes, outdoor games

Make a purchasing list

Using the information gained from your above assessments, do the following:

1. Brainstorm. Write down everything that you see in catalogs, stores, etc. that you think you would like to add to your program.
2. Put the list aside for a couple of days.
3. When you have a quiet moment, take out your list and place each item in one of these three categories: Essential, Not Sure, Superfluous But Nice.
4. Meet with your teachers during a quiet time of the day (perhaps nap time) and explain that you are planning future purchases and want to avoid impulse buying. Have the teachers outline any changes or additional purchases that they would like for their classroom areas.
5. Plan time, perhaps a week later, to sit down and discuss the teachers' wish lists, explaining what monies will be available this year for purchasing.
6. Put together all your information and set up a game plan for purchasing, as below.

Make a game plan for purchasing

1. Look first at your "Essential" list. Divide it into two groups— immediate and long term—as follows:

    Immediate—If you don't purchase the items on this list, the overall program will deteriorate rapidly.
    Long Term—This group would include equipment that has some remaining value or supplies that you still have enough of. However, replacements or replenishments will eventually be necessary—for example, a swing set that will need new seats by next year, sand for the sand box, bookcases that have been repaired but should be replaced and so on.

2. Consider the "Not Sure" category next. For this area, ask yourself the following questions: Will the program fall apart without this item? Can the purchase be deferred until next year? Will the staff be upset if the purchase is not made now? And most important, will this item contribute to the development of the children and/or the total program?

3. Finally, consider the "Superfluous But Nice" category. Purchasing items on this list will be determined primarily by your cash flow. However, you should divide this list into two groups. First, which items are educationally and developmentally beneficial for the children? You might have plenty of puzzles and manipulatives, but you may remember seeing a new and exciting set of floor puzzles at a conference display. Second, what items would be physically attractive additions to brighten the environment? This could include—but not be limited to—bulletin boards and material, posters, new carpeting, etc.

Evaluate your lists and make purchases for the area of your program that is the weakest. In other words, ask yourself, Are we providing a quality program for the children educationally and developmentally? Is the facility attractive and inviting?

Management of Purchasing

Once you have your purchasing game plan, consider the following strategic management questions:

1. Is there equipment that is not being used? Could it be sold to raise cash?
2. Are there areas that are obsolete and uninviting to the children? Would a paint job help?
3. Are there enough small-motor coordination toys and educational materials? Are these appropriate for each age level?
4. Are the arts and crafts supplies sufficient for the teachers to do exciting activities with the children?
5. Does the center have a reliable supplier of essential products, i.e., paper cups, toilet paper, paper towels and so on?
6. If meals are supplied, does the center buy in quantity, thus cutting costs? Would it be better to consider a caterer?
7. Is the storage space sufficient, safe and efficient?
8. Is too much time spent running to the store for individual items? Is weekly shopping for supplies becoming too time-consuming and aggravating?

9. Is the outside equipment safe, in good repair and an attractive advertisement for our program?

Purchasing Shortcuts and Budget-Saving Ideas

The following tips can make purchasing more effective and can save you money. Remember! Avoid impulse buying at all costs.

1. Establish a work area near front desk where current catalogs and price lists are available.
2. When you are ordering, consider one item at a time. Compare prices, including shipping costs. Check shipping charges, especially on large items, as this may add considerably to the cost.
3. If you need several pieces of large equipment, try to order them at the same time. This way you may be able to negotiate a discount on the price or the shipping from either the distributor or manufacturer.
4. Look for durability in most items. But, for example, if you are just starting out, you may do better to buy less-expensive playground equipment with a life span of two or three years so that you can buy more variety.
5. Whenever financially feasible, try to order arts and crafts supplies such as paint, paper, etc., by the case as this procedure usually saves money. For everyday items such as paper goods (cups, toilet paper and towels), shop for a wholesale supplier. Occasionally, you might be able to arrange for quantity discounts.
6. Whenever possible, order supplies like paint, paper, etc., for the coming school year in the spring when prices are generally better and you can be sure of prompt delivery.
7. If you are unsure about a piece of equipment, ask your colleagues at other centers or call a child care consultant.
8. If feasible, set up a cooperative buying system with other centers for common supplies. Although this has obvious advantages, someone will have to organize such a venture, keep it running and assume financial responsibility. If you foresee that you are going to be the coordinator, consider the value of your time spent compared to the savings. You may find that you actually lose money in the long run.
9. Be sure to have quality, convenient storage space for games, puzzles and arts and crafts supplies. This is the

best possible way to protect your investment in small materials.

10. Small equipment (games, puzzles, toys, books) may often be purchased locally at prices lower than those offered by distributors. Ideal sources are tag sales and church fairs.

11. To save time and often money, set up a monthly account from petty cash for the head teacher of each class to use for special occasions. For example $20 a month could be set aside for the teacher to use for birthday parties and other events.

12. Do not order over the phone unless you are sure of the business that you are dealing with. Several highly questionable operations are currently calling child care facilities throughout the country.

13. Learn to say no forcefully to any impulses unless your budget allows it.

Phone Solicitations and "Super Bargains"

Nearly every child care center in the country has received calls at one point during the year from high-pressure salespeople offering a limited-time-only "super bargain" on supplies or equipment. If this should happen to you, be very careful before placing an order. Watch out for sales pitches such as:

"We are overstocked on certain items. Our warehouse is full so we have special discounts if you buy in quantity."

"If you buy a certain quantity of pens or construction paper, then you will get a special offer on other items."

"All you need to do is take one set of pens in order to get your special buy." "One" may actually mean one dozen, one case or one gross. Make the salesperson be specific.

"If you buy a certain dollar amount you will get a free gift." Ask for specific details about the quantity and the gift!

In many cases you will find that the cost is higher than what you would pay in a top retail store in your area and certainly more than what many of the catalogs charge. Make sure you carefully calculate the dollar amount and do the following:

1. Write down as much information as possible, i.e., prices, brands, etc.

2. Do not order immediately. Ask for the phone number and a name to call back if you are interested. Often this will turn off disreputable salespeople.
3. Ask questions. Don't let the sales pitch go on indefinitely. Interrupt and explain that you do not order over the phone from unknown sources.
4. Compare prices with those in catalogs or with those of local retailers.
5. If you are suspicious of the company, contact your local Better Business Bureau or your state attorney general's office to see whether any complaints have been filed against them.
6. If you have placed an order already, remember you do not have to accept it; you can refuse it upon delivery or send it back. And finally, do not accept any partial orders for which you are asked to pay the full amount COD.

Over time, you will no doubt find that your purchasing game plan will have to change. Distributors and manufacturers will offer you different types of deals, and you must know how to evaluate the offers. If you ever have questions, call your local professional associations or management consultants. Often networking with other managers will help you track what is happening in the field.

PART TWO
FLEXIBLE PROGRAMS THAT AIM FOR PROFIT

• •

To insure the profitability of your child care center, you need a well-run, flexible program that fills your center as close as possible to its capacity.

A flexible, cost-effective program requires that you plan your new facility—or scrutinize your current center—with the various needs of the three age ranges in mind. For each of the groups (infant/toddler, preschool and school age) you'll need specifically designed indoor and outdoor spaces, appropriate equipment and materials and a carefully selected staff to plan and implement an excellent curriculum. In addition, good summer programs will help make your center a year-round success.

Chapters 6 through 10 guide you through the process by dealing with:

6. How to increase profits and better serve your community by implementing a flexible program.
7. How to deliver safe, hygienic infant and toddler care with correct staff ratios and group sizes while still making a profit.
8. How to create a quality, flexible preschool program that assures you a large number of clients even though care for this age group is generally the most widely available.

9. How to establish an innovative before- and after-school program either in a separate or shared space.
10. How to maintain your profits during the summer months by competing effectively with seasonal programs.

THE FLEXIBILITY FACTOR[1]

Whether you are opening a new center or already have one in operation, you can insure your business's profitability in a shorter time with flexible programming. This management technique can increase revenues, and as a result improve teachers' salaries, maintain parents' current tuition rates and improve the overall quality of the care your center delivers.

FLEXIBILITY DEFINED

The basic principles behind flexible child care are a radical departure from what is usually taught about child care delivery systems, but both profit and nonprofit centers have been using this method with great success. In some cases owners and directors have increased their profits by 30% to 40% in less than a month; new centers run with flexibility typically reach their break-even in less than eight weeks.

To successfully implement a flexible program, you must first understand the principles behind it and then apply management techniques with tight controls. Flexible child care, by definition,

---

[1] Parts of this chapter were originally published in an article entitled "Flexible Programming (Your Key to Increasing Revenue)" by Nan Lee Howkins, which appeared in David Pierson's *Child Care Review* in the February/March 1989 (Volume 4, Number 2) issue on pages 8–16. Reprinted here by permission of the publisher, *Child Care Review*, P.O. Box 578, Metarie, LA 70004, tel. (504) 831–9662.

is providing child care on a flexible, hourly basis to parents who preregister their children. This system contrasts not only with preregistered full-day and part-day care, but also with what are commonly referred to as "drop-in" programs. A drop-in program implies a baby-sitting service where there is no preregistration and no commitment by the parent to a set number of hours each week. That is not what flexibility is about. In a flexible program, parents must preregister but may use the center for whatever hours and days they need provided there is space for their children. If they want to be certain of having a set day and time available, they may reserve the slot on a permanent basis.

This is significantly different from the way most centers now package their child care services. Most centers offer only full-time care five days a week. Some centers will offer part-time care, but they dictate the hours and the days that part-time care is available and will not adapt to an individual client's schedule. This type of rigid programming can cost you, your teachers, your center, your parents, your children and your potential customers dearly.

The key to your center's profitability is to make it as flexible as possible so that more parents—including those with irregular work schedules such as nurses, grocery store clerks and parents with part-time jobs—can afford to buy your center's services for the hours per day or week that they need child care coverage. By accommodating this type of client—who may only need the center, let's say, between three and 10 hours per week—you can increase the profit margin, because the fewer the hours a parent uses the center, the higher the hourly fee they will be charged. Since licensed hourly care is so difficult to find, parents are willing to pay more to use your center on a part-time, hourly basis. Obviously, a program run exclusively on an hourly basis and charging top hourly rates would bring the largest profit, but the market will generally not bear this type of fee structure. For a parent using a center 40 to 45 hours per week, the costs would be far too expensive.

There are a number of other reasons as well for offering a flexible program. For one thing, you can serve more families, thus reducing parents' reliance on the nonregulated forms of child care that now fill the void as a low-cost flexible alternative. Another valid reason affects you and your center more directly. If profitability is not one of your center's principal goals, you will not be able to provide quality child care over the long term. The economic realities of child care are such that in order to provide a quality child care program, a center must be cost-effective. And a flexible program is cost-effective as well as profitable.

Flexible programming essentially means using your center to its maximum capacity, which is *not* the same as your licensed capacity. The term "capacity" is generally used to refer to licensed capacity—the number of children a center is allowed to care for at a given time. This figure is determined by the number of usable square feet per child that your state requires. It is also affected by fire, building and zoning requirements on both the state and local level. As a general guideline, the national fire code, which is used in many states, requires 35 square feet per child.

If at any given hour you have the maximum number of children allowed, you have reached the highest possible percentage of occupancy. With flexible programming your goal is to operate at maximum capacity where you have all portions of the program full to the licensed capacity every hour that the center is open. To calculate your maximum capacity, first calculate the total number of hours per week that your center is open. If, for example, you are open from 7 A.M. to 6 P.M. five days a week, that would be five days times 11 hours, or 55 hours. Then take this number of hours and multiply it times your *licensed* capacity to get the *maximum* capacity of the center. It has been our experience that most for-profit centers are only operating at 65% of their potential maximum capacity, and nonprofit centers at an even lower 48%. *If a facility is licensed for 50 children, this could mean it is potentially losing at least $100,000 per year in revenue.*

HOW TO SET UP A FLEXIBLE PROGRAM

How do you start a flexible program at a new center or implement one into your on-going operation with the minimum amount of time, money and energy? To give you an idea of what is involved, we have described the steps taken by one existing child care center that switched to a flexible program. This center, which had a licensed capacity of 50 children, had been in operation for five years and was moderately successful. However, the owner/director had drawn only a small salary and had not yet recouped her initial investment. She did not have the funds available to replace worn equipment inside or to update the playground. The owner realized she needed to make changes but was unsure where to start. As a result, she hired a consulting firm that guided her through the following steps to flexible programming.

To begin, the consultant had the owner critically look at the reasons the center was only marginally profitable. She studied expenses, looking for areas where she might save money. As in most centers, there were a few adjustments she could make but none were substantial enough to make continuing the struggle to stay in business seem truly worthwhile. Expansion was also a possibility since there was room for reconstruction, but this approach seemed inadvisable given the financial troubles of the current program.

Finally, she examined the actual gross income to see if there were any changes that might result in increased revenues. The center had a total of 47 children enrolled in the program and interviews set to fill the final three slots. To her, that meant the center was currently operating at 94% capacity.

The center only had full-time students, since the owner felt it was much better to have 50 full payments than to risk having part-time slots empty, particularly in the afternoon.

Actual Time Usage

At the recommendation of the consultant, the owner completed two different Time Usage forms for all the center's hours of operation for one week (Table 6-1). On one form she entered all the children's names in a given classroom and marked off when each child was *scheduled* to be in the center's care. She called this the Estimated Time Usage.

On the second form each classroom teacher wrote down the *actual* times each child used the center that week, This was the Actual Time Usage (Table 6-2). The teachers did the Actual Time Usage because they were aware of the subtle changes in parents' schedules. The children's absenteeism rate for the week was not factored in.

The result was a *15% difference* between the owner's Estimated Time Usage chart and the teacher's Actual Time Usage chart.

Next, the owner calculated the total number of hours the center was in operation per week. It opened at 7 A.M. and closed at 6 P.M. for 11 hours a day or 55 hours a week. She then multiplied this total by her center's licensed capacity to reach the center's Total Child Hours Available (55 hours a week multiplied by 50 licensed slots equals 2,750 Total Child Hours Available).

She then divided the Actual Time Usage (in this case, it was 1,650 child hours per week) by the Total Child Hours Available.

TABLE 6-1 ESTIMATED TIME USAGE

NAME	7:00	7:30	8:00	8:30	9:00	9:30	10:00	10:30	11:00	11:30	12:00	12:30	1:00	1:30	2:00	2:30	3:00	3:30	4:00	4:30	5:00	5:30	6:00
Bradford, Thomas	X				X	X	X	X	X	X	X	X	X	X	X	X	X	X	X	X	X		
Darby, Erika		X	X	X	X	X	X	X	X	X	X	X	X	X	X	X	X	X	X	X	X		
Emmery, Elizabeth		X	X	X	X	X	X	X	X	X	X	X	X	X	X	X	X	X					
Grant, David			X	X	X	X	X	X	X	X	X	X	X	X	X	X	X	X	X				
Masterson, Joe					X	X	X	X	X	X	X	X	X	X	X	X	X						
Netherling, Adam				X	X	X	X	X	X	X	X	X	X	X	X	X	X						
Potter, Allison	X	X	X	X	X	X	X	X	X	X	X	X	X	X	X	X	X						
Pratt, Jeanne							X	X	X	X	X	X	X	X	X	X	X	X	X	X	X	X	X

TABLE 6-2 ACTUAL TIME USAGE

NAME	7:00	7:30	8:00	8:30	9:00	9:30	10:00	10:30	11:00	11:30	12:00	12:30	1:00	1:30	2:00	2:30	3:00	3:30	4:00	4:30	5:00	5:30	6:00
Bradford, Thomas					X	X	X	X	X	X	X	X	X	X	X	X	X	X	X				
Darby, Erika				X	X	X	X	X	X	X	X	X	X	X	X	X	X	X	X	X	X		
Emmery, Elizabeth		X	X	X	X	X	X	X	X	X	X	X	X	X	X	X	X	X					
Grant, David			X	X	X	X	X	X	X	X	X	X	X	X	X	X	X	X					
Masterson, Joe																							
Netherling, Adam					X	X	X	X	X	X	X	X	X	X	X	X	X						
Potter, Allison	X	X	X	X	X	X	X	X	X	X	X	X	X	X	X	X	X						
Pratt, Jeanne							X	X	X	X	X	X	X	X	X	X	X	X	X	X	X	X	X

This calculation gave her the center's Percentage of Occupancy. To her surprise, she found she was actually operating at a capacity of 60%! In other words, while the owner thought she was operating at 94% capacity (47 of the 50 licensed slots filled), she was, in fact, operating at 60% capacity!

She started to see how to change her center's fortunes. Her battle with a tight budget, her inability to replace equipment or raise her teachers' or her own salaries—all of this was the result of operating at 60% capacity. To continue in the same manner, she concluded, would handicap the center and prevent it from being the profitable venture it needed to be.

Objectives

As a result of her analysis and with the help of the consultant, the owner decided to set two objectives:

1. Increase the gross income by increasing the Actual Time Usage by clients per week.
2. Use the licensed capacity to its maximum by keeping careful track of Actual Time Usage and absenteeism.

The owner projected that, if she accomplished her objectives, she could achieve her larger goal of increasing her center's gross income.

She was charging $55 a week for full-time students, which averages out to $1.22 per hour for 45 hours of care. But few full-time children actually come to a center every hour of every day. If the center knows when a full-time client will not be there, those hours can be filled by another child. And experience with a flexible program has shown that a center can sell its unused child hours at a premium, that is, at a higher rate than what is charged full-time students.

After reviewing the market rate in the area for hourly care, the owner decided to charge $2 per hour for 11 to 25 hours of care a week and $2.50 per hour for 10 hours or less. Anything over 25 hours of care per week would be at the full weekly rate. She then had the parents of her full-time children indicate which hours their children would use the center. With this information in hand, she could proceed with selling the unused child hours.

At the same time, she examined the current absenteeism rate. This was unpredictable, of course, but if she *could* determine which scheduled children were going to be absent, she could resell those slots at the higher hourly rate to those parents who would preregister their children on an "occasional, space-available" basis. Because parents of children who used the center full time were required to pay for sick days, she started an incentive program to encourage parents to notify the center if their child was going to be absent on a day she/he was scheduled. If the parents notified the center, the child care bill for that day would be discounted by 10%.

She wasn't sure it would be much of an incentive, because a 10% credit on one day's tuition for a full-time student came to slightly less than $1 (98 cents, in fact). But it worked! Parents started calling in to report when their sick child would not be using the facility the next day. This allowed the director to resell that space at the premium hourly rate.

Focusing now on selling her unused child hours, the owner projected she could sell 90% of her Total Child Hours Available. Operating at a 90% capacity, the owner projected a 20% to 30% increase in gross revenue.

Test Class

To implement the program as quickly as possible with a minimum capital investment, she tested it with the three-year-old class, which seemed the easiest to work with.

Table 6-3 shows the initial three-year-old enrollment with the classroom capacity at eight full-time children. (The 1:8 staff–child ratio, by the way, will remain constant.) In this particular case, the classroom was actually being used during only 60.5% of the child hours the center was open each week. With a flexible program (Table 6-4), the owner was able to fill several unused slots, and increase usage in the three-year-old class to 82.3%.

The center also accepted additional children on an occasional, space-available basis. Parents who had preregistered their child would call ahead to see if illness or vacations had left a slot open. Further, a logging procedure was instituted so the owner or her staff could accurately address inquiries about space availability. Table 6-5 shows how these additional children were served by substituting them for students who were absent.

The center's gross income quickly increased after it began using this method in all classrooms. Empowered by knowing exactly what the Actual Time Usage was for each hour of every day, the owner added a before- and after-school program to fill in early

TABLE 6-3   ACTUAL SPACE USAGE*

This table shows enrollment in the center's three-year-olds class before instituting the flexible program. All children are full-time students. All children's names are fictional. The center's hours of operation are 7 A.M.–6 P.M. The total child-hours available is 440 (11 hours × 5 days × 8 children).

Name	Mon	Tues	Wed	Thurs	Fri	Hours	Other
Bradford, Thomas	X	X	X	X	X	9–5	
Darby, Erika	X		X	X		7–5	
Emmery, Elizabeth	X	X	X	X	X	7:30–3:30	
Grant, David	X	X	X	X	X	8–4	
Masterson, Joe		X	X	X		9–3	
Netherling, Adam	X	X	X	X		8:30–3	
Potter, Allison	X	X	X	X	X	7–3	
Pratt, Jeanne	X		X	X	X	10–6	

Actual Space Usage: 266 Child Hours
Actual % Usage: 60%

*This table originally appeared in "Flexible Programming (Your Key to Increasing Revenue)" by Nan Lee Howkins, which appeared in David Pierson's *Child Care Review*, February/March 1989 (Volume 4, Number 2) issue on pages 8–16. Reprinted here by permission of the publisher, *Child Care Review*, P.O. Box 578, Metarie, LA 70004, tel. (504) 831-9662.

and late times. This additional business moved the center into the 90% space usage range.

Financial Projections

Within the first month, the center's profits had more than doubled. Further, the improved profit picture made the prospect of investing in expansion, which a month ago seemed unwise, very attractive indeed.

These are the financial calculations that rejuvenated the center:

> Current Annual Income: $124,080 (47 students at $220/month × 12 months)
> Total Child Hours Available: 2,750/week (50 children × 11 hours x 5 days)
> Actual Time Usage: 1,650 child hours/week
> Percentage of Total Capacity Used: 60% (1,650 child hours/ week actual time usage divided by 2,750 total child hours)

TABLE 6-4   ADDING PART-TIME STUDENTS*
This table shows the same class after part-time students were included.
Note the increase in the percentage of Actual Space Usage.

Name	Mon	Tues	Wed	Thurs	Fri	Hours	Other
Bradford, Thomas	X	X	X	X	X	9–5	
Darby, Erika	X		X	X		7–5	
Emmery, Elizabeth	X	X	X	X	X	7:30–3:30	
Grant, David	X	X	X	X	X	8–4	
Masterson, Joe		X	X	X		9–3	
Netherling, Adam	X	X	X	X		8:30–3	
Potter, Allison	X	X	X	X	X	7–3	
Pratt, Jeanne	X		X	X	X	10–6	
O'Leary, Cindy	X	X			X	7–12:30	
Ashbee, Jennifer	X	X			X	12:30–6	
Williams, Mark	X	X	X	X	X	3–6	
Shelberth, Sarah	X	X	X	X	X	3–6	
Morton, Melanie		X			X	7–1	
Burnside, Ben		X			X	1–6	
Carter, Michael					X	7–6	

Actual Space Usage: 362 Child Hours
Actual % Usage: 82%

*This table originally appeared in an article entitled "Flexible Programming (Your Key to Increasing Revenue)" by Nan Lee Howkins, which appeared in David Pierson's *Child Care Review* in the February/March 1989 (Volume 4, Number 2) issue on pages 8–16. Reprinted here by permission of the publisher, *Child Care Review*, P.O. Box 578, Metarie, LA 70004, tel. (504) 831-9662.

Available Number of Child Hours/Week for Hourly Children: 1,100

Projected Occupancy: 2,475 child hours/week (2,750 total child hours × 90% projection)

Increased Occupancy: 825 child hours/week (projected occupancy minus actual time usage)

Projected Weekly Revenue Increase: $1,650 (increased occupancy of 825 child hours × $2/hour)

Projected Annual Revenue Increase: $85,800 (1,650 × 52 weeks)

In actual practice, the increase in income will probably be larger because some children will be at the $2.50/hour rate rather than the $2/hour rate. Also, some hours will be "sold twice," since the full-time parent will call in to report their child will not be attending that day, thus allowing the center to resell the time slot.

TABLE 6-5 ADDING HOURLY SPACE-AVAILABLE STUDENTS*

This table shows the same class after the occasional (but preregistered) children were admitted on a space-available basis. The circles are children who, though registered, will not attend that day. Note again the increase in the Actual Space Usage percentage.

Name	Mon	Tues	Wed	Thurs	Fri	Hours	Other
Bradford, Thomas	X	X	O	X	O	9–5	
Darby, Erika	X		X	X		7–5	
Emmery, Elizabeth	X	X	X	X	X	7:30–3:30	
Grant, David	X	O	X	O	X	8–4	
Masterson, Joe	O	O	X			9–3	
Netherling, Adam	X	X	X	X		8:30–3	
Potter, Allison	X	X	X	X	O	7–3	
Pratt, Jeanne	X		X	X	X	10–6	
O'Leary, Cindy	X	X			X	7–12:30	
Ashbee, Jennifer	X	X			X	12:30–6	
Williams, Mark	X	X	X	X	X	3–6	
Shelberth, Sarah	X	X	X	X	X	3–6	
Morton, Melanie		X			X	7–1	
Burnside, Ben		X			X	1–6	
Carter, Michael					X	7–6	
Porter, David	X	X			X	9–1	
Aarons, Sara		X				8–5	
Eakins, Natalie				X		8–2	
North, Joshua			X		X	9–3	

Actual Space Usage: 393 Child Hours
Actual % Usage: 89%

*This table originally appeared in an article entitled "Flexible Programming (Your Key to Increasing Revenue)" by Nan Lee Howkins, which appeared in David Pierson's *Child Care Review* in the February/March 1989 (Volume 4, Number 2) issue on pages 8–16. Reprinted here by permission of the publisher, *Child Care Review*, P.O. Box 578, Metairie, LA 70004, tel. (504) 831-9662.

As part of the changed management, the owner took two other steps to increase revenue. While analyzing her business, she realized she was losing four weeks of revenue per year by charging a monthly fee (of $220) based on a four-week month. In fact, each month has 4.3 weeks. So she switched to a weekly basis, which netted the center an additional $18.33 per full-time child per month. Since the owner also planned to increase her tuition rates in six months, she also felt her parents would object less to an increase if it was measured on a weekly basis.

TABLE 6-6   YOUR 9-STEP WORKSHEET*

Use this worksheet to calculate your potential increased revenue. The 90% (or .9) projection in Step 6 is based on the experience of programs currently using the flexible program system. In Step 8, "your hourly fee" is what you plan to charge hourly students for less than 25 hours care a week.

1. **Your Annual Tuition Income**
   Total licensed capacity × weekly tuition × 52 weeks

   $_____

2. **Your Total Child Hours Available**
   Total licensed capacity × total hours of operation × 5 days

   _____
   child hours a week

3. **Your Actual Time Usage**
   Grand total from all classroom teachers' Actual Time Usage forms

   _____
   child hours a week

4. **Your Percentage of Total Capacity Used**
   Your actual time usage (Step 3) ÷ your total child hours available (Step 2)

   _____%

5. **Available Number of Child Hours for Hourly Children**
   Your total child hours (Step 2) − your actual time usage (Step 3)

   _____
   child hours a week

6. **Projected Occupancy**
   Your total child hours available × .9

   _____
   child hours a week

7. **Increased Occupancy**
   Your projected occupancy (Step 6) − your actual time usage (Step 3)

   _____
   child hours a week

8. **Projected Weekly Revenue Increase**
   Your increased occupancy (Step 7) × your hourly fee

   $_____

9. **Projected Annual Increase**
   Projected weekly revenue increase (Step 8) × 52 weeks

   $_____

*Your 9-Step Worksheet" originally appeared in an article entitled "Flexible Programming (Your Key to Increasing Revenue)" by Nan Lee Howkins, which appeared in David Pierson's *Child Care Review* in the February/March 1989 (Volume 4, Number 2) issue on pages 8–16. Reprinted here by permission of the publisher, *Child Care Review*, P.O. Box 578, Metairie, LA 70004, tel. (504) 831-9662.

The second step she took was to charge the hourly care students an extra $15 fee at the time of enrollment to help defray additional bookkeeping costs.

Record Keeping

As you might expect, a flexible program does require a very accurate bookkeeping system. Keeping such records on a greater number of students can be a pure nightmare, especially if paperwork is not your strong point. But the problem of additional paperwork is not a good enough reason to turn your back on an additional $100,000 a year. The flexible program is readily adaptable to a computer system, but fortunately it can also be effectively handled with a good manual system.

The forms in Tables 6-7 and 6-8 show a good basic format for tracking daily enrollment. Each classroom should have its own color-coded forms for enrollment, registration and sign-in. You should keep the enrollment forms for all classrooms on a clipboard at the main sign-in desk and note any changes in scheduled hours immediately on these master sheets, such as a child who is out sick or absent due to a trip. The simplest procedure is to circle the mark by the child's name for the day involved (see Table 6-9). Note any changes in the attendance time at right in the column titled "Other."

If you have a very large enrollment, you may have to use legal-sized paper or even have a morning clipboard and an afternoon clipboard. Whatever system you use, make sure it is easy to tell at a glance if you have space available, so you and your staff can answer inquiries immediately.

All information should be entered on the permanent records at the end of each week, and an accurate running account should be kept for each child. In your account book, keep a single page for each child. With the flexible program, this can mean hundreds of pages but is an absolute necessity. See Chapter 11 for more on organizing and keeping records.

Staff Orientation

To run effectively, the staff must thoroughly understand the purpose of a flexible program and how it will directly and indirectly affect their classrooms. If your center is already in operation, explain that this program initially will make their classrooms more hectic, but that they will receive assistance where necessary. Also, assure them that they will still have the same number of children

TABLE 6-7 ENROLLMENT TRACKING FORM

NAME	7:00	7:30	8:00	8:30	9:00	9:30	10:00	10:30	11:00	11:30	12:00	12:30	1:00	1:30	2:00	2:30	3:00	3:30	4:00	4:30	5:00	5:30	6:00
Bradford, Thomas	X				X	X	X	X	X	X	X	X	X	X	X	X	X	X	X	X	X		
Darby, Erika		X	X	X	X	X	X	X	X	X	X	X	X	X	X	X	X	X	X	X	X	X	
Emmery, Elizabeth		X	X	X	X	X	X	X	X	X	X	X	X	X	X	X	X	X	X	X	X		
Grant, David			X	X	X	X	X	X	X	X	X	X	X	X	X	X	X	X	X				
Masterson, Joe					X	X	X	X	X	X	X	X	X	X	X	X	X						
Netherling, Adam				X	X	X	X	X	X	X	X	X	X	X	X	X	X						
Potter, Allison	X	X	X	X	X	X	X	X	X	X	X	X	X	X	X	X	X						
Pratt, Jeanne							X	X	X	X	X	X	X	X	X	X	X	X	X	X	X	X	X

Day of the week: Monday

TABLE 6-8 SIGN-IN SHEET

Name	Monday		Tuesday		Wednesday		Thursday		Friday		Totals
Bradford, Thomas											
Darby, Erika											
Emmery, Elizabeth											
Grant, David											
Masterson, Joe											
Netherling, Adam											
Potter, Allison											
Pratt, Jeanne											

in their classroom at any one time, and that the core of the children in each classroom—60%—will be attending on a regular basis. As the director, you must make sure the staff incorporates the hourly children into all activities and projects. When hiring staff for a new center, explain the flexible program and the fact that staff members will see many different children each week, and that their own schedules need to be flexible.

Occasionally, there will be a teacher who is unable to accept this flexible situation. As in all other management situations, you will need to make your position very clear and help the hesitant employee understand that the new system is staying, and to continue employment she must adjust. Your staff manual should clearly state that a condition of employment is adherence to the philosophy and goals of the center, so if an employee does not conform, appropriate disciplinary action can be taken. (See Chapter 13.)

However, any new program will not work if the staff does not believe in it and does not incorporate it into the classroom. The new program will mean an increased workload for your staff at

TABLE 6-9 ENROLLMENT TRACKING FORM WITH SCHEDULE CHANGES

Day of week: Monday

NAME	7:00	7:30	8:00	8:30	9:00	9:30	10:00	10:30	11:00	11:30	12:00	12:30	1:00	1:30	2:00	2:30	3:00	3:30	4:00	4:30	5:00	5:30	6:00
Bradford, Thomas	X				X	X	X	X	X	X	X	X	X	X	X	X	X	X	X	X	X	X	
Darby, Erika		X	X	X	X	X	X	X	X	X	X	X	X	X	X	X	X	X	X	X	X	X	
Emmery, Elizabeth		X	X	X	X	X	X	X	X	X	X	X	X	X	X	X	X	X					
Grant, David			⊗	⊗	⊗	⊗	⊗	⊗	⊗	⊗	⊗	⊗	⊗	⊗		⊗	⊗	⊗	⊗				
Masterson, Joe					X	X	X	X	X	X	X	X	X	X	X	X	X						
Netherling, Adam				X	X	X	X	X	X	X	⊗	⊗	⊗	⊗	⊗	⊗	⊗						
Potter, Allison	X	X	X	X	X	X	X	X	X	X	X	X	X	X	X	X	X						
Pratt, Jeanne							X	X	X	X	X	X	X	X	X	X	X	X	X	X	X	X	X

times. The most important thing is to explain everything to them during the transition. Assure them that the extra effort will also benefit them if it results in improved business.

Have individual meetings with each staff member within a week of the new program to hear any problems. Group staff meetings are usually not a good idea at the start of a flexible program as issues can be easily blown out of proportion; it is easier to diffuse worries on an individual basis.

Plan, by the way, to hire a "floater"—this is someone who "floats" between two or three classrooms helping with snacks, lunches, changing and outdoor play and also helping to introduce children who arrive at odd times. Typically, a floater is needed for only three hours per day—10 A.M. to 1 P.M. are the most predictably busy times. When hiring the floater, look for someone who could "find the glasses in your kitchen on her own." She should have a keen sense of humor and should be self-motivated.

When first instituting a flexible program, the director and office staff should expect to also help with the floater's chores one or two busy days a week. During the initial weeks of the new program, the director should always be at the center at the busy times and ready to lend a hand or offer advice.

And a final word of caution: Experience has shown that, for every increase of 10 registered children, the staff will have to make major adjustments. This is the time when a manager must have a clear vision of the goals and be very calm. The resulting success will be well worth it.

THE ADVANTAGES OF A FLEXIBLE PROGRAM FOR YOUR COMMUNITY AND YOUR CENTER

With a flexible program, you will provide a service that accommodates the needs of many more children and parents from the community. Previously, parents who could not afford or did not want full-time care may have been left with undesirable choices—non-regulated child care, latchkey situations for their children or their own unemployment. With this program you are helping these parents buy the few hours of coverage they need for their children. They can be at ease, knowing their children are in a licensed facility with a quality program, instead of in an unregulated baby-sitting service.

Within the first year you can realistically expect, for a licensed capacity of 50 children, to be serving at least 150 different children in the facility each week. If your licensed capacity is 75, you can expect weekly usage by at least 325 different children. If you later increase your licensed capacity, your weekly usage increases exponentially, because you have more possible combinations to accommodate parents' child care needs.

You must be committed and your approach must be positive to make flexibility work. Immediately address any inquiries regarding your program with an eye toward reaching a satisfactory solution for that parent. Make it clear to everyone—the parents, your staff and yourself—that your center is not there to serve just the needs of a few parents for full-time child care, but that you intend to provide a quality program that serves the varied needs of the community.

If you are implementing flexibility into an already operating center, marketing will be a major concern for you for the first few weeks. The steps you should take to introduce the program to your community are fully detailed in Chapter 15. They include creating and distributing a brochure, having tours of the center and contacting local realtors, school guidance departments, hospitals, businesses and the local press.

By increasing your center's profits, thereby making available more money, a flexible program can substantially improve salaries, purchase supplies and equipment and generally enhance the quality of your child care service. As with constructive change and growth in any business, there will be a transition period that may be difficult. But remember that your positive management and a true commitment by your staff can mean the difference between success and failure, not just with the flexible program but with your child care center.

7
INFANT/TODDLER CARE
• •

In nearly every community there is a critical need for quality infant and toddler care, perhaps because this is the most difficult age group for which to provide child care services. Infants are defined as children from birth to 12 months, and toddlers as those 13 through 35 months. To effectively care for both these groups, low staff ratios must be strictly adhered to and very hygienic conditions maintained. In addition, although the business of child care is generally very labor intensive, the care of the very young child requires especially large numbers of caregivers. In this chapter you will learn how to provide top-quality, consistent infant/toddler care using a flexible, cost-effective program.

Most child care centers that provide infant and toddler care do not allow the children to attend on a flexible basis. This is primarily because administrators think that the risk of infection is too great and the maintenance of hygienic conditions too difficult to justify the convenience for parents or even the increase in income to the center.

However, good infant and toddler care can be provided on a flexible, hygienic basis with minimum risk to the children. Many centers that offer such a program have had tremendous success; their clients have been pleased and do not object to the higher hourly cost for the convenient scheduling. Most important, centers using this method are actually encouraging the parent—the primary caregiver—to be with their young child as much as possible, an extremely important concern in this age group.

PHYSICAL ARRANGEMENTS

Sleeping Areas

Traditionally in the infant section, rest areas are kept separate from play areas, because infants' schedules vary and some babies take two naps, others one. Some centers attempt to maintain a group sleeping schedule geared to the needs of the largest number of babies; however, this is usually not in the best interest of the infants. If you allow for individual differences in personality and sleep patterns, letting each infant choose his or her own schedule, the infants will usually be more content.

In order to accommodate individual schedules, you will need to make some philosophical and practical decisions; namely, do infants really need total quiet in order to sleep properly, and if so, can you actually separate the sleeping area from the play area without decreasing the supervision? As every provider who has cared for infants knows, one of the main fears is that an infant will become ill while napping and a supervisor won't notice. In truth, there may be little one can do to save an infant from sudden infant death syndrome, for example, but nonetheless infants should be directly supervised at all times while in a child care facility and this includes their naps. Therefore, your sleeping areas should not be separated by physical and acoustical barriers unless you intend to have a caregiver in the napping area at all times.

Changing and Toileting Areas

Each infant and toddler room must have a sink near the changing area that is totally separate from any meal, snack or formula preparation surface. The following precautions will minimize the risk of infection:

- Either elbow faucets or faucets operated by electronic pedals wherever possible.
- If this is not feasible, a paper towel dispenser next to the sink. Train the staff to use the paper towels to turn the faucet on and off, thus keeping the germs from the diaper area from spreading.
- An exhaust fan installed above the changing area and in all toileting areas to remove germs and fumes.

- Well-covered dispensers for the soiled diapers and changing table liners right next to the area. Remove these regularly during the course of the day.
- All toddler areas should have small accessible toilets. NEVER use potty chairs, because in this setting they cannot be sanitized and have been known to contribute to the spread of hepatitis among staff and parents. (Children rarely show signs of this disease but are carriers).

When constructing the toileting areas for toddlers, you should use a low wall with a Plexiglas window for easy supervision and a dutch (half) door. If possible, place the toileting area between two toddler rooms so that they can share the space, and a common supervisor can lend a hand during hectic times. It is usually best to have the sinks located just outside the toilet area for supervision purposes. This also encourages the staff to help the children learn that they should always wash their hands before eating, which will cut the infection rate way down in your center.

"Floor" Plan

Infant/toddler areas should have as much floor space as possible for crawling and exploring. About 60% of the room should be carpeted with the other portion tiled, especially in the feeding area where it is important for easy cleaning. This percentage may vary for very young infants who are held for feeding rather than being placed in a high chair. Conversely, in the toddler area, it is easier to have only a small carpeted area for books and quiet time as the toddlers need space for eating, painting, using Play-doh and being the messy young explorers they should be!

Storage for Belongings

Provide convenient storage for each child's belongings with plenty of space, especially if the parents provide their child's diapers. (With flexible scheduling, it is better for the center to provide the diapers to save confusion and space; just build the additional cost into the price.) The storage area should be near the entrance to the room so there is as little disruption as possible when infants arrive and leave. Be VERY careful to put the storage area out of the babies' reach and secure it so that objects cannot fall out on their heads. For this reason a small closet may be best.

Label these areas clearly so that important items do not get mixed up. Movable containers or bins can be labeled on each side and rotated for different children, or you can use stackable containers that can be readily interchanged. You may find that parents are not terribly diligent about taking the child's belongings home each day, but this should be a requirement. Particularly with a flexible program where there are many children using the center, personal belongings should be taken home each day to avoid a cluttered, disorganized atmosphere. Parents should also be required to label all items brought with the child to ease the burden on the teachers.

Toddlers each need a storage area for both changes of clothing and their outer gear. The changes of clothing can be managed with bins as in the infant areas, but because many toddlers are starting to dress themselves, hooks for their outdoor clothes are needed to encourage independence. Most important, these areas should be close to the entrance area of the room so that the children's activities are not disrupted by individual arrivals and departures. This is particularly necessary in a flexible program where a classroom that accommodates eight toddlers may easily have as many as 16 different children in it each day.

Storage for teachers' belongings should be well out of sight and reach since, for example, there are often dangerous pills or objects stored in a teacher's pocketbook.

Toy Storage

Two or three storage shelves for toys are all that is needed in the young child areas as this age range has difficulty even removing toys from the shelves. Particularly with infants the teachers make the choices of play materials and place them within easy reach.

As the children reach the toddler age, there should be some low shelving with a few play things on each shelf but not so much as to confuse the child. Make it easy for the children to remove and return toys to the shelf; if the teachers are constantly correcting the toddlers, the arrangement and materials in the room are not working *with* the teachers. The teachers should rotate the materials regularly. Be certain that all shelves are securely anchored and that no heavy toys can fall on the children's heads.

Use of Lighting and Colors

Keep in mind when designing your space that color, light and texture are important considerations for the very young child. You might decide to use indirect lighting or have alternative forms of lighting available for different times of the day. Most centers use only harsh overhead lighting which does not create a soft, comfortable atmosphere for young children. The addition of track or spot lights can add to the feeling of the room.

Recent studies have shown that infants are stimulated more by vibrant colors such as red and orange rather than pastels. Since you will be responsible for the major growth and development of many of the infants and toddlers in your care, you might want to try new design techniques to tastefully incorporate stimulating color schemes. Remember too that the very young child needs a variety of textures and should be encouraged to explore new horizons safely in his surroundings. Using color and texture is an easy way to establish a noninstitutional, welcoming atmosphere.

Room and Staff Continuity

When planning or renovating space for infants and toddlers, keep the importance of continuity in mind. As infants grow older, it is best for them to have the same caregiver in the same space whenever possible until they move into the preschool area. If you are maintaining the same space for the very young children, it will only be necessary to rotate the materials and equipment so that both are age appropriate as the children grow and develop. For example, it would not be desirable or practical to have eight high chairs in a space now being used by children who have turned two and are learning to use a table and chair and, more important, need as much space as possible.

In some instances, keeping the same staff throughout the very young years may not be practical. For example, you may have a caregiver who is really excellent with very young infants and should be left with that age group. If a caregiver will not stay with a group of children, then on a gradual basis introduce the children to the new caregiver, physical space and other new children they will be with. This can be accomplished by having the infant(s) who will be moving make "visits" to the new situation.

Obviously, if you have built-in cribs, you move the children and the caregiver. Also, if you have one infant who is "borderline" or develops more rapidly than the group, and a space in the next age range becomes available, you should move that one child.

EQUIPMENT

Infants

All basic equipment—cribs, cots, high chairs, walkers, etc.—should be easy to sanitize daily with a diluted bleach solution or suitable industrial cleaner.

Portable cribs are the most common in child care centers because they are small and easy to store when not in use. You may opt to use the mesh-type play pen as a sleeping place with a thicker mattress. Some centers are even using wall unit cribs with storage space underneath; this makes for both an efficient use of space and a less institutional appearance.

Infant seats and high chairs should be sturdy and easily stored when not in use to allow more space for crawling and walking. All surfaces should be easy to clean yet have contrasting textures. There should be no sharp corners or edges.

You will need a way to take the infants outside daily for fresh air. You can use play pens, a small fenced-in, secure area or a screened-in porch. There are also delightful new strollers that can seat four infants safely at the same time.

In infant areas, there should be a rocking chair or comfortable seating area for each caregiver. This will encourage individual feeding of the infants and help the staff to relax; a calm caregiver is more comforting to an infant. For the same reason, soft music may help create a relaxed atmosphere—all children seem to respond well to occasional, quality background music. Use tape cassette players to provide appropriate music for the individual rooms.

A small hot plate or a microwave in the room is necessary to heat formula. If you decide to use a microwave, the staff must be very careful as it is easy to overheat the formula, which can seriously burn a child's esophagus.

To further reduce the risk of infection, reserve an area for a washer and dryer. Having these appliances at the center will not only save hours of work at home or the expense of a laundry service, but will also make it easier for the staff to change bedding between children when several children are using the sleeping area during the week. The area for the washer and dryer does not need to be large and can fit in a closet next to the cleaning or supply storage closets.

Toddlers

For the 13- to 35-month-olds, you may decide to use cots, especially the shorter ones designed for this age range. Cot storage can be a major problem. For example, cots stored in a pile in the classroom can be a real eyesore and take up valuable floor space that will not be considered "usable child space" for licensing requirements. Here are two alternatives. A table built at a height at which the toddlers can stand (which they sometimes prefer anyway) can accommodate the cots slid under one side. At least one manufacturer has developed such a table. There are also cots and mats available that can be hung on a wall. Their drawback is they can be unsightly, and you must make certain that they cannot fall onto the children. Before ordering mats, make sure that your state allows mats for sleeping.

The toddler rooms should have several small tables so that a few children at a time can work and play together. Having eight toddlers eat or do an art activity at one table does not encourage individual growth or stimulation. Plus you are pushing the patience of a two-year-old, if you expect him to wait while six or seven other children use the paste first. Your staff will find it much easier to work with two toddlers at a time on an activity while the others are using different materials. At eating times, two or three tables of four toddlers each—with a caregiver at the most disruptive table—is much more manageable.

As you would with older children, divide the toddler room into activity areas. If your state requires toddlers to be in groups of eight but your room is large enough for 16, you may decide to divide the space into two varied areas and rotate the children between them. Toddlers love make-believe and dress-up areas. A small indoor activity space to release some of their excess energy and develop large muscles is a good idea as well.

The number of materials accessible to the toddlers should be limited and easy for the child to take care of. Do not have wooden blocks as these can be lethal in the hands of a toddler. But you should have cardboard blocks and soft blocks. See Figure 7-1 for an example of areas in a preschool room.

In addition, toddlers love any manipulative materials that they can nest, bang or experiment with. These can be as simple as pots, pans, spoons and an egg beater or quality puzzles and hardcover books. Arts and crafts materials add interest and provide a challenge. Remember that this is a stage of very rapid growth and development so there should be a wide variety of materials to stimulate each individual child.

OUTSIDE PLAY AREAS

Outside play areas for the very young child must be adjacent to the room. Many centers have found that it is easier to keep the infants (up to 13 months) and toddlers totally separate when they

FIGURE 7-1   3-D DEPICTION OF A SAMPLE PRESCHOOL ROOM

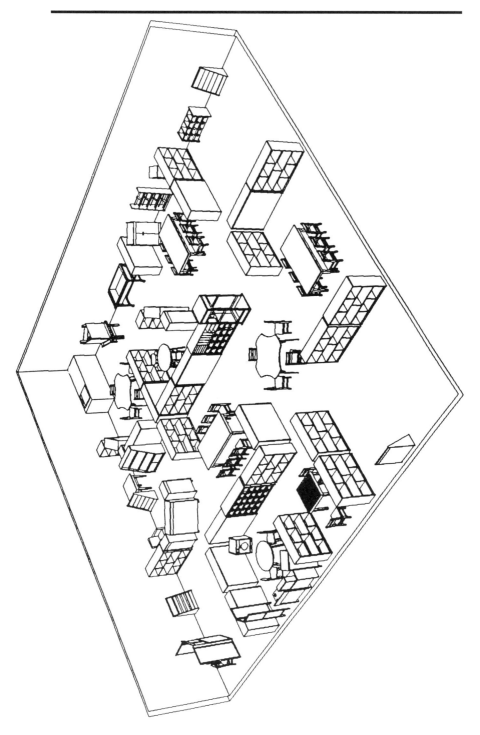

Educational Design drawings compliments of Kaplan School Supplies, Louisville, N.C.

are outside. This will depend upon the number of infants and toddlers that you are caring for; however, each area should be visible from the other since young children love to watch the activity of other children.

When you install climbing equipment, remember that a child can be easily injured in a fall from twice his height! Swings, climbers and slides should have a sand, crushed rubber or other alternative surface underneath to a depth of eight to 12 inches to minimize the risk of serious injury. When designing the play area, remember to include plenty of running and exploring space for the toddlers.

No matter what climate your center is in, there will be times of the year when it is difficult to get the children outside for a portion of the day. If it is too cold to take the very young infants outside since they are not very mobile, consider having inside/outside play time. Dress the infants in their outside clothes and open all the windows. Conversely in very hot, humid climates, go out early or late in the day for everyone's comfort.

Environmental concerns in some areas may limit the outside play options. For example, if your center is in an urban setting, only filtered air in a covered area may be safe for young children. As the infants grow and begin to crawl, they want to explore outdoors and watch birds, insects, leaves, flowers and nature. A simple ground covering or net pen will suffice to protect them from insects.

Toddlers love balls, objects to crawl on and through and walks in strollers and carriages. They enjoy a regular swing with a toddler seat at this stage, but would rather be on the move. Older toddlers love to use their newfound strength to climb and run and explore as much as they can.

STAFFING

The caregivers in the infant and toddler areas need as much support as possible from the administrative staff to avoid burnout, an all too frequent problem. The turnover rate for staff in infant care is often very high, and unfortunately this lack of continuity can be disastrous for the very young child.

To alleviate burnout, consider implementing a four-day work week. On such a schedule each staff member works four days a week, nine hours per day with a half-hour lunch and two 15-minute breaks. Scheduling may seem difficult, but if you think of each group of teachers in units of four it becomes easier. For example, if classrooms A and B need two teachers each, schedule each of the four teachers for a day off each week and hire a fifth teacher to work with this "unit" of teachers and cover the days off. This system can also reduce the need for substitutions as the teachers can substitute for each other, thereby keeping the staff consistent. The children get to know the five-member teaching team well and feel more comfortable. The director of one large center, who has been using this method for eight months, said she has needed a substitute teacher only two times! Plus her turnover rate is way down, and the teachers seem less stressed and much happier. In most cases, the teachers love having a day off for personal chores or time with their families.

Since you will not need a full staff for all hours, stagger the work schedule according to the number of children and the times they arrive and depart. Again, the centers that have used this staffing method have found that the parents like seeing the same caregivers in the morning and the evening. An extra bonus in this type of set-up is that the age of the caregiver is generally older, alleviating the need for large numbers of "fill-in" high school and college students in the late afternoon. Statistically the late afternoon hours are the most dangerous of the day, and a more experienced staff can mean safer care.

The qualities one looks for in caregivers of young children are somewhat different than those needed in the preschool and school-age areas. All caregivers must be patient and have a basic knowledge of the developmental stages of infants and toddlers. Chart 7-2 may be helpful in your search for the appropriate people. It is also advisable to require that all staff members receive training in both first aid for young children and in infant/toddler CPR.

If your state does not have a specific requirement about the staff ratios for infant/toddler care, establish good ratios yourself and use this as a selling point. Better ratios are also an excellent reason for charging more. According to the accreditation standards of the National Association for the Education of Young Children, infants should have a staff ratio of one to three and toddlers, one to four (the latter depending on the qualifications of the caregivers, with one to six being the highest acceptable ratio). Remember that the ratios you decide to use must also coincide with the licensing regulations. If the lower ratios are not feasible, consider adding a "floater" to the staff at peak activity hours to assist the regular caregivers. (See Chapter 6.)

Finally, you will want to encourage professionalism. There are many excellent courses at community colleges, and early childhood conferences usually have excellent speakers; you and your staff should take advantage of them. Your staff should have at least one teacher who is well trained in developmentally appropriate practices for infants and toddlers, because good training in infant and toddler care is difficult to find. Establish a dress code and at the very least provide smocks that make each staff member feel a valued part of the team. For their comfort you might also consider having a shower available if the center has large numbers of young children so that the staff can clean up thoroughly when there's an accident.

COMMUNICATION BETWEEN PARENTS AND CAREGIVERS

Since young children cannot communicate other than by crying if something is wrong, you need complete information about their care; the most effective way to obtain it is via forms. For each child you must have thorough developmental charts, health forms and permissions on file. If a parent has not filled out the forms completely, you should refuse to accept their child until they have done so.

In addition, both the caregivers and parents will need detailed, daily updates. Each morning, the parents should talk to the caregiver about what kind of night the child had and any special scheduling or feeding considerations for that day. Without this knowledge, the staff will have no idea of how to treat the child during the day and what to watch for. Throughout the day, the staff should keep track on a form of what has happened to the child, i.e., how many times fed, changed, bathed, what the child ate, likes and dislikes and new activities. This bolsters parents' confidence and makes them feel better about the care the child is receiving.

Speaking of communication with parents, there is one certain but unwritten rule to insure parents' happiness—the young child NEVER does anything first at the center. We jokingly say that no child has ever taken his *first* step at a child care center! But many times you will hear a staff member say, "I think that Johnny is about to walk. . . . Keep an eye on him!"

CURRICULUM

In a quality infant and toddler program there will not be a curriculum per se. However, the staff must understand the develop-

CHART 7-2   CHARACTERISTICS OF COMPETENT INFANT CAREGIVERS*

Desired Caregiver Characteristics	Cues to Desirable Caregiver Characteristics
I. Personality Factors	
A. Child-centered	1. Attentive and loving to infants. 2. Meets infants' needs before own.
B. Self-confident	1. Relaxed and anxiety free. 2. Skilled in physical care of infants. 3. Individualistic caregiving style.
C. Flexible	1. Uses different styles of caregiving to meet individual needs of infants. 2. Spontaneous and open behavior. 3. Permits increasing freedom of infant with development.
D. Sensitive	1. Understands infants' cues readily. 2. Shows empathy for infants. 3. Acts purposefully in interactions with infants.
II. Attitudes and Values	
A. Displays positive outlook on life	1. Expresses positive affect. 2. No evidence of anger, unhappiness or depression.
B. Enjoys infants	1. Affectionate to infants. 2. Shows obvious pleasure in involvement with infants
C. Values infants more than possessions or immaculate appearance	1. Dresses practically and appropriately. 2. Places items not for infants' use out of reach. 3. Reacts to infant destruction or messiness with equanimity. 4. Takes risks with property in order to enhance infant development.
III. Behavior	
A. Interacts appropriately with infants	1. Frequent interactions with infants. 2. Balances interaction with leaving infants alone. 3. Optimum amounts of touching, holding, smiling and looking. 4. Responds consistently and without delay to infants; is always accessible. 5. Speaks in positive tone of voice. 6. Shows clearly that infants are loved and accepted.

B. Facilitates development

1. Does not punish infants.
2. Plays with infants.
3. Provides stimulation with toys and objects.
4. Permits freedom to explore, including floor freedom.
5. Cooperates with infant-initiated activities and explorations.
6. Provides activities which stimulate achievement or goal orientation.
7. Acts purposefully in an educational role to teach and facilitate learning and development.

*Reprinted by permission of the publisher, the National Association for the Education of Young Children, 1509 16th St., N.W., Washington, D.C. 20036-1426.

mental stages of the young child and have appropriate materials ready and available for each stage of development. This is a very important period of growth as 30% of our total knowledge base is accumulated before the age of three (50% by age five)! The center should have an excellent reference library for your staff (see Appendix F) and a list of resources to call when you suspect that a child may be showing a developmental delay or has a hearing problem or is even being abused.

In conclusion, encourage your staff to treat each child as an individual with varying growth patterns. The supervisors of the infant/toddler areas should be able to demonstrate new methods to use in the classroom or have someone available who can do so. The care of infants and toddlers can be most challenging, but also extremely rewarding.

8

PRESCHOOL CHILD CARE

Preschool programs located in a child care center are probably the most available form of child care; in fact many communities have a surplus of care for three- and four-year-olds. When planning this part of your program be certain there are enough preschool children needing care. Your market analysis should have indicated if too many openings already existed for this age group. During the start-up phase and summer months of your center, you should be certain you have enough potential enrollment.

Fortunately, there is almost always a need for *flexible* care for the preschool child, and you will be able to sell the *hourly* program at a higher rate in nearly every community at any time of the year. If you could analyze the number of hours existing centers are used, as outlined in Chapter 6, you would probably find that for this age group there is the most inefficient use of available child hours.

PHYSICAL ARRANGEMENT

Designing the Activity Space

The arrangement of the rooms will set the tone for the whole preschool program. A good rule of thumb to use when designing quality space is that the children should easily be able to understand the purpose of each area and how to use it with as little teacher direction as possible. Because a child may be in the space for up to 10 hours each day, the activity areas in each preschool room should offer a wide variety of choice. Children at this age should be on their own—learning, exploring, questioning and reasoning. The teacher role, for the most part, is to facilitate this learning and to direct some curriculum activities during the morning hours.

In the design phase it is useful to draw the room to scale on graph paper and actually place scale drawings of the dividers and large equipment onto the plan. This will help you see how much space there will be between dividers, tables and shelving. The activity areas in each room will vary with your program philosophy. Some areas can have a dual purpose especially where space is limited; however, in general a good preschool area needs spaces for the following:

Entrance
Circle or meeting time (carpet)
Block building
Arts and crafts, Painting
Library
Audio/Visual equipment
Manipulatives
Kitchen/Dress-up
Indoor games/Music
Science/Animals
Quiet Area

Keep in mind that the children will need to eat and rest throughout this same space. Some states require cots rather than mats for rest time, and your fire marshal may have some definite opinions about how far apart the cots must be, so try to check this out discreetly. Snack and meal time can take place at the tables in most activity areas, but at least one table should be on a tiled, easily cleaned surface for messy eaters. More information on each of these areas is provided below.

Good physical planning is important, because a poorly designed entrance or misplaced furniture and materials can create a chaotic and hectic atmosphere.

Entrance and Storage for Belongings

The entrance into the room must facilitate the flow of children in an orderly, nondisruptive manner. In a classroom designed for a maximum of 20 children at any time, a flexible program can easily have as many as 50 different children using the room during the week. Of course, there will never be more than the maximum capacity of 20 children at any given time, but the entrance area must accommodate shared individual space for the total number of children using the classroom. It's best to create a little entrance area where personal belongings can be stored. A separate entrance provides an extra bonus of giving children a more private place to say good-bye to their parent. There are some children who have trouble with transitions, and this space will allow them to make a more gradual entrance into the room.

In some centers the owners have opted to have hooks and shelves just outside the classroom. A hall should be about five feet wide to facilitate traffic flow. Also, be sure to check the fire codes in your area for regulations on hallway widths.

Cubbies for personal storage do not work very well in flexible programs, because it is difficult to make certain that each child removes all belongings as he leaves each time. In many centers, too, the cubbies are a constant source of irritation for the management, because teachers rarely clean them out and they always look a mess when you enter the room. If you *do* opt to use cubbies, be sure to bolt them securely to the floor.

Whether using hooks with shelves or cubbies, you should NEVER put the storage units along the wall in the classroom. This arrangement takes up too much valuable space, and arrivals and departures make for constant disruptions.

Circle Area

The carpet area for classroom meeting time or circle time should be well away from the entrance area. A corner area is usually best where there is little interruption. Also, it's useful to attach a piece of plain carpet to the wall or the back of a bookcase somewhere in the carpet area for a flannel board. If you use a block storage bookcase (bolted for safety) as a room divider, this area could double as a space for block building.

Block Area

The block area should be separate with plenty of space to build in. If the space is too near to the center of the room's activity, the children won't be able to build without being disturbed. One child's creation in a high traffic area is an invitation for another child's destruction. Once, when helping to redesign a center, we met with a group of teachers and had the director pretend to be a child building a wonderful structure while the head teacher was a child playing with a baby buggy. The "head teacher-child" crashed through the "director-child's" structure and there ensued a terrific argument to the delight of the staff. Suddenly there was a hearty laugh in the doorway from the three-year-old child of one of the teachers who was thoroughly enjoying the scene! Provide enough space on the shelves for the blocks to be stored logically and for auxiliary articles such as small cars, people, animals and other "props."

There should be another block area in the room for the larger blocks to create really big projects. The least expensive, quietest and most enjoyable type of block for this area is the cardboard, brick-patterned block and, again, you will need to have a neat storage area for these.

Arts and Crafts

The arts and crafts area should be large enough to house both an easel and a wide table for activities. There may be a smaller table or shelf off to one side on which the teacher can place different materials (such as collage items) for the children to use at their leisure during the day. To help with clean-up, this area should definitely NOT be carpeted and should have plenty of storage for the materials.

Drying space for projects is always a problem, but here are some ideas:

- Hang strings from cup hooks across the corners of the room above the adult's eye level for hanging paintings and other art activities.
- Use traditional clothes-drying racks.
- Transport the projects on old cookie sheets to a higher shelf or space not being used.
- Have special racks and shelves built on the walls near the arts and crafts area for drying.

Library

The children in your care need good books available to them at all times. To encourage good reading habits and a respect for books, you should store the books on a book display rack—a *few* at a time—and rotate them regularly. As with many types of equipment, children cannot take care of the books properly if the storage space is not well designed. In many centers the books are destroyed in a very short period because they are not stored properly and too many are put out at once. Unfortunately, directors often don't replace them because they feel the money is wasted if the books aren't taken care of. Tragically, the children are being penalized because the adults have mismanaged the storage concepts!

Audio/Video Area

In many child care centers there are also areas where the children can use head sets to listen to tapes. This should be a quiet space with interesting art on the walls that you can change frequently. Use your imagination to create an interesting environment for the children to listen to various types of music and stories. Borrow new tapes regularly from your local library so that the children are exposed to different things.

You may choose to have a TV/VCR cabinet in the listening area for showing tapes. This can be combined with the audio area since it will not be used every day. The television and VCR may be portable and brought into the room on a cart. If you leave the television in the room, be sure to have it concealed except when in use. There are now special media centers made for child care centers and schools that centralize the storage of the materials and equipment needed to listen to music. However, you can just as easily use an accessible area of the room and arrange the material and equipment attractively.

Many excellent videos have been developed for use with children. But in an educational setting, a world of caution is in order. Be very selective about the use of the VCR and make certain that video viewing is a supplement to your quality curriculum, not a substitute for program activities. Using the television and VCR too often will not encourage the children in your care to develop and use their imagination, creative thinking and problem-solving skills.

You may be tempted to rent entertainment videos that are currently popular with children, but again be very cautious; many of these are violent and not appropriate for the young child. Nearly every preschool teacher knows their effect on the children; violence becomes an accepted behavior in the classroom shortly after the viewing.

Assure parents that television is used only as a supplement on a limited basis. Many parents are concerned with what their children view, and it is a good idea to post a list of what the children have been viewing.

Manipulatives

Manipulative areas should be well divided from the active play areas and encourage children to concentrate on a given activity. Tables in these areas should generally be smaller, with seating for not more than six children at a time per table. Encouraging children to work in small groups will enable each child to use materials creatively and give the teacher a chance to teach more easily on an individual basis.

Storage areas should be easily accessible and make sense to the child. For example, piling wooden puzzles on a shelf makes it impossible for a young child to remove one from the bottom or to return the puzzle to its proper place. Children enjoy logic and order, and the storage methods used in your classrooms should emphasize this. The preschool child does not mind taking care of materials as long as the adults in his world have designed the storage areas to encourage his efforts. This will mean—above all else—that there should be only a *few* materials on each shelf. For example with puzzle storage, it would be far better to use a small puzzle rack or to simply lay out four puzzles on the shelf side by side. As a general rule, you should decide how many manipulative materials you want to display on each shelf (two or three is usually a good number), and ask your teachers to rotate the materials on a regular basis. For this reason the manipulative area should be close, if possible, to the storage closet in the room.

Kitchen and Dress-Up

The kitchen is a key area for make-believe and creative role-playing. All objects should be as realistic as possible so children can easily relate to the roles they play in the surroundings. For example, children react better to modern kitchen sets because they are more like the appliances at home. One unit even has a wall telephone on it, and you'll often see a child cooking while talking animatedly with the phone on his shoulder! The more traditional wooden sets are sturdy but not nearly as attractive to the young child in either color or form.

The dress-up area should be adjacent to the kitchen to encourage role-playing. If possible, mount a nonbreakable mirror nearby. Dress-up props should also be realistic, with plenty of sports jackets and clip-on ties as well as wonderful dresses for the ladies. All sorts of wigs, hats and helmets are fun too. As your collection grows, rotate the various pieces to keep interest. (By the way, if your center has an outbreak of lice, don't throw your valuable dress-up collection out; just place all clothes and headgear in a black plastic bag and seal for 48 hours.)

Indoor Games and Music

Some centers have incorporated a special space in their facilities for indoor active games and music. This is a nice addition particularly in northern climates where it sometimes gets too cold for outside play. The area must be designed carefully in order for it to be safe. For example, if the floor surface is hardwood, an indoor climbing frame would be especially dangerous if a child should fall. If riding vehicles are used, the room can get extremely noisy, and again can be more dangerous because of the confined nature of the space.

The area must be wisely used and very well supervised by the teachers. One of the best and safest uses are for activities such as "Farmer in the Dell," "Duck, Duck, Goose!" or music using such props as rhythm sticks or instruments.

However, if you decide to include a space like this as part of your center, be sure to make it "convertible"; you may soon need it for regular classroom space. One way or another, you will pay the square footage cost for this space and it may be a luxury you cannot afford. With good classroom planning, the teacher can provide indoor, large motor activities and music within the normal classroom setup.

Science/Animals

The science area can be incorporated anywhere in the room; it is most often placed on a surface adjacent to the manipulative area. If you don't position the area near a window, have a "grow" light handy for planting. There should be space enough to spread objects out and encourage touching and exploring. Place animals where children can easily observe them and take part in their care each day, with teacher supervision only. One teacher found a dead goldfish beside the fish tank; a child had removed the fish to "pet" it because he felt it needed love—very appropriate behavior under other conditions!

Quiet Area

In a quality child care center, there should be a "quiet" space for a child to just be alone or talk with a friend in some privacy. This space can be created in unusual ways that will enhance the variety and interest of the room. For example, you may be able to make a "house" under a staircase with carpeting and a light. Install a vandalism-proofed, exterior light like the ones outside apartments that are difficult to break. Perhaps there's a fireplace in the room that you can block off and make cozy. Or set off a small separate place with a short wall and cover it and the floor with soft carpet. These areas may double as a reading or listening area.

Toileting and Sinks

To promote good hygiene and personal habits, there should be at least one toilet adjacent to each room. Be sure to check on licensing standards for the number of children allowed for each toilet. If, for example, the requirement is one toilet for every 15 children and you have two preschool rooms with 20 children each, you may decide to put a common toileting area between the two rooms with access from each room. Plexiglas windows cut to adult eye level are advisable in order to supervise activities inside at all times. Sinks should be in the actual classroom but adjacent to the toileting area for convenient hand-washing. One option is to incorporate one deeper sink for water play at certain times. This deeper sink will also help the teachers with paint clean-up.

Time for Change

Once the center is in use, you may need to adapt the physical design occasionally. The best indication that a change is needed is when children become argumentative. This nearly always means that they are bored and that the spatial arrangement and materials are not working WITH the teacher to promote the interest and active participation of the children. As the director, you will want to work with the classroom teacher to improve the layout of the space so that once again there are happy children actively enjoying the space. While you and the teacher evaluate the floor plan and make positive changes, you may find that the equipment and materials have to be reconsidered as well.

EQUIPMENT

In order to have developmentally appropriate equipment in the preschool area, you must carefully plan for the various age spans and for individual differences in growth and development. For example, you can have a three-year-old child who is reading and a five-year-old child who doesn't know his basic colors. It won't take long for an experienced teacher to identify the strengths and weaknesses of each child, but it is your responsibility to have the materials available that the teacher needs for each child. Encourage your teachers to rotate the materials in the room frequently so that the activities available grow with the children and keep their interest.

Storage Units

As mentioned before, each area should have a limited number of well-arranged materials on each shelf or surface. Above all, there should be a certain order to the room so it doesn't look confusing. There should be plenty of shelf space in each area of the room at the child's level. Children should be able to remove and replace items from the shelf very easily; they will need to take an active part in taking care of the materials in order to learn responsibility.

Tables and Chairs

When choosing tables and chairs for the space, make sure that they are the correct height and size. Your distributor or consultant can assist in this decision, but here are recommendations for the various age ranges:

Age	Height of Chairs	Height of Table
1	8"–10"	15"
2–3	8"–10"	15"–20"
4–5	12"–14"	20"–24"
6–8	15"–16"	24"–26"
8 and up	16"–18"	26"–30"

The optimum seating capacity is no more than six children at a table. Keep each group small, and the children will be less intimidated, find it easier to develop at an individual rate and make friends more easily. But be sure to have enough seating at snack and lunch time for the total room capacity. For example, a room with a licensed capacity for 20 children at one time should have at least three tables for six children and one table for two children. The popular kidney-shaped tables are wonderful for teaching; however, they are usually quite large and rarely fit well into preschool spaces.

Cots and Mats

In ordering cots or rest mats, shop around for the best price and quality. If your available space for the preschool children is small, remember to consider how much the legs stick out from the cot and whether the walking space between the cots meets the fire codes in your area.

Another important consideration is storage of the cots. Nothing looks worse in a child care center than a stack of cots going every which way in a corner of the room; it is unrealistic to expect your staff to be neat with the cots using the stacking method of storage. There is a unit available that stores the cots under an attractive usable table. (Normally cots stored in a corner are not allowed in "usable child space".) There are also mats and cots that are designed to hang on the wall, but these can also be unsightly and even unsafe.

Manipulatives and Art

Manipulative materials are very important to your program and will help keep the interest of the children who are at the center for 10 hours a day. Make sure that the materials are age appropriate and rotated often to alleviate boredom. If you are on a limited budget, there are many games and activities that you can make inexpensively. (See Appendix for Reference Material.)

As the children in the preschool area progress through your program, they should be exposed to more self-directed activities. Display activities for the children to choose from and have all the materials needed to do the activity. For example, during a certain portion of the day the children can elect to paint at the easel, and so the necessary materials should be arranged conveniently and ready to use.

Blocks

The preschool children need to have blocks to build with and a logical storage system for them. The traditional wooden blocks are wonderful for developing spatial conceptualization, so have a large supply in the room. It's best to store these blocks by shape and size, with a picture of the appropriate block drawn in each storage space. Also provide colored blocks and some with curved surfaces since girls are more attracted to different shapes and softer textures. It is important to sell the building concept to the girls as well as the boys, since this skill is fundamental to development of math skills.

Clays

Every preschool area should have a wide choice of play dough, plasticene and modeling clays to develop strength in the very small muscles of the fingers and hands. Without strength in these muscles, a child has a more difficult time later with writing in elementary school. It is particularly important for preschool boys to use the clays extensively as their small-muscle strength is usually not properly developed. Have equipment that sells the activity: Various props such as rolling pins, plastic knives and cookie cutters will help.

It is useful to place a large tray on the table when the clays are out. This will define the area of use and limit the amount that falls on the floor. There are excellent plastic trays for this purpose available from several manufacturers and distributors. As an alternative, kitty litter trays work just as well.

When purchasing equipment for the preschool rooms, refer to Chapter 5. It is very easy to fall into a quick-fix spending pattern for equipment and materials for this age group if you don't have a long-range purchasing plan.

OUTSIDE PLAY AREAS

For the preschool child, the outside play areas should be readily accessible with plenty of room to run and play. The equipment should encourage the development of all of the large muscles in the body. Be certain to provide lower-level skill activities and equipment for the child who is slow to develop in certain areas. For example, many children have difficulty with jumping, so you may want to provide a piece of jumping equipment that provides optimal security. Riding a vehicle (e.g., a tricycle) may be very difficult for some children so you may want to have a community vehicle.

Provide a variety of balls and bats and goals for learning basic ball game skills. The preschool child develops these skills rapidly, and it is a wonderful way to build self-esteem. However, before the age of five, children generally will not be ready to participate in a team ball game because their coordination—and patience—will not be sufficiently developed.

Playground design is very important in terms of safety. The playground is the most hazardous area, and there must be constant supervision by your staff. You can alleviate the major cause of serious and fatal injuries on playgrounds by providing eight to 12 inches of sand under climbing and moving equipment. Other substances, such as crushed rubber or wood chips, are available if you are in a climate where fungus infections are spread in the sand. When designing climbing areas, try to have them expand *outward* rather than *upward;* limit the height from which a child could fall to no more than twice his height.

To have developmentally appropriate and safe equipment for all children, divide playgrounds into age groups with the preschool through kindergarten children in one area. If you decide to have swings, be sure to provide cones or some other visual barrier so that the children will not run near the moving swings. Also, to accommodate different stages and sizes, it is a good idea to have the capability of raising and lowering the level of the swings.

Children love a sand box so it's a nice addition to any playground. Place a cover over it, especially if there are animals in the area. If the box is large, you can use pieces of lattice work; it's easy for teachers to remove, allows rain to drain through, is inexpensive and available at most lumber yards. When installing the box, line the bottom surface with a large piece of plastic before adding the sand to keep the sand clean. Sand-box toys should be free of sharp edges and checked regularly for broken bits and pieces. Provide different digging objects too for added interest. Old kitchen pots and pans are always popular, and water from a nearby fountain can be very enticing.

Wherever possible, have an area blacktopped for the riding vehicles. Paths around the perimeter may look attractive but can be dangerous if they intersect the flow of play or go too near to swings or climbing frames. Keeping activities separate is generally safer. Check riding vehicles regularly for safety. Also, try to avoid the traditional tricycles that sit high up since they are more likely to cause injury in the event of a fall. Instead use the variety that has a big wheel or the vehicles that stay low to the ground and do not tip over easily. Wagons seem to work fairly well in the toddler areas but not in the older preschool areas; children tend to get too wild with them and tip them over.

Maintenance of the playground equipment will be your best method of accident prevention. If you have a regular schedule for checking the equipment and have told the staff what to watch for, your risk should be minimal.

STAFFING

The teachers and assistants in the preschool classrooms, for the most part, establish the tone and reputation of your program. Unless you have training in child development or early childhood education, you should have a head teacher or educational coordinator to assist with curriculum development. The individual in this position should agree with your overall philosophy and be able to assist with hiring staff and implementing a quality program.

When staffing your preschool program, remember it is the teachers that will give your center an edge over the competition, which is generally more intense for three- and four-year-olds than for any other age group. It is true that your infant and toddler program will act as a "seed" for the older preschool children, but initially you will have to provide a very attractive program for preschoolers with top teachers. Once the program is established you will have to maintain the quality to keep the younger children with you.

The four-day work week as described in Chapter 7 for infants and toddlers also works well with the preschool teachers. In this age group, more than any other, encourage team teaching in the preschool classrooms with each teacher doing an equal share of the work. This can often prevent conflicts and burnout, while enhancing the atmosphere in the classroom.

To attract staff for this age group you need to offer good benefits and salaries. In addition, regular staff training sessions often attract teachers and assistants, especially if you build in an incentive system for attendance. In some centers the management gives a 10-cent-per-hour raise up to $1 per year for every workshop or course attended. The incentive system also seems to decrease the burnout rate.

DAILY ATTENDANCE SCHEDULING

Accurate daily scheduling is very important. Try not to allow too many parents to sign up their children for just the morning program slots or you'll have too many openings in the afternoons. This problem can be alleviated by offering a morning and afternoon preschool program if space allows. Try to encourage more parents to use the "odd" hours for their own shopping or appointments.

Each morning be sure to tell the classroom teachers who will be attending for the day so that they know what to expect. Most teachers who teach in flexible programs find the work challenging but rewarding; many actually enjoy the variety. Also, the flexible programs in preschool usually have a core group of 60% of the children who come regularly, so that only 40% attend on a flexible basis. Most teacher realize that the different mixes in personalities are good for the children. The method also builds the self-esteem of the "regulars" as they get to show the newcomers the ropes.

CURRICULUM

The quality preschool program should have a curriculum that is age appropriate for the developmental stages of each level and that promotes the philosophy of the center. The parents should understand your philosophy and know what curriculum is used in the classroom. In most classrooms the parents are kept up-to-date through a parent bulletin board at the entrance area to the room or through monthly newsletters that list the activities. An informal discussion or conference time should be held with each parent during the course of the year unless there are difficulties that need immediate attention. (See Chapter 14 for more on Parent Relations.)

The day's schedule should be clearly outlined and posted. Two issues of major importance arise here. First, most centers decide not to have children arrive after the preschool program begins at, say, 9 A.M. However, if you are actively promoting the program in a highly competitive market, you should definitely accommodate the parents who might want to bring their child at, say, 10 A.M. Have an office staff member or floater assist in integrating the child into the program.

Second—and this is perhaps the most controversial issue for parents, children and administrators—is nap time policies. When asked what they remembered liking the least about child care, most high school students today will say, without hesitation, "Nap time!" Many parents dread having their children nap at the center, because they know that as a result their child may be up until 10 o'clock that night. It truthfully seems "abusive" to force a child who is not sleeping to stay on a cot or mat for two hours or more. Most state regulatory agencies require a rest time, but the wise administrator will divide the children into two groups—the "nappers" and the "resters"—in two separate rooms. The observant teacher will know which children need to sleep and which can just rest. A rest time of 30 to 40 minutes is tolerable for the resters and can be followed by quiet activity times and indoor board games. This policy alone, if publicized, may bring you increased enrollment if your competitors refuse to change their scheduling.

In formulating or evaluating any policies concerning scheduling and curriculum in the preschool classrooms, your best guide will be the children's reactions. If the children are happy and content, the room will hum with activity and cheerful voices. But if there is discontent, the children will be argumentative, bored and listless.

If you run into difficulty at any point in the set-up or operation of your preschool program, consider whether the room is inviting enough. Go outside and enter the area on a child's level. Physically and mentally, pretend that you are a young child entering for the day and that you may be there for 10 hours. Is the entrance inviting? Are the teachers friendly? Are there enough activities? Would you feel bored quickly? Can you go outside as often as possible? Do you feel good about yourself? You will better understand the course of action you should take to make improvements if you can enter the world of the child.

9

SCHOOL-AGE CARE

As with infant care, there is usually a critical need for quality school-age care in every community. An attractive before- and after-school program can be an asset to any center. Filling some of the odd child hours available can bring in significant additional income, and there may be an increase in preschool enrollment as well because parents often like siblings to be in the same center.

As with younger age groups, materials and supplies as well as the arrangement of space must be absolutely age appropriate. Careful planning is a must, but interestingly, the larger the program for this age group the easier it becomes to run efficiently.

There are basically two types of school-age programs: one is added to an existing child care program, and the other takes place in a totally separate facility or room. Most programs will be additions, because there is generally not enough income from a before- and after-school program alone to support a separate facility unless there are many kindergarten children who need a supplementary program in either the late morning or early afternoon, or if you have space that is very inexpensive.

PHYSICAL ARRANGEMENT

The design of the area for school-age children will largely be determined by whether the same space is used by children of other ages during the school day. But the concerns regarding specific areas and atmosphere apply to both shared and non-shared space.

First, determine what ages will be served in the school-age program and how you will divide the groups. Most centers serve children ages five through 10 and divide them into two basic groups: five- through seven-year-olds (kindergarten through second grade) and eight- through 10-year-olds (third grade through fifth grade). There is room for variation within this scheme, but these age groups seem to be the most compatible.

Activity areas should be well defined by the spatial arrangement so that the children can choose to work individually, in small groups or in a large group. For each age group of school-age children, you'll need the following areas:

     Storage
     Quiet area
     Homework
     Arts and crafts
     Special interests

Atmosphere

Make each interest area visually appealing so that the children will want to go there. A homelike atmosphere will also help the school-age children relax after a long day at school. Create this atmosphere by decorating with a soft touch, using carpet, tablecloths, bean bag chairs, draped fabric, centerpieces, pictures, sculpture and wall hangings. And finally, remember to rotate the materials and interest areas regularly so that the children do not become tired of a particular activity.

When arranging a shared space, try to use decorative materials that are not too young for the older children. For example, instead of using cute preschool animals on the wall, cut out animal pictures from *Ranger Rick* or discarded *National Geographic*s. Another time, decorate the walls with pictures of athletes that will serve a different purpose for each age group. For example, with the school-age group, you could encourage an active interest in sports, while with the younger children you can identify what individual sports are being played. Admittedly, this takes imagination and planning, but the extra effort will be well worthwhile.

Non-shared Space

If you can use space in a separate facility or room, you have more opportunities for individual planning. The truly excellent, independent before- and after-school programs that do not share space are usually subsidized either with space or direct funding from industry or government. These programs generally endeavor to offer a variety of choices for the children. They include the basic activities in the same type of areas described above but on a much larger scale. For example, a program that has four rooms may have the activities divided like this:

Room One: Program Home Base—Meeting Room
Room Two: Gross Motor—Ping Pong, Punching Bag, Mats, etc.
Room Three: Quiet Room and Homework—Reference and Games
Room Four: Arts and Crafts—Painting, Cooking, Sculpting, etc.

There may also be a computer area in the first room near the administrative space.

Shared Space Considerations and Scheduling

If you are adding before- and after-school care to an existing program, you will probably be using shared space, that is, the school-age children will occupy the same room used by younger children during school hours. Planning space so that it is appropriate for the two age groups can be a big challenge.

As with all areas of child care, you have to be flexible because some children may not fit the categories exactly. You may be able to justify a room of their own for the younger age group of five- to seven-year-olds if there are enough kindergarten children to occupy the space during the school hours, either in a supplementary or private kindergarten program.

Another option would be to have a schedule such as this for the room:

7 A.M.–9 A.M.: kindergarten through second grade
9 A.M.–11:45 A.M.: three-year-old nursery school program

12 P.M.–3 P.M.: supplementary kindergarten
3 P.M.–6 P.M.: kindergarten through second grade

If the public schools offer a full-day kindergarten program, then consider offering an afternoon three-year-old nursery school program in the space. There are other possible variations; consider your market analysis and how your enrollment is building for the school year to determine the best scheduling approach and room usage.

The eight- to 10-year-olds can usually share space with a two-session, four-year-old nursery school group.

If you run a traditional center without a separate preschool room, you can combine the four-year-olds with the three-year-olds in the three-year-old room in the early morning and late afternoon hours. The before- and after-school children of all ages then go into the four-year-old room before school. At nine o'clock the school-age children leave, and the four-year-olds go into their room until the school-age children arrive after school.

If you have a supplementary kindergarten program in the early afternoon, you can divide the preschoolers once again with "nappers" in the three-year-old room and "resters" with the kindergartners in the four-year-old room. This second group has a rest time for 30 to 40 minutes and then an activity time and outdoor play time. After having a snack, the before- and after-school groups are separated from the younger children. The younger children then play inside first while the older children are outside, and then they switch areas.

Storage for Belongings

Providing storage for personal belongings becomes more difficult if different age groups are sharing the room as a home base. One way to alleviate the confusion is to have the older children use hooks and shelving in the hall area and another is to provide a second shelf that is higher for the older children. Also encourage each child to use a backpack for his belongings.

Quiet Area

The same area used by the younger children for their "circle time" can be transformed into a quiet area for school-age children with bean bag chairs and low tables for games. Incidentally, convenient storage of the games is very important; provide shelving that enables the children to stack the games individually. Some popular music that can be played at a low volume or with head sets adds to the atmosphere along with appropriate posters and magazines especially for this age range.

Homework Area

The homework area may be more difficult to create in a room designed for younger children. However, the tables that seat six preschoolers will encourage the school-age children to sit in smaller groups of four, which will help them concentrate on homework. Usually the manipulative area for the preschoolers works best for this function. As described in Chapter 8, this area is probably near a closet and so the encyclopedias, dictionaries and other reference materials can be stored on an accessible shelf in it.

Arts and Crafts and Special Interests

School-age children can use the same arts and crafts area but more choices of media should be available. Have display areas for the older children's art within the room; children enjoy each other's art work and the younger children will love checking out the older children's newest ideas.

Set up specific interest areas throughout the room as you have for the preschoolers, adapting them as necessary to match the interests and abilities of the older children. You may, for example, have larger sets of Legos for the older children and allow them to build on a project throughout the week. Keep the work on a plastic tray and store it in another room at the end of each day.

The older children can contribute to the younger children's ideas or projects in, for example, science or math. School-age children love to cook and feel very special when they are allowed to make snacks for the younger ones. And, of course, this age group loves creative drama and needs little encouragement to stage wonderful plays and skits for the center and the parents.

EQUIPMENT

The equipment in school-age child care programs will have to be inviting, yet sturdy. For seating in the quiet areas, try couches and soft chairs. However, many directors have found that these do not hold up to the excessive amount of use in the center and have searched for other options. The best to date seems to be bean bag chairs, which are relatively inexpensive, colorful, comfortable and readily replaceable when necessary. They can also be used by any age group. The tables in the quiet area should be relatively low and invite two to four children to play cards or board games. If the space is shared with another age group, these tables will have to be portable and stored in a closet at certain times of the day.

Storage of Materials

Storage of materials becomes a major issue in the before- and after-school programs, because although there must be a large choice of games and books, these should not interfere with the other programs using the space. Also, the materials must be stored in an orderly manner so that the children can take care of them easily, and they are not ruined in a short period of time. For example, traditional board games are often stacked 10 deep on a shelf in a closet. When a child removes a game from the middle of the pile or the bottom, the other games are moved about or, worse, knocked over. A solution to this problem is a storage cart that is actually made for the art area to separate and store paper. The individual shelves are just right for board games, and the whole unit can be wheeled out of the room for storage elsewhere during the day. Or you could have a carpenter make dividers for the shelf space so that each shelf will only hold one game.

Storage containers for the materials should be large and easy for the children to open. Each deck of cards, for example, should be in an individual container or held together with a rubber band and then placed in a larger storage box. Some centers color-code the storage containers according to age group for ease in locating the materials quickly in shared space. Be certain to plan the storage so that the school-age children can obtain and return things independently.

Materials for Play

Materials for hobby and art projects need to be available and accessible to the children. The art area will need to have the right-size materials such as smaller crayons, brushes and markers than, say, the ones three-year-old children traditionally use. Be sure to store any on-going projects by the older children out of reach of the younger ones who share the space, and mark all projects clearly with the owner's name. For display purposes, you may want to encourage the older children to contribute art work for the entrance area or for the hallways. This can be a wonderful self-esteem builder for the school-age children.

Older children still love to build, and there should be woodworking materials and blocks for them. The use of tools in a woodworking area will need careful supervision and may need inspiration from an outside source such as an elderly volunteer.

Dress-up clothes and make-up encourage dramatic play—the children will find props everywhere! And cooking materials should be provided often, as this promotes independence and teaches a valuable life skill—plus the children love to cook and eat!

Homework Supplies

For the homework area, there should be a set of encyclopedias, a dictionary, pens, markers and pencils, paper, maps, a globe, a thesaurus, an atlas, pencil sharpener, rulers, etc. A nice addition here or in the quiet area is a small library of quality books for the children to read at their leisure; you may even decide to allow the children to sign out books for reading at home. Some centers are also providing computers to assist with homework.

Indoor and Outdoor Equipment for Active Play

For the outdoors, active play equipment such as balls and bats, kickballs, soccer balls and goals, chalk for hopscotch, hoops and bases are needed. Larger equipment may be difficult and expensive to provide since, for example, any climbing equipment that is appropriate in height for the school-age children will be dangerous for the preschool children. Some swings are adjustable to accommodate older children. Other equipment, such as a sand box, may be enjoyed for short periods of time. In general, the older child needs to be much more active and is more likely to enjoy noncompetitive games and sports. In fact, the main ingredients for the school-age outdoor program are a teacher who can guide the children and the right props and equipment.

An indoor play area (for exercising large muscle groups) is important for the school-age children and will require some extra equipment, depending on the space you have available. If, for example, you have a gym, you may want to invest in mats for basic gymnastics or a basketball or indoor volleyball set. Instead of providing these activities on site, you may decide to take the children to gymnastics, dancing, etc. If you do not have space for, say, gymnastics, there are innovative gymnasiums that are creating portable training areas out of empty school buses to bring the activity to you!

STAFFING

The staff for school-age programs must be selected very carefully. It's advisable to have a head teacher with extensive experience with this age group who can both supervise the program and plan activities. In addition, this individual should have excellent organizational skills to assist the administrative staff in keeping track of the children's various departures and arrivals from the different schools.

Caregivers in the school-age programs have to assume diverse roles. When the children first arrive, they need a trusting adult with whom they can talk about their school day and share their joys and frustrations. As they get into activities, the children need someone to encourage their ideas, help solve their problems and sometimes act as a mediator in conflicts with their peers, should they arise. The caregivers should take pleasure in each child's accomplishments and cheer each individual on to try and reach new horizons. And finally, the adults in the program need to be role models who can set positive examples for the children.

The head teacher's primary job responsibility should be the school-age program; he or she needs plenty of time during the day for planning and, if space is shared, preparing the rooms for the older age group. A well-coordinated program will run smoothly and maintain the children's interest levels; however, to do this takes a great deal of time and effort on the part of the teachers.

The remaining staff can generally be younger adults, but each staff member must have the maturity necessary to be a good role model for this age group. In some centers directors have used an intergenerational approach, "adopting" grandparents to assist with special activities and skills such as sewing, woodworking, knitting, model building, tutoring, speaking foreign languages, etc. This method can obviously be advantageous for both age groups.

In some areas of the country, there are shortages of qualified teachers. This scarcity can intensify the search for quality employees for school-age care. Community colleges, universities offering education degrees, private schools and even the public schools may be good sources to explore. If your local high school offers a child development course, you may find students who have an interest and a natural talent with children. Again, they must be sufficiently mature to be a positive influence on the children. (See Chapter 12 on staffing for additional suggestions.)

CURRICULUM

The activities for this age group must be fun and relaxing and not a repetition of the courses the children have experienced during the school day. At the same time, the projects should be engrossing, not simply entertaining. The various choices should promote a child's positive self-esteem, curiosity, creativity and sense of responsibility. Individual projects should encourage the development of life skills and enhance small and gross motor skills, balance and coordination. The projects should also augment the child's language, reading and writing skills as well as promote creative problem-solving.

Many programs have supplemented their special interest areas by bringing in special teachers from the outside to teach, for example, tap dancing, ballet, gymnastics or tae kwon do. The possibilities are limited only by your imagination and the expertise you can find in your vicinity. Most centers pass the extra charge along to the parents, but you may decide to pick up the tab initially to help promote your program.

Some centers offer other organized activities such as Brownies and Cub Scouts, Girl Scouts and Boy Scouts, Campfire Girls, 4-H Clubs and even religious education. These are optional and can be successful depending upon the interest level of the children and their parents. The philosophy behind offering them is that each child should have the same opportunities that he would have if he were at home with a parent. Frankly, in most centers the options available are better than those he would have if he were to go home each day after school.

TRANSPORTATION

A major consideration for a school-age program is whether or not to offer transportation. If so, should you charge a fee? A word of caution: first contact your state department of transportation regarding public service vehicle regulations and talk with your lawyer about the liability implications. While offering transportation may increase your enrollment, providing it is costly and full of scheduling hassles.

Therefore, explore all possibilities of using the existing public school transportation system. Perhaps an incident in the area has shown the importance of school-age children being supervised. Use this concern as a negotiating tactic. Or try to get the backing of a local superintendent of schools. Use these or other factors as leverage in negotiating an agreement with the company providing transportation for the public schools. If the bus company is private and the schools don't cooperate, another option is to make a special arrangement with the bus company: you provide a certain number of hours of child care per week for their employees' children in return for transportation.

If none of the above prove successful, probably the only way that you can offer a school-age program is to provide transportation yourself, since the schools that the children attend are not usually close to the center. You have the option of purchasing or leasing a van, or even a few vans, if the program is large enough. Leasing has become more popular recently, especially when the program is on a trial basis. Also, in some instances the leasing company assumes the liability. Check your own liability insurance policies carefully if you are purchasing the vehicles, because most policies exclude transportation. In addition, a center is put into another insurance and registration category if it charges an extra fee for transportation, so look into all restrictions before setting the fee schedules. Generally, centers that provide transportation either absorb the cost or make an across-the-board increase to cover the extra expense.

Having a van or two can make field trips for the older fours and special events for the school-age children much more feasible. Drivers are usually not too hard to find, and many centers that do provide transportation hire retired people. Have a radio system in each van that connects with the center to handle emergencies or changes in schedules.

SPECIAL CONCERNS

With this age group you will find a great diversity in the strengths and weaknesses of the children. Also you and your staff will be challenged by some children who are under great stress and emotional strain. The wise director and head teacher will decide ahead of time what methods of discipline to use in the school-age programs and explain them thoroughly to the caregivers. They will also decide in advance when and how referrals will be made to outside resources for children with problems that are beyond the expertise of the staff (See Chapter 14, Parent Relations). It is the job of the head teacher to train the caregivers in how to use techniques that assure a happy classroom.

If the head teacher has a particularly challenging group of children in the program, it may be advisable to have the prime caregiver set up a contract system with the children before things get out of control. For this, each child writes down or dictates what he or she expects from the caregiver, and the caregiver writes a contract stating what is expected of each child. The contract should not be broken by either party, but if it is, both parties have to sit down again and find out what happened. The expectations may have been too high and the contract may have to be modified.

As with the other age groups, a good clue that a program is not working is a restless, bored, argumentative group of children. When this happens, take action immediately and either bring in new interest projects or rearrange the schedule. You may find that the caregiver is just wrong for the particular group.

Above all else, the administrators, head teachers and caregivers must command the absolute respect of the children. Without this, the school-age program cannot succeed.

10

SUMMER PROGRAMS

Summer programs for a child care center can be a marketing, management and programming challenge. Many centers find that the summer brings a large drop in enrollment with a consequent decrease in income. You may need to try several different methods to keep enrollment up during the 10 to 12 weeks that the schools are closed.

Marketing becomes crucial as the competition from many other sources increases. Scheduling and management must be efficient in order to plan and coordinate additional, interesting activities and field trips. Summertime can be a fun time for everyone, and you can have a successful center if you plan properly, approach the summer with enthusiasm and use your imagination to its fullest. Remember, you have something unique to offer the parents and children of your community!

MARKETING

Planning how to maintain enrollment during the summer months should begin in January, thus saving you from panic once the competition begins promoting their programs. Focus on new ways to convince parents that their child should come to your center.

Assess the Competition

Your primary competition will come from the following:

1. Town-run programs: Parks and recreation departments and other municipal organizations often run low-cost programs that have access to swimming and other town recreation facilities.
2. Private, nonprofit programs: These will include programs such as those run by the Boys Club and Y's that, because they are heavily subsidized and may provide scholarships, can be more competitive in price. They also generally have access to more recreational facilities.
3. Private local day camps: The day camps often have large facilities, market aggressively and, in recent years, have extended days with increased child care capabilities.
4. Family day care homes: There seem to be more of these during the summer when some employees have the opportunity to stop work and be home with their children for the summer.
5. Home care: During the summer months, high school and college students can accept full-time jobs caring for children at the child's home, which is more convenient for the parent.
6. There may also be alternative summer care programs particular to your area, so be sure to do a thorough search.

One advantage that nearly every one of these programs will have over yours is that each will be underregulated, if it is even regulated at all. They will be able to have, for example, more children per staff member. Their staff requirements may be much less strict, and qualifications, including age, may be much lower, if they exist at all. Some will be able to use swimming facilities and will charge reduced rates or provide free transportation. Since they do not have to conform to the same stringent health and safety requirements as a child care facility, their standards may be much lower. For example, in some camps and recreation programs there may only be one bathroom area available for over 100 children from ages three to 10.

However, one problem many of the summer programs have is rainy day activities or indoor play. Camps and recreation programs are planned to take place primarily outdoors, and when the weather forces play indoors, the children are often jammed into an inadequate space with no age group separation and few activities for the whole day. So when you are considering marketing strategies for your center, you need to understand the competition thoroughly and pinpoint their weaknesses. Then you can build on your strengths and tailor your summer program to offer advantages the others don't.

To plan a marketing strategy, you need a clear picture of the advantages and disadvantages of each of the other programs. Gather as much information about them as possible by looking for articles and advertisements in last summer's newspapers in the library and calling for their new brochures.

Next make a chart on a large piece of paper or a chalkboard and fill in the following categories:

> Name of Program
> Type of Activities
> Advantages to Parent/Child
> Disadvantages

Then have your staff look over the information you've gathered and have a brainstorming session. When doing this exercise, encourage your staff to put down all ideas no matter how silly they seem. Organize the ideas by the same categories as you've used for the competition. From the pattern that emerges, you'll find needs not currently being met by the other programs, like noncompetitive sports, innovative science and math activities or nature studies. More on program specifics is included later in this chapter. Also, your marketing strategy may include some form of continuing parent education.

Parent Education

Following are some ideas to use with parents. As you can see, they emphasize your advantages without directly critizing another program.

1. Throughout the year gently remind the parents who currently use your center of the high standards of safety that are maintained day in and day out. Explain to them that numerous summer programs crop up between the months of May and August, and that these programs are not as well regulated as year-round programs, and may in fact be potentially dangerous. This is also a good time to remind the parents of the high qualifications of your staff.

    Another option is to purchase inexpensive, yet professional, name tags for each teacher to wear. This makes them appear professional and insures that parents know the name of their child's teachers. Or you may want to have a special newsletter about the teachers and staff.

2. Next, join with other child care and educational professionals to inform the community about summer options. For example, bring representatives from the different programs together at a "Camp Night" at your community center or local gym to talk about and give out materials on their facilities. As a long-term goal, for the protection of the children, you and the other professionals may even be able to improve the regulatory standards that govern all summer programs.

3. Create a brochure or flier that explains how to choose a summer program. Include a section that raises questions about issues such as safety and distribute it free to parents. Use it, first, to educate the parents at your own center. For example, you might have a simple list of thought-provoking questions such as:

Did you know:
- That our fine staff ratios stay the same during the summer?
- That there will be special activities for each age group . . . even on rainy days?
- That each week we will have a field trip for the older children?
- That, even in the summertime, our staff will meet our strict training requirements, including knowledge of first aid?
- That all of our staff are 18 or older?
- AND FINALLY, that the space is LIMITED so that there isn't overcrowding?

Above all, your approach should be aggressive. (See Chapter 15 for further suggestions on marketing.) The first factor that parents look at will be price, and nearly without exception, the competition's will be lower because they are under less stringent or nonexistent regulations. This issue is difficult, but not impossible, to combat.

RESERVING SPACE

First, determine how many slots you expect to have empty for the summer. Take an enrollment (see Chapter 11) from the existing clients no later than the end of March. Based on enrollment, you'll know how many additional children you'll have to enroll in the various age groups to assure a steady income to the center throughout the summer months.

Make clear to parents in your center that if they take their child(ren) out for the whole summer, their child's spot may not be available in the fall. Usually you can guarantee slots only for those who use your service on a yearly basis. Obviously, this policy can be adjusted for a seasonally employed parent such as a teacher; however, try explaining to the parents how their child would benefit from a part-time attendance in the summertime. You could even be more aggressive and require it.

With care of infants and toddlers, it will be almost impossible to reserve the slots since the strict staff ratios and group sizes will strain your budgeting for a classroom that is not at capacity. To compensate, you may be able to increase the number of flexible, occasional uses in these age groups during the summer. Another possibility is to require half payment to reserve a slot. Be sure not to guarantee a slot if you will be taking a loss by doing so.

PROGRAM ACTIVITIES AND FEATURES

You can gain an advantage over your competition with a special program or extra-exciting field trips and activities for the children. These can vary from a theme-oriented curriculum to having special field trips once a week or providing transportation to the local park for swimming lessons. The purpose of designing and publicizing each special feature is to convince parents that your program offers something to their child that is worth the extra cost over other summertime activities.

Themes

A theme-oriented curriculum can vary from a set topic such as "Circus," "Beach" or "Flying Objects," to exploring a different country and cultural background each week. All activities should relate to the central theme and be age appropriate.

For example, during a Circus Week you might do the following:

Monday—Make clown hats with glitter and sparkles.
Tuesday—Decorate large balloons with funny faces.

Wednesday—Make a Popsicle-stick cage and a pipe cleaner animal.

Thursday—Pretend you're tigers and make masks.

Friday—Have a circus carnival for the whole center in the late afternoon. Include face painting, bean bag toss, water splash, etc.

Supplementary Activities:

Have an elephant water fight with water bottles or water balloons.

Make candy apples and popcorn.

Color circus pictures with magic markers.

Sing "Old McDonald Had a Circus . . ." or "The Farmer at the Circus" (instead of "The Farmer in the Dell").

Have a hot dog stand for lunch or make pigs-in-a-blanket.

Have the children pretend they are monkeys, elephants, snakes, etc.

Create a "tight-rope" with a balance beam or rope.

Other options for programming are: a science and nature program with subjects such as marine life, rocks, printing, space, cinematography or bones.

Multiculture Themes

Another theme could center on the culture of a specific country. For example, if Mexico is the choice for one week, have tacos for lunch, make piñatas and sombreros, do the Mexican hat dance, teach a few Spanish words for simple objects, do colorful paintings with fluorescent paint and pretend they're on bark, etc. By the end of the week, the children will have an introduction to the culture of Mexico. Be sure to gear each activity to the age of the children. Place simple information about the theme weeks in your promotional literature and post information or art work from each week's activities for the parents to read and admire.

Theme-week ideas and related activities are only limited by your staff's imagination and the amount of time the days hold. Encourage your staff to use reference books for ideas or create new ones on their own. Remember with children there is no right or wrong way to be creative—it is usually only an adult who perceives the distinction between right and wrong. Be sure your teachers value the child's judgment and let creativity come from within the child.

Special Activities

Instead of using theme weeks, teachers can plan more general activities and then punctuate the program with special treats for the children. Some ideas:

> Attend special children's shows at a nearby theater.
> Go to the zoo.
> Take a hike through a local park.
> Visit the library weekly for a special event.
> Swim daily at a town- or city-sponsored area.
> Go to an amusement park.
> Have a magician come to the center.
> Bring in a children's theatrical group.
> Present a play done by the older children.
> Encourage your teachers to use modern music and let the children dance and do "free-form" creative movement.
> Have the older children present a puppet show.
> Make ice cream with the children and have an "ice cream social."
> Do face painting.
> Let the children create a village with refrigerator boxes.

As you can see, imagination and availability of props are the only limits.

Another option is to bring in a special teacher for the summer months on a part-time basis. An art teacher could introduce the children to sculpture, ceramics, batik, etc. A teacher trained in physical education could teach basic gymnastics, soccer, and baseball. If you do this, try to find a teacher who does not emphasize competition and winning, since many children react negatively to competition and show increased signs of stress.

Programs for School-age Children

In some centers the number of school-age children attending will increase during the summer months, and you will want to plan carefully for this age group. In particular, once the school year is over, regular program activities should be more relaxed. There are several excellent reference books on programs for this age group. (See Appendix F.)

Learning life skills in a fun way can be fascinating to the children. For example:

> Encourage the children to *cook* regularly by following recipes.
>
> Teach *woodworking* so that the children learn to use the basic tools.
>
> *Sewing, knitting and crocheting* can also be fun with a pillow or wall hanging as an end product.
>
> The children could plant a *garden* and cook the vegetables they grow.
>
> A weekly trip to the *library* for the children to take out books or join in for the library's story time can be very rewarding. Many have special programs that the children can take part in.
>
> Children could bring in their *bicycles* and have them checked by the local police department for *safety* with an informal discussion on rules of the road and the importance of helmets. You could follow this by taking short bicycle trips once a week.
>
> *Hiking* skills can be taught, with the children planning the menu and preparing supplies for a full-day hiking excursion.

School-age children love to work on longer projects with visible results, so plan activities that can be finished over a period of several days. Some planning guidelines for this age group in the summertime are:

1. Have adequate choices for activities.
2. Plan activities that encourage release of extra energy.
3. Allow some free time for simple, nonstructured activities such as playing board and card games or just reading a book.

Swimming

Swimming is often a concern for the year-round child care center. Nearly every director would like the children at the center to learn how to swim and be able to cool off. Although each child should have this opportunity, swimming is perhaps the most dangerous activity of a summer program. If you are going to use a public swimming area, try to go in the morning when there are fewer people. This will make supervision much easier, and it is the time when swimming lessons are usually given. In some centers, the owners have installed their own pool. Before you think of doing this, check your insurance policy for coverage and weigh the additional costs against the benefits carefully. It will be necessary to have qualified staff to act as lifeguards as well, and the cost may be prohibitive.

MANAGEMENT ISSUES

Staffing

Finding staff for the summer months is usually easy as there are many college students looking for employment. However, be sure to assess carefully the student's maturity and patience with children. If possible, have the prospective student employee substitute for a regular employee before the summer program begins and observe their attitude toward children. Get a firm commitment from the student about when he or she must leave for college so that you aren't left without staff at the end of the summer. Also, do not hesitate to fire a summer employee who is showing any signs of abnormal behavior to the children. Try to use these temporary employees only as a supplement or aide for the younger age groups in your center. The younger the child, the greater the need for consistency in staffing throughout the year. However, the older children seem to really enjoy a change in staff, and the fresh energy and outlook of college students can give the program a boost.

Health and safety become major issues in the summertime, so conduct a thorough orientation session with the staff before the program begins. Scheduling, accidents, discipline, parent relations and material and classroom organization should all be addressed thoroughly during the meeting.

Because the daily chores of the summer programs are generally more demanding, preparing the staff in advance, at the orientation session, can bring fewer headaches and less confusion. To help with organization, prepare separate lists of chores and assign one to each teacher so there is no confusion. For example, the list may include covering the sand box, refilling the paper towel dispenser, making the juice, taking the garbage out and wiping off the tables. In making the list, think of chores that will aggravate you if they are not done daily/weekly and give the staff their choice of which they would like to do. They may even suggest other jobs. Post the finished list in an inconspicuous place so that the staff can refer to it as necessary. If these chores are approached in a positive manner, no one usually minds and they can make each teacher feel more a part of the team.

Transportation

Several of the program ideas detailed earlier in the chapter require transportation. If you are going to use your own or your teachers' vehicles, make certain that the insurance coverage is adequate. For example, if you have an insurance policy with $500,000 liability, this will be the amount available for claims *per occurrence.* So if there should be an accident in which five children were injured, you would only have, on average, $100,000 available per child. Check details of your coverage carefully with your insurance agent and lawyer. With the current costs for medical care, this coverage could be inadequate; the parents would have no choice but to go after the vehicle owner's assets, as well as the center's.

However, most liability insurance for child care centers will have an exclusionary clause for transportation. For these reasons it is usually better to secure transportation from a school bus company or lease a van through an agency dealing with schools.

PART THREE
EFFICIENT ORGANIZATION AND MANAGEMENT

• •

The day-to-day operation of a child care center requires expert management in order to maintain quality and maximum profitability. Chapters 11 through 14 deal with basic aspects of an ongoing operation with particular emphasis on communications and organization skills.

To be an effective manager, you also need to understand all aspects of bookkeeping, purchasing, enrollments and records maintenance. Administration of a staff requires your knowing how to recruit and hire employees, write a staff manual, motivate and even terminate employees. And creating and maintaining a good relationship with parents who use your center is a crucial aspect of child care center management.

These chapters explain:

11. How to organize your center and maintain an efficient system for records and finances.
12. How to recruit quality employees and substitutes, conduct an effective interview, make hiring decisions and train new staff.
13. How to motivate your staff and manage even the most difficult employees.
14. How to use sales techniques, handbooks, resources, and referrals to keep your relationships with parents positive and protect yourself from unnecessary problems.

11
ORGANIZATION

. . . .

Excellent management skills are needed to run a successful child care center. Identifying your own strengths and weaknesses is a good first step. You may find that you have a natural talent for some of the required tasks, but that for others you need to get training or hire someone else to do them.

There are many good books available on management, so the focus here is on child care center–related issues. In particular some of the critical keys to management success, with emphasis on programs implementing flexibility, will be addressed.

The average child care manager comes to the position with limited business training or experience in child care management. You may have just been promoted to management or decided to start your own business, because you are a very good "doer" of a particular job. Suddenly, as a manager you no longer *do* the tasks yourself but instead *delegate* the responsibilities to others. Your effectiveness as a delegator will often determine your success as a manager.

First, you need a thorough understanding of the jobs involved in running a center and how they relate to each other in an organizational structure. Only then can you determine what support people are needed both in the office and throughout the center. And finally, to have the center run smoothly you need well-designed forms and procedures.

MANAGEMENT BY DELEGATION

The larger the center, the more important your ability to delegate; but even in small centers you must be familiar with the tasks at each level so that you can make appropriate decisions about delegation. First, determine the overall categories and decide which are your direct or indirect responsibility. One way to do this is to design a diagram like this:

OPERATIONS OVERVIEW

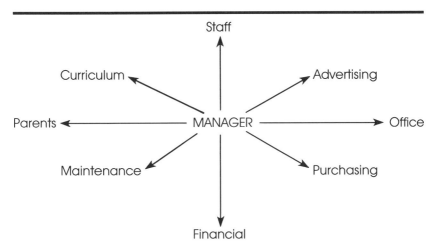

Your expertise will determine the areas for which you take responsibility; for the remainder you have to decide whether to allow someone else to take responsibility or whether you can gather the necessary knowledge and skill to do the job efficiently.

Begin by making a more detailed list of the specific tasks in each category. Then determine whether the tasks must be handled on a daily, weekly, monthly or seasonal basis. For example:

Category	Specific Tasks	Frequency
Curriculum	infants/toddlers	Weekly/Monthly
	preschool	Weekly/Monthly
	before & after school	Weekly/Monthly
Staff	recruiting	Seasonal
	hiring	Seasonal
	training	Seasonal
	firing	As needed

Advertising	newspaper ads	Seasonal
	public relations	Monthly
	brochures/fliers	Seasonal
Office	physical plant	Daily/Weekly
	forms	Seasonal
	staff	Daily/Weekly
Purchasing	classroom equipment and materials	Seasonal
	consumables—	
	paper goods	Monthly
	snacks & meals	Weekly
Financial	accounts receivable	Daily/Weekly
	accounts payable	Monthly
	taxes	Monthly
	budgeting	Seasonal
Maintenance	interior	Daily/Weekly
	exterior	Seasonal
	improvements	Monthly
Parents	conference	Seasonal
	resources	Weekly
	education	Monthly

Next, decide what specific tasks you have the skills to do and which you will need help with. These guidelines can be used as a starting point for your own planning.

After these initial steps, you may recognize that the size of your organization warrants having an assistant director, a manager or an administrative assistant. Or you may choose to act as the administrator, with limited day-to-day responsibilities, and have both a director and assistant director under you. If the facility has a large number of children flowing through it each week, you may decide to have departments for each age level with a supervisor or head teacher for each. No matter what your particular scenarios, the task overview that you create will be useful in writing precise job descriptions. (More on job descriptions in Chapter 12.)

Finally, add a fourth column to the chart indicating who will be primarily responsible for each task. Although you may delegate many tasks, you still have to establish the objectives for each task, and their relationship to the total organization; you should command at least a working knowledge of the skills necessary to complete each task. Without this understanding, you can't determine whether a delegated job is being done properly.

Once you have determined the major jobs and the delineation of responsibility, design your staff structure. For example:

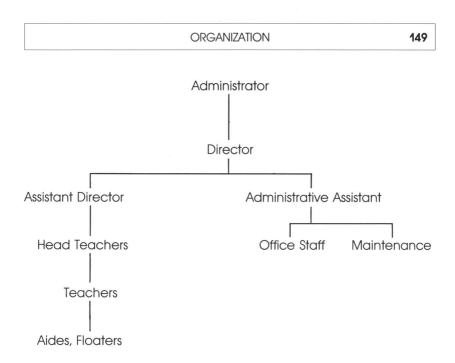

REGISTRATION MATERIALS AND FORMS

To insure the health and safety of the children and the financial stability of the center, you must obtain and maintain accurate records on each child. Also, it is helpful to provide parents with well-prepared materials so they understand—from the start—that certain forms are absolutely required by the center and that all accounts must be kept current.

Cover Letter

When a parent expresses interest in enrolling a child in your center, a well-planned registration packet of materials should be ready for them. First, there should be a friendly cover letter that welcomes their interest in your center and *briefly* explains your programs and fees. It can also include information about the head teacher for the program and any assistants. In the closing, be sure to invite the parents to call you if there are further questions and include your phone number.

The registration packet should contain all necessary forms.

Enrollment Form

The enrollment form for each child indicates what specific periods of time and which program the child will be attending. Taking enrollments is often done on a seasonal basis, with separate enrollments taken for the summer and school year programs. If done early enough (in February for the summer and in May for the fall), this information will significantly help with projections for the upcoming season.

If you decide to have a separate enrollment for the summer program, be sure to do three things:

1. Start to enroll your current students for the summer early so that you know whether you need to do extra advertising.
2. Have parents indicate on the form which weeks the child will be attending during the summer so you can plan staffing and map out available openings.
3. Have an attractive brochure or flier detailing the program ready for your current clients.

You may also need to take an additional enrollment when you add programs. For example, if you are thinking of adding a supplementary kindergarten program to augment the public school program, take a special enrollment to determine the interest level.

Some owners have a no-fee "pre-enrollment" when they are first considering starting a center. This procedure can help you assess the immediate market if your advertising reaches a large portion of the potential clients. If there are indications that a flexible program would be in great demand in the community, the pre-enrollment form may help to convince a potential funding source that your business can support a loan.

Registration Form

The registration form that accompanies the enrollment form should concisely provide identifying information, necessary emergency information and release signatures and a schedule of the days and hours of the week that the child will be attending. You may offer parents the option to state that the child will be attending "occasionally" on a space-available basis.

Operating Policies Statement

As part of the registration procedure, give parents a formal statement of your operating policies. Clearly indicate the fees for which parents are responsible and require that parents sign and return an acknowledgment agreeing to the fees and assuring that they've read the policies. The issues that should be covered include:

Scheduling Details
Tuition—method and time of payment
Enrollment Fee
Registration Fee
Absenteeism and Vacation
Holidays (when center is closed)
Termination of Service by Parents
Termination of Service by Center
Illness (when child may attend)
Emergency Procedures
Weekly Tuition Schedule
Signature of Parent(s)/Guardian
Signature of Director

A copy of this form or at least the last page detailing the weekly tuition schedule with the proper signatures should be kept in the child's file at the center, and the parents should be given a completed copy for their records. When creating your operating policy statement, make it thorough so that it protects the center legally, but simple enough for the parents to understand and adhere to. If the statement is too lengthy or complicated, parents may feel threatened and even question using your center. (More on the Operating Policy Statement is covered in Chapter 14 and a sample is included in Appendix E.)

Medical and Emergency Information

Your initial package for the parents must include a medical form to be signed by the child's physician certifying that the child has had the proper inoculations. You may also decide to include a developmental form that indicates when the child reached various stages of development. For infants you will need a schedule of approximate nap and feeding times.

An additional form that is very convenient both for emergencies and for field trips is the Emergency Card. This card should have the necessary information and signatures if the child should require medical treatment or evacuation. File the card in a separate card box that can be easily transported. Keeping all these cards together saves time in an emergency, and a teacher can just take the cards for an individual class on field trips. As an added bonus, the confidentiality of the main files is maintained, because there is no reason for anyone other than the administration to have access to them.

TRACKING ENROLLMENT AND ATTENDANCE

An efficient method for accurately tracking the enrollment is essential to determine where there are spaces in your program to fill. With a flexible program, accuracy becomes particularly important, since the number of children using the center during any given week is apt to be large. (See also Chapter 6, The Flexibility Factor.)

The simplest way to track enrollment is with a computer; however, you have to thoroughly understand what the computer will be doing for you. For example, if you need to know the number of children in each class on an hourly or half-hourly basis, and the computer program will only indicate the daily or half-day enrollment, you won't have the information necessary to maximize your enrollment.

To understand scheduling well, begin by doing the enrollments by hand. There should be an enrollment sheet for each class—a well-designed form that clearly indicates when each child is scheduled. This information will also help schedule staff.

Next, you need a simple procedure to indicate on the enrollment sheets when a child will be absent. The simplest way is to circle the X'd-in area if the child is not attending. (See Table 6-9.) This method will help you ascertain at a glance where there are openings for children using the center on a space-available basis. Obviously this information must be kept near the office telephone and all staff should understand the procedures.

Finally, there must be a sign-in sheet where a parent will sign the child in and out each day. This sheet is very important, because it is the verification for the fees charged, and in some cases the number of hours used will determine the fees charged. Since this is an administrative responsibility, the sign-in sheets should NOT be in the classrooms but rather should be kept at the front entrance desk, where you can also readily accept payment and review charges with the parents. This can dramatically improve your cash flow if it's done properly.

Keeping track on paper of attendance and enrollment will eventually become obsolete as computer systems become more sophisticated. There will probably be key-cards that automatically enter each child's hours directly into the computer, which will calculate the fees and print the bills. However, a word of caution—the computer output will be only as good as its input, so you must thoroughly understand the methods first and have manual backup procedures until you feel confident of your computer system.

SETTING THE RATES

Setting correct, competitive rates will be very important in achieving success. Also, the fee structure should be concise and very easy to understand.

In the first portion of the book, we covered how to study the competition and determine where and what type of market there is for additional child care in your area. We also pointed out the need for flexible child care services throughout the country. Now, if you assume there is such a market that you can reach, you must determine what price that market will bear for your services. And, more important, can you charge a higher rate for the hourly program; if so, how much higher?

Take into account the professions of your clients, their relative incomes and ability to pay. For example, one owner I know insisted that the parents just couldn't afford to pay more than they were paying. However, it was obvious from the vehicles the parents were driving that the majority were well-paid professionals. The owner surveyed her clients' occupations and analyzed the latest statistics for their income levels. Then she computed what percentage of income each was paying for their child care expenses.

Ask parents' occupations when they register so that you can find the median income line for pricing. This should range between a minimum of 5% and a maximum of 15% of the gross family income. The lower income families pay a higher percentage of their gross income, but they pay a higher percentage for many necessities such as fuel, transportation and food. But don't price child care services based on the lowest-income earner; instead, find the median of the center.

In the example above, the owner found that on average her clients were spending 3.5% of their gross incomes on child care and could afford to be paying at least 5%. She decided to raise the rates based on the ability of the parents to pay and lost only two children in the process. It should be added that she also gave financial assistance to one family and obtained help from the state for two others.

When establishing the fee structure for your center, first determine what rate will be competitive in the market for full-time infant/toddler care. If the going rate in the area for infant/toddler care is $170/week, you could start at $160/week to be competitive. If you take this route, be certain, of course, that you can afford to charge a lower amount and that it doesn't make your program appear cheaper in more than just price.

Once you have established the weekly fee, establish what the hourly, flexible fees will be. The rule of thumb in setting hourly fees is that *the more hours the client uses your center, the lower the hourly fee.* To calculate the "base" hourly fee, assume that a full-time client will be using the center for approximately 45 hours/week (average work week of 40 hours plus one hour per day of commute time) and divide the full-time fee by 45. Continuing the example above, the cost per hour of full-time care is:

$$\$160/45 \text{ hours} = \$3.55/\text{hour}$$

The moderate hourly fee—for clients using the center between 11 and 35 hours per week—should be based on what your market analysis showed clients are paying elsewhere. For the example above, the fee would probably be $4.50/hour; this will be in line with using 35 hours as the "cut-off" time for full-time services. The cut-off point for full-time care would be determined by dividing the full-time fee by the hourly fee:

$$\$160/\$4.50/\text{hour} = 35 \text{ hours}$$

In other words, anyone using the center for more than 35 hours would pay the weekly rate.

Finally, set the maximum fee for a client who will use the center for only a few hours per week—usually 10 hours or less. This is between $.50 and $1 per hour higher than the moderate hourly rate:

$$\$4.50 + \$.75 = \$5.25/\text{hour for 10 hours or less per week}$$

This is a premium price because clients have the privilege of using the center for a limited number of hours. Thus, when you present your fees to the parents, the rates for the infant/toddler program would be listed as:

Full time (36 hours or more per week)	$160/week
11–35 hours/week	4.50/hour
10 hours or less/week	5.25/hour

To set the rates for a center with different age groups, decrease the rates for the children in older groups because the staff ratios will be lower. (The one exception to this rule may be the kindergarten program if you have decided to offer a private kindergarten for children outside of the center's school district.)

An example of a center's fee structure is:

Age Group	Weekly	11–33 Hours	<10 Hours
Infant/Toddler	$160	$4.50	$5.50
Preschool	125	3.75	4.25
Kindergarten*	125	3.75	4.25
School Age	125	3.50	4.00

*These rates are not for a private kindergarten, but instead for care of kindergarten-age children before and after school. The fee for a private kindergarten would be the same as or slightly lower than the infant/toddler fees.

The rate sheet should present the information in a positive and upbeat manner. For example, "We are pleased to announce at Creative Child Care Centers the addition of an infant/toddler program and hope that you will enjoy this service. Since the staff ratios are lower, the fees are slightly higher, but we are offering hourly scheduling to meet your work needs. The remaining fees are as they were before, although some of you may see a slight decrease in your fees due to our increased flexibility! If you should have questions, please call." The message to parents is positive and not apologetic in any way.

ACCOUNTS RECEIVABLE

Your accounting will be simpler if you use one of the new improved computer systems; initially, however, you may want to use a manual accounting system. Set up an account book with an individual page for EACH family. At the top of the page, include the parents' name, address, phone number, rates charged, hours, class and child's birthdate. Make the initial entry of the enrollment and registration payments. Also, keeping the individual family's payments separate helps to maintain some confidentiality and makes it easier to provide each family with its total annual payments (along with your Federal Tax Identification number for the business) for the parent's income tax forms.

If you use this system, billing should be unnecessary because you can easily approach parents as they sign their child in or out. With a flexible program this collection method increases the cash flow dramatically; try to collect the fees for children who use the center on an occasional basis on the *same* day that they attend. If you absolutely must bill a client, keep the billing system simple and send the bills out on a regular basis. Some directors prefer to hand the bill to the client to avoid postal delays.

If a client does not pay a bill, have a set procedure to start collection for past-due amounts. For example, if a bill is more than two weeks overdue, first speak to the parents when they come to pick up their child. If payment is not received within a few days, send written notification (by certified mail, return receipt) that the child may not continue to attend if the arrangements for payment are not made. Then, if no response is made, stop the child from attending. If you resort to legal action (such as small claims court), you need to have clear documentation of the client's use of your services and proof that the parent has received the bill(s), such as a certified mail receipt.

Another aspect of accounts receivable is the amount of cash that may be in your office at any given time, especially if you have a large percentage of flexible and occasional clients using the center. Cash can be tempting to even the most trustworthy employee, and you don't want to be at risk. You will need to establish a system of checks and balances. Your best insurance to guard against theft will be your own supervision and knowledge of procedures and your ability to estimate income on an on-going basis.

Some centers require payment of the fees a month in advance and then use this money to earn interest for the center or to gain extra leverage when applying for a loan. In other words, if your gross monthly accounts receivable is $20,000 and you collect this amount on the first of the month, you can earn interest on the money for the full month. You will also gain financial leverage with the banks when they study your average monthly bank balance during any loan application process. However, as the fees for child care increase, this method of payment can be difficult if not impossible for parents. And of course, monthly payments discourage flexibility and the more profitable hourly use.

ACCOUNTS PAYABLE

Decide the best time of the month to pay the center's regular bills. Depending on the cash flow from your accounts receivable, it might be the end of the month, or the beginning. It is most efficient to collect all the bills in one area and pay them all at one time. This saves time and effort. Try to pay all bills on time to avoid interest charges and late payment penalties. This is particularly true of federal tax deposits and unemployment compensation fees, for the interest and penalty fees are very high.

Sound management systems and simplified and accurate bookkeeping will certainly help your business succeed. However, it should be emphasized that you will need excellent organizational skills so that you run a "tight" business. When a business has tight controls there is very little room for error, and staff, children and parents know exactly what to expect in advance.

12
RECURITING AND HIRING EMPLOYEES

The degree of professionalism projected by your center, which results from your management and the staff's attitudes, will contribute significantly toward the development of a quality child care service. Recruiting and hiring the best possible staff for your center will reduce many personnel problems later. Having an adequate roster of reliable substitutes will also keep your center running smoothly.

JOB DESCRIPTIONS

Accurate job descriptions help not only in selecting the person best suited for a given position, but also in evaluating that person's performance later. In fact, if you give a prospective employee a copy of the job description, he or she may be able to judge whether he or she should even be applying for the job.

The following points should be considered in preparing a concise, complete description:

1. Briefly describe the primary function of the position within the structure of the center. If the position is administrative, list the major responsibilities of the position and the other employee(s) he/she will be supervising.
2. List other specific requirements. For example, keeping his/her space in good order, returning materials or attending staff meetings and workshops.

3. Indicate how much time the job requires and whether the position is for the school year, the summer or year-round. State whether the employee is expected to spend preparation time outside of the specified hours.
4. State what background is required, including any required education, experience or supplementary courses, such as first aid.
5. Describe the starting salary, payment basis and salary review procedure. (This is optional, but some centers prefer to include these items up front.)

RECRUITING

Finding staff can be a major undertaking, especially if the labor market is tight and the starting salary you are offering is relatively low. The higher the starting salary, the easier it will be to attract applicants.

If your budget prohibits you from offering a higher salary, there are other ways to make a position more attractive. For example, offer flexible working hours. This may mean allowing two employees to share a given position, or offering a four-day work week as described in Chapter 7 or working around an employee's school schedule. By accommodating the needs of individual employees you help them to help you. Another option is to offer extra perks, such as time off to care for sick children, expense-paid trips to conferences or holiday parties for the staff and their guests.

Your benefit package is especially important when the majority of the employees are single. (Married employees are likely to be covered by a spouse's benefit package including health insurance.) A good health insurance plan will be invaluable to them. And clear, fair policies on vacation, personal days and sick pay can often attract a good employee.

Advertising for new employees can be tricky, so be careful what you say in your ads; and of course, you are not allowed to discriminate on the basis of age, sex or race. Emphasize the most important factors from the employee's point of view—usually the ability to work with children and the hours. You may want to mention a salary range (rather than a specific salary) as well as the benefits, flexible working hours or availability of training. Many employers don't quote a starting salary over the phone and don't even discuss it until the second interview.

Keep the ad *simple*. Don't overwhelm the reader with too many facts. As with marketing to prospective parents, your goal is getting the top prospects in the door! Write short, two- to three-word lines in **bold** print wherever possible, and include your phone number and the hours to call. Then, read the ad objectively and have a friend or colleague do so too. Place the ad in the classified section of the newspaper. If your first few ads don't bring in applicants, try church bulletins or supermarket bulletin boards. A call to a nearby part-day preschool program may bring leads, since the director may know of parents who need work, have an aptitude for teaching or are highly qualified.

However, your most effective "advertising" may be word of mouth. Some directors offer their staff a bonus if they find someone for a given position. You should also consider the parents who are using the center as potential employees. Generally, this does not pose a problem in a larger center where the parent can easily work with a group that is not close in age to that of his or her own child. Although you do not want to use this method and lose a client, you may find that a parent is making a career change anyhow. The only way to determine this is by getting to know the parents well enough to have them confide in you and share their plans for the future. Remember to establish a policy for employees whose children attend the center, particularly whether to charge the same rate that everyone pays or make reduced child care costs part of the employee benefit package. In any case, you must be up front with the prospective parent/employee and treat all your employees consistently to avoid potential disputes.

INTERVIEWING

The way you conduct the interview will determine that employee's perception of you and your business and to an extent your future relationship with the employee. For this reason keep the goals of the interview clearly in mind.

Remember that you are not trying to *sell* your business to the applicant, especially if the applicant has answered an ad. (The situation is a bit more difficult if *you* made the initial contact and requested the interview, basically, because you have implied that the person may have special qualifications for the job. Unfortunately, if this applicant becomes an employee, he or she may also be the most difficult to manage.) Your basic goal during any interview should be to determine whether the applicant is the right person for the position, and you can only do this by being a good *listener.*

Setting

The location of the interview and even the position of the chairs is important in a professional center. For example, if you use the couch in the staff lounge, you will be next to the applicant; this position will make it difficult to see all her reactions and you may miss some innuendoes. However, if you feel uneasy about an applicant and want to get her to open up about sensitive issues, then the informal atmosphere may be preferable. Many child care managers insist that the only way to conduct an interview is in a formal office setting. This may be appropriate when interviewing administrative and clerical staff, but may be too intimidating for teachers or assistants, and prevent you from getting the answers you would in the more informal setting. As an alternative you could use a round table with some basic materials such as a center operating policy, brochure, pens and paper. This setting is businesslike but also gives you a chance to steer the conversation to more casual talk when necessary and enables you to easily observe the applicant's reactions and body language.

Preliminaries

Before beginning the interview have the applicant fill out a job application; hopefully, they will also have given you a resume or letter describing their experience. Have this material in front of of you during the interview, where you can easily refer to it for formulating questions.

Next, make sure that you are not interrupted during the interview unless it is absolutely necessary. The applicant needs to feel valued, and you need to concentrate on the job at hand. If you must leave, excuse yourself politely and return as quickly as possible.

First interviews

Begin by outlining the basic requirements of the position, and then steer the conversation toward the applicant's goals and philosophies and attitudes toward children. For example, ask the applicant what she thinks her main goal would be if she were in charge of a class for a year. Or what she feels a teacher's relationship should be with the parents. To determine if she feels comfortable with children, you might ask what she would do with a child who is upset about Mom leaving or a two-year-old who is biting.

Remember that there are *few* direct questions that you can legally ask about an applicant's age, sex, race, marital status, children or physical ability to do the job, and you cannot refuse employment on the basis of these factors. If the position requires that the employee keep to a particular schedule, try to ascertain whether the person can handle it. For example, assume you have a position that begins at 7 A.M. If the applicant's last position was at night and the hours were not the reason for leaving the job, try to determine through casual conversation whether the applicant will be dependable during the early morning hours. If the applicant mentions that her husband was able to care for the children after school because of his working hours, you may have reason to suspect she would have difficulty being in at 7 A.M. due to child care conflicts. You might suggest that if there is a problem, you may be able to make some arrangements, but first make sure they would be within the guidelines of your employee policies.

Many interviewers have difficulty getting an applicant to open up about themselves. A good way to do this is to make statements that begin with, "You seem to . . ." In this way you are making a positive comment about the applicant; only a very shy person would not pick up on the cue to talk about themselves. A sentence beginning with "Could you explain about . . . ?" will encourage further conversation.

Flattery will usually help a person to relax. For example, if you were to say, "You seem to have enjoyed all your different jobs with children," the applicant may readily talk about her experiences at various centers, and in the midst of this you can pick up on why there *were* different centers. This way you will gather much more information than if you asked the applicant why she worked at so many centers in three years!

Occasionally you will find a potential employee who is very shy and unconfident with adults. This person may be excellent with children but would not be suited for a head teacher position where parent relations are crucial for maintaining clients.

During the interview assess how well the applicant reacts during a crisis and how well he or she might be able to handle emergencies by asking a sudden, difficult question. For example, what would she do if she were placed in a classroom with only a table, chairs, paper, water and a mixed group of eight two- and four-year-olds? Or how would she decide what to do first if three infants woke up at once? What would she do if one toddler was constantly biting an infant? Or what type of activities would be appropriate for eight- and nine-year-olds? There are many possibilities, and this type of question will help you assess not only the applicant's thinking and coping skills but also whether her ideas are compatible with your philosophy.

Remember to limit the length of the interview, and give only a brief overview of your center. If possible, have an assistant give the applicant a short tour and ask for further feedback from this staff member.

If you think a person is absolutely great, let them know that they are one of the leading candidates for the position so that you keep them interested. Mention that you have a few more interviews to conduct and that you'll call to set up a second interview. Then, you can think about all the candidates objectively once you've finished the first round of interviewing. Remember that there is always more than one solution to a problem, and this is particularly true with the hiring and firing of staff. If you remind yourself that *no one* is irreplaceable, you'll keep many of your staff problems in perspective.

Second interviews

After the initial interview, the second and more serious interview will be a time for sharing more information about your center and its benefits. If you are unsure whether the match is right, ask a trusted staff member to conduct the second interview. If after this second screening process you are still hesitant, it is usually wise not to hire the applicant.

If you are in the unfortunate position of being desperate for an employee, hire the best person on a trial basis and continue looking just in case.

No matter what your decision, be sure to reply to each applicant promptly. Your efficiency and courtesy in this area is important for creating and then maintaining your reputation in the business community. Be polite to each applicant, and explain that although there is not a position available at present you will be keeping their application on file. And then file each applicant's information with all of your comments—you may find that the "perfect" employee did not work out, and you'll need the backup immediately!

REFERENCES

Until recently, contacting references was a valuable way to ascertain a potential employee's value. However, new laws often dictate that the reference only has to verify dates of employment.

Of course, even dates of employment may be crucial. For example, you may find that someone's last position was indeed as head teacher for an after-school program but lasted for only two months!

You should always call the references as they may be unaware of any changes in the law or may just decide to give you information. If your community is not too large, knowing your fellow directors is extremely helpful. In some instances, initially attractive employees have skipped from center to center leaving behind a trail of unhappy children. A well-coordinated child care community can stop this.

Perhaps the most controversial reference for child care employees is the police check required by some states during the regulatory process. For the protection of your business, you will want to ascertain that an applicant does not have a criminal record, especially one involving child abuse. Usually the easiest way to do this is to establish a working relationship with the detectives in your local police station by calling and introducing yourself and making your child care expertise available if needed by the department. You might decide to offer a discount to policemen's children. If your state requires that all employees' names be submitted for a criminal record check, you should insist on receiving verification from the state that the records have actually been checked and that there is not a problem. And of course, being part of a professional network in your area will provide access to information you might not be able to obtain elsewhere.

HIRING

If you are serious about an applicant, ask him to work at the center for a few hours to give you a sense of the applicant's abilities in the classroom and his effect on the teaching team at your center. This may be with or without pay but explain the terms up front either way.

Once you decide to hire an applicant, you should inform him as soon as possible, preferably in person. Outline the pay scale, benefits and your expectations. This process is best done in a formal setting with the necessary paperwork ready. If for any reason the applicant is indecisive, give him a short time period to respond to you—usually not more than 48 hours.

When the employee accepts, you may want to have him sign a form saying that he has read the job description; some managers prefer to have employees sign a form saying that they have read the staff manual and agree to the conditions of employment and the description of the job all at once.

Some even enter into a contract with the employee, but be *very* careful here: experience has shown that contracts in the child care profession should be used for only the most crucial positions, if at all. In a service-oriented business that involves children's happiness, you should reserve the right to dismiss an employee who cannot maintain the goals you have clearly established and create a happy, safe atmosphere for children. If your management options are hampered by contractual obligations, you may find it difficult or impossible to take appropriate actions. Also, it is usually better to have an unhappy employee feel that he or she may leave without the restrictions of a contract. Above all, creating a cooperative, pleasant atmosphere is easier to accomplish with an "open door" policy that swings both ways!

If you are worried about an employee leaving without sufficient notice, include a period of appropriate notice in your terms of employment. As a further precaution, you can include a non-compete clause especially for key administrative staff. This will at least encourage an employee to consider the ramifications of leaving your center and setting up their own child care business with your clients.

ORIENTATION

Orientation will vary according to your management style. At the very least, introduce the new employee to the staff and make him feel comfortable. To work efficiently in the classroom, he must be able to locate materials and resources easily. For safety, he must know all first aid procedures and emergency evacuation methods in case of fire. Some centers require that each employee take a first aid course within the first three months of employment; this would give you some peace of mind during a crisis and would also be a selling point with parents.

If you hire several employees at once, you could conduct an extended orientation for all of them together. However, you will usually hire only one or two employees at a time and then orientation should be individualized. In either case review with the new employee the center's staff manual, emphasizing key issues that you know have been most difficult for other employees. Pay particular attention to those points that affect the quality of your center such as punctuality, consistency, cooperation and cleanliness.

Finally, let the employee know that the first three weeks are a trial period for both of you. In other words you are finding out whether the new employee fits into your center, and equally important, the employee is deciding how he or she likes the job. Experience has shown that three weeks will be sufficient time for the initial determination. This period also coincides in some states with the time period within which you are allowed to fire an employee without having your unemployment rating jeopardized. Be sure to explain to the employee that at the end of the three weeks you will both sit down and evaluate the results.

SUBSTITUTES

Directors have come to dread the phone calls between 6:30 and 8:00 in the morning that mean someone—for some *excellent* reason—will not be at work! As soon as your center opens, you should have substitutes hired and procedures in place to get them. Below are some possible solutions:

Guaranteed Salary Substitute

Hire a person as a substitute and guarantee him/her a minimum number of hours of employment per month, usually 20 to 30 hours. This person is paid a slightly higher hourly rate than the normal starting hourly wage. Since this employee is on call, you must agree on the number of times the employee can decline to substitute without jeopardizing the arrangement.

Flexible Hours

As described in Chapter 7, instead of hiring full-time staff for the regular eight-hour schedule, consider a three- or four-day work week with the employee working 10 hours per day. This will necessitate hiring an extra person to cover the one or two days for that particular classroom—and this supplementary staff person can have an extra "substitute" day where needed.

Job Sharing

In several industries, young mothers are "job sharing"; in other words, dividing the number of hours required for a particular job between two people. The two employees are responsible for covering a given position and can shift days when necessary. Obviously, this can decrease your substitute requirements if they can cover each other's work time when one needs to be absent.

Bonus System

Some directors give a year-end bonus for substitutes who have responded 90% of the time when called. Alternatively, you could invite the substitutes to the special staff dinner, retreat or theater outing. Any form of visible appreciation, such as a small pin or charm, will encourage responsiveness and loyalty from a substitute employee.

School Year Moms

During the school year you will find Moms who would like to work on a flexible basis while their children are in school. These individuals can substitute during the busy middle-of-the-day hours and can also act as the valuable floater employee during times of peak enrollment. Contact the elementary school guidance department or local part-day preschools for people who may be interested. Also, advertise in the classified section of your local newspaper for "occasional" help between the hours of 9 A.M. and 3 P.M. This will usually get a good response, especially in September, December and January.

Floaters

Hire a "floater" for every second or third classroom for the busiest hours (usually 10 A.M.–1 P.M.) to assist with snacks, outdoor play, lunches, hand washing, etc. This person's primary job will be to float between rooms and help wherever necessary. At the time of hiring, make it clear that this person's hours need to be flexible when necessary to cover the hours between 9 A.M. and 3 P.M. (or longer if at all possible). The person hired for this position should be self-motivated and adaptable to new situations; additionally the floater can be an excellent substitute who will be well acquainted with your facility.

Office Staff

Often a center is not large enough to justify hiring a full-time secretary or bookkeeper. In this case, you could hire someone for the office who would enjoy substituting in the classroom when necessary. This practice should NOT be extended to the administrative staff, such as director or assistant director, except when absolutely necessary. Especially in a center with a staff of over 25, the primary office positions will be too demanding to allow these staff members to help out in the classroom.

Teacher Responsibility

Directors sometimes give each *teacher* a list of three substitutes available for their position, and then the teacher is responsible for contacting the substitute directly. This system decreases the pressure on the administrative staff and can decrease the expense where the absent teacher is expected to pay a percentage of the substitute's salary. However, most centers have policies that allow a maximum number of sick days with full pay for full-time staff; the employee is charged only when this number is exceeded.

Staff Bonus

When the labor market is tight, some centers offer a monetary bonus for the staff member who locates a substitute or employee. This is not only advantageous for current employees but also can bring in excellent new people.

Sick Child Sitter

Some centers have found it advantageous to hire a person to care for teachers' sick children at the teachers' homes. If you have hired someone to care for children outside your facility, you may extend your liability. However, most liability insurance does not cover you off-premises (except, of course, for field trips).

College Students

Centers near colleges and universities sometimes find substitutes from students majoring in such areas as early childhood, child development, education, recreation and physical education. Speak directly to professors, give out fliers and be sure to keep the hours under 12 per week and the salaries attractive (slightly above the going hourly rate in the area). Remember that junior colleges and two-year programs often have early childhood concentrations and may also be a resource. College students may also be interested in working extended hours over the summer and midterm breaks, and they can also be a real help during the holidays.

Using the above suggestions should make the search for substitutes easier and certainly less time-consuming for the administrative staff. However, in some areas of the country, finding potential substitutes may still be a problem. If so, the following ideas may help:

1. Sponsor (individually or with other early childhood professionals) a workshop designed to train or introduce prospective child care employees to the profession. Use speakers and have hand-outs. Suggest substituting as a way to enter the field gradually and to find the program the employee would most like to work in.
2. Start a "surrogate grandparent" program to supplement staff on difficult days. Remember that many retired people would love to feel needed and desperately need to supplement their fixed incomes. Volunteer to speak to senior citizens' groups. Set up a slide presentation and video or have a cooperative art day with the children to promote the seniors' interest. Be sure to explain that there are many areas to which they can contribute and that their expertise and love are badly needed!
3. Implement a "work study" program with your local educational institutions. This will generally be free labor though you will need to complete evaluations. Motivate your work/study students by giving short, informative talks about the profession and making them feel a part of the staff!
4. Consider hiring substitutes for part days rather than full days if no other alternative exists—some help in a crisis is better than none!
5. Place notices in local religious newsletters and speak to clergymen and social workers. Put up notices at local supermarkets. Make the position sound attractive by stressing flexibility or scheduling.
6. Contact the local unemployment bureau and list the substitute positions. Mention that you may be able to provide job training and opportunities for extended employment.
7. Hand out fliers to part-time preschool programs in the area advertising for occasional and substitute help.

In far too many child care centers, the director has to substitute in the classroom. While this can occasionally be advantageous, the director cannot manage a child care center and be in the classroom several times a week. To solve the substitute problem, always remember that, except in dire circumstances, *you, the director, are not the solution!*

You might even consider contacting other directors in your area if recruiting employees has become a crucial problem for your center.

If you can set a high standard of employment and maintain a loyal, well-motivated staff, you will soon find that you have a list of individuals who would love to work at your center for both occasional and full-time positions.

13
MOTIVATING AND MANAGING EMPLOYEES

• •

One of the most important factors determining the quality of your child care program will be the management of your employees. If you provide each employee with an accurate job description and comprehensive staff manual and set up an effective system for motivating and evaluating staff, you will have satisfied employees, happy children and contented clients.

STAFF MANUAL

The staff manual, a vital management tool, should be a brief and clear statement of what you expect and what benefits you offer. Your own management style will determine the details of the manual, but, it should contain, at the very least, the following:

Philosophy and goals of the center
Brief description of the programs
Explicit rules of the center
Overview of job descriptions
Explanation of benefits
Expectations of management, including grounds for termination
Description of discipline and termination processes

Remember when you are designing or revising your manual to keep it as simple and clear as possible. As the center grows and you gain experience you may be tempted to try to cover every possible employee problem within the confines of the staff manual. Of course, this is an impossible and probably not even a desirable goal: in the process of covering all the bases, you'd create a complicated, lengthy manual that could be a confusing turn-off to your staff. The purpose of the manual is to clarify the employees' *major* concerns, state your benefit policies and share the goals and philosophies of the center. You want a manual that your staff reads thoroughly and understands easily, one that encourages them to work as a positive, cooperative team.

To assist child care centers with the task of creating an effective and correct staff manual, some law firms offer a service whereby they will take the outline for your staff manual and incorporate the necessary employment guidelines on a state and federal level. This service can assure that you will be kept up to date on any changes in state or federal employment laws and also that your manual follows any regulatory requirements in your state with regard to staff.

MOTIVATION

In order to have a quality child care program, you must have staff who are motivated to do an excellent job and who enjoy their work. There are many incentives that you can use to encourage your staff. Some centers have an "Employee of the Month," posting her picture in a prominent place with some background information about her and praise for particular portions of her job. Others give cash bonus awards at the end of the year. Nearly all centers have employee parties at the holidays or dinners at the end of the year. And at these times it's nice to award employees for the number of years they've worked or for a special job done. Some centers also give cash incentive awards equal to the amount of money they have not had to pay a substitute because the employee didn't take personal and sick days.

However, on a daily basis encourage a professional atmosphere with ideas such as these:

- Buy permanent name tags with each employee's position included (this helps parents too).
- Include all employees' names in any newsletter to the parents.
- Get aprons or cover-ups with the center's logo.

- By your example, encourage your staff to take pride in themselves, their work and their appearance.
- Discourage staff from wearing jeans except on one day a week—your staff will no doubt plan the extra messy activities for that day!
- Plan to have the monthly staff meeting at the end of the day and bring in dinner or special treats.
- At least once a year have a surprise, non-serious staff meeting! For example, one director hired a specialist to come in and demonstrate how to choose colors for each person's skin tone—a fun meeting and a self-esteem booster.

When you attend professional conferences, share ideas with other managers and watch for little extras for your staff. For example, buy decorative lapel pins with figures of children or holidays symbols or attractive, sturdy bags that help your teachers to organize the materials that they carry between the center and home. Many conferences have vendors who offer wonderful sweatshirts with appropriate sayings that your teachers will love.

Finally, the best motivator of all employees is praise! If your style is too critical, your employees will be easily discouraged and unmotivated. On the other hand, if you temper criticism with praise, your staff will be more motivated and accepting of your suggestions.

EVALUATIONS

Use annual evaluations to help determine salary increases or to decide whether or not to retain any employees in particular. In most centers, the true evaluations are done on an on-going basis; the competent manager is continually aware of all components of the center including the performance of the employees.

Make a file for each employee and add to it both positive and negative comments. If problems with an employee should arise, this documentation becomes very important. Keeping track of the positive aspects of an employee's performance is equally important to jog your memory during evaluations and to let the employee know that you recognized and remember their successes.

When conducting annual evaluations, have the employee fill out a self-evaluation before meeting with a supervisor. The supervisor may or may not use the form during their meeting, but this process is usually very revealing to the employee and supervisor alike. Most employees who take their job seriously can recognize their weaknesses through a self-evaluation and are willing to discuss them and come up with possible solutions. In this way the valuable employee takes responsibility in solving any difficulties he may be having with the job and sees ways to try to correct weaknesses. The process also helps the supervisor spot an employee who does not take the job seriously and does not assume responsibility for his or her weaknesses. This type of employee will usually be unreceptive to change and may not warrant a raise or the opportunity to continue working at the center.

The self-evaluation form should be designed to cover the following areas:

- How well the teacher understands children's needs
- Use of materials in the classroom
- Relationships with parents
- Cooperation with other staff
- Ability to accept direction
- Loyalty to the management and program
- Adherence to the philosophy of the center

Remember too that an employee may change with time. When you hire an employee, you bring into your business not only the person in front of you, but also the people and environments that shape his sense of well-being. As time goes on, a person's circumstances may change adversely so that even a model employee may begin to have problems. When this happens, you may be able to weather the storm, but if the person becomes so distracted or displays such a change in attitude that children and other staff are affected, you will need to consider disciplinary action. Often just giving the employee a few days off to think things through, or a leave of absence, may help. But you must help the troubled employee face the particular issues that affect his work.

TERMINATION PROCEDURES

If you have exhausted all channels of communication with an employee, then you have reason to take the unpleasant course of dismissal. Use appropriate procedures to eliminate any hard feelings among the staff and make the transition as smooth as possible for the children and parents.

When you have a problem with an employee, sit down and make an objective, concise list of the issues. Beside the issue make a note of what could be done to resolve the problem and then take the action that you have recommended. For example:

Issue	Solution	Action Taken
Jane late on M, T & Th	Speak to Jane directly	Spoke on Friday
Jane yelled at child	Remind Jane of staff policies.	Done 2/26/91
Jane left children alone	Cause for immediate dismissal	—

The above is a typical scenario of an employee who is not acceptable and probably not suited for the child care profession. Often the problem is that the director of a center has not taken the action necessary to comply with the legal requirements for dismissal of an employee.

Although the state requirements can vary somewhat, in most cases employers should attempt to give three written warnings to an employee to justify dismissal with the labor relations board. Thus, to protect your business interests, you should generally give *written* warnings in cases of serious employee difficulties. Naturally, if the children's health and safety are at stake, immediately take whatever measures are required to protect the children.

The first time that you have to dismiss an employee can be traumatic. It can be helpful to discuss the situation with a colleague in order to alleviate some of the pressure and clear your thinking. This colleague should not be someone directly involved with your business, since all employee relations within the center should be kept confidential. Once you have made the decision to terminate the employee, do so as discreetly and quickly as possible. It is unwise in a service as personal as child care to retain an employee once she has been given notice; the chances are high that any bitterness on the part of the employee may filter down to the other staff members, or, worse, to the children and parents. To eliminate this possibility, you must act decisively. Your timing will be critical and you should always do the following:

1. Make the announcement to the employee when there are few parents at the facility.

2. Do NOT go into long explanations; make the meeting brief. Have any forms required by the Labor Department ready.
3. Don't apologize; you have made a management decision and should not have any regrets if your assessment is accurate. You would not be doing the employee a favor by excusing her adverse behavior.
4. If the employee has personal belongings in the classroom or in other areas of the center, request that she return after hours to remove them. Ask that she send you a list so that you can have the materials waiting.

To assist the transition for the children, have someone who is familiar with the employee's group remain with the children for the day. Introduce the new staff member as quickly as possible. If you have had time, try to have the new employee with the children prior to the dismissal, and above all, do not allow anyone at the center to make the children unduly sad over the departure. Children are more adaptable than adults usually give them credit for and will quickly adjust to the new teacher, assuming the issue has been dealt with positively and briefly—and that the new teacher is good!

As soon as an employee has been dismissed, you should inform your staff members individually—again, do not discuss details. This is a confidential matter, and the staff only need to know that they are not affected and that you need to have quality staff to have a quality center. You should also ask the staff not to discuss any difficulties they may have had with the dismissed employee either inside or outside of the center, as the issue is now history.

Announcing the change to the parents is usually easiest in writing, unless the center has undergone several recent changes, in which case you should approach each parent individually. In either case, make your explanation brief and positive. First emphasize how pleased you are to have the new teacher on your staff and describe a little about her background or her positive ways with the children. When referring to the dismissed employee, it is best to be vague and state that you wish her the best of luck in her new endeavors. Do *not* discuss details with the parent, but if asked directly for an explanation, state, in general terms, that you made a management decision for the best interests of the children and the center. And, always reiterate how excited you are about the new staff member.

If you don't have someone waiting in the wings to take the position, you will have to interview quickly. But don't hire someone inadequate—who may have to be let go soon—just to fill the void. There should be as few changes in the classroom as possible. So if you do not have someone available, have your most positive teacher fill in on a temporary basis (preferably a teacher from another classroom that the children already know) and explain to the parents that you are in the process of screening potential employees. A substitute can fill in for the temporarily moved teacher so that the children in the dismissed teacher's class see fewer "new" faces in a short period of time.

As your management style develops and your skills improve, you'll find your employee problems will diminish. At some point you may even be able to spot problem employees before you hire them, but if you can do this with 100% accuracy, you should probably be managing an employment agency instead of a child care center!

If you have followed the proper steps in the employment procedure, given your staff appropriate training for the job, included incentives and motivation and watched for opportunities to praise, then you will generally have happy, content and productive employees. In turn your employees will work with you to create the relaxed, professional atmosphere that will make a quality child care program thrive.

14
PARENT RELATIONS

• •

In order to have a successful child care center, you have to have
an excellent relationship with the parents who purchase its
services. From explaining the center's policies and keeping parents up to date on what's going on, to the more difficult issues of
handling complaints and outside referrals, you'll need to master
the art of positive and effective communication.

ATMOSPHERE

Throughout this book there's been an emphasis on the importance of a center's physical atmosphere. However, equally important is the issue of the *emotional* atmosphere. During the
developmental phase of your business, you establish the tone of
your center and this includes how you communicate with parents.

If you're just starting out, visit other centers to get some idea
of their tone. Do you feel there's a "heart" in the business, or do
things seem businesslike and "cold?" Does the management make
you feel welcome, or do you feel you are intruding? Do you feel
at ease with the staff, or are they too stiff or formal? Are the children happy and relaxed or overly quiet and regimented?

These aspects determine the emotional atmosphere of a center
more than any single factor. You must decide whether the tone
that your management style produces is attractive to current and
prospective parents.

As we have discussed, a profitable child care center will incorporate flexibility. To encourage flexibility, the most successful centers promote a relaxed atmosphere with evident, but not overwhelming, organization. This means that the flow of parents and children in and out of the center will seem natural without undue stress, and that the systems for tracking and billing the clients are efficient and easy to use. The staff is not overburdened with unnecessary paperwork and tasks, and are consequently relaxed and friendly even after a long day. Finally, the children sense that the center was created for *them,* and as a result, the rooms are full of happy faces waiting eagerly for the next opportunity to play and learn. If parents sense this wonderful atmosphere, you will have happy clients and a prosperous business.

As your business grows and more children use the facility each week, it will become more difficult to maintain a comfortable atmosphere. You will also have more difficulty remembering every parent and child. Many directors find it helpful to trigger their memory about each family by making note of a special feature. For example, you may remember Mrs. Jones by her red-headed child, whereas Mrs. Smith has brought in twins with black hair. Also be sure to greet each parent and child individually and have a special but sincere comment for each.

OPERATING POLICIES STATEMENT

Perhaps the most valuable management tool for a center is the statement of its operating policies. Like the employee manual, your operating policy statement will provide parents with all the center's guidelines and inform them about the following areas:

Flexible Scheduling

Explain flexible scheduling and what its parameters are. State what hours are available and what must be done to reserve space. For example:

> Parents are allowed flexibility in scheduling. You may schedule your children part time or full time for hours most convenient to you. Please enroll your children for specific days/times in advance; you'll then be responsible for payment for those days/times. The exception to this is the "occasional child." In this instance the parent can call the center to see if there are any slots available on a daily/weekly basis.

Tuition

Explain how the fees will be charged (daily vs. weekly vs. monthly) and when the fees are due. With the "occasional child" described above, payment should be due when services are rendered. For children who are signed up in advance, the fees should be paid at the beginning of each week, and any payments for additional hours that they may use the center should be made the following Monday. If you give a discount for additional children in the same family, explain the percentage in this section. This is also the place to mention any scholarship funds that may be available.

Enrollment Fee

Here you explain your policy regarding the fee charged when a child is enrolled. Usually the fee is minimal and only signifies a commitment on the part of the parent. You may also choose to have separate enrollments for the school year and summer programs. This is a good planning tool for you, especially in an uncertain economy. Enrollment also reminds parents to let you know in advance when their vacations will be. This section might read as follows:

> For planning purposes, each child will need to enroll separately for the summer and school year programs. For each segment, a $10 enrollment fee will be charged.

Registration fee

Describe your registration policy and what fee is charged to register. Most centers find that they need a registration fee equal to at least two weeks tuition. This provides a cushion if the parent withdraws the child without the required notification or gets behind in payments. For the "occasional child," the fee is usually at least $25 to cover the added bookkeeping. Inform your clients in this section that all registration fees will be applied to the last two weeks of final use of the program, assuming termination has been made in the proper manner. (See Termination sections below.) Here is a sample registration description:

> All children must be registered in advance and must comply with the state regulations with regard to physical examinations and inoculations.

Absenteeism and Vacation

To write this portion of the policy statement, you must decide whether you can afford to have the parents *not* pay for time when the child does not attend or when the child is ill or on vacation. Most centers have a firm policy for these circumstances and cannot afford to have no pay for an absent child all of the time. Your policy might be as follows:

> Each child registered for 52 weeks will be allowed a one (1) week vacation without tuition charge as long as the center is notified two (2) weeks in advance. Additionally, there will be a 10% reduction in fees for absenteeism for all children, if the center is called before 8 A.M. on each day that the child is absent. (This reduction will be credited to the following week's tuition.)

Indicate here your payment policies for days that the center may be closed due to bad weather. If your center stays open and the public schools are closed, there is usually a 10% reduction in the normal fees if the child does not attend.

Holidays

List the holidays on which the center is closed and what the policy is about payment for those days. Many centers feel that since full-time employees are paid for the holidays, the parents are responsible for payment for holidays that fall during the working week. State your policy clearly to avoid any misunderstanding with the parents about what days you are officially closed and what their payment responsibilities are for those days.

Termination of Service by Parent

This should be a simple statement of the amount of notice needed for termination of service. The time should coincide with the amount charged for the registration fee—usually two weeks. Always state that earlier notice, if possible, would be appreciated.

Termination of Service by Center

Clarify your position in advance regarding what will be done if a child is disrupting the program or has needs beyond what the center can provide. An example might be:

> The center reserves the right to re-evaluate the continued participation in the program of any child who has special needs

that the center cannot meet or that may be detrimental to the health or progress of the other children. The center may, under these circumstances, request withdrawal of the child from the program. The center will be happy to recommend suitable alternatives that may better suit the child's needs. Unless the child is an immediate danger to himself or others, two weeks' notice will be given should the center request withdrawal of the child from the program.

Illness

Explain the policies on accepting or refusing ill children into the program. It is also advisable to request that the parents pick up an ill child promptly and to state your policy about the administration of medication. For example:

> Please do not send your child to the center with a fever, sore throat or other suspicious symptoms. However, please do not feel that it is necessary to keep your child home with allergies or a case of the sniffles. If your child develops a contagious disease, please inform us immediately so that other children in the class can be watched for symptoms."

You also want to include attendance guidelines for typical childhood diseases:

If your child has:	May return to school:
chicken pox	6 days from onset of rash
German measles	5 days from onset of rash
measles	10 days from onset of rash
mumps	when swelling stops
strep throat	2 days after antibiotics are given

Emergency

What will happen in the case of a medical emergency if the parent cannot be reached? It is a good idea to outline your procedures and inform parents that they are responsible for any expense incurred.

Parents' Signature

Most centers require that parents sign a form stating that they have read and understood the operating policies.

EVENTS FOR PARENTS

Nearly every successful center has functions for parents so that they feel part of the program and consequently part of their child's care and education. With this in mind, you should design events that are enjoyable and not at all stressful for the parents. At least one function during the year should be for the parents *only* so that they have a chance to see the center and visit the teachers and staff informally. To encourage attendance, show a video of the children or have a dynamic speaker. Plan to serve wine and cheese or coffee and sweets. Try to make the event as informal as possible and encourage your staff to attend as well.

You may also decide to have several functions involving the parents, staff and children. Outdoor events like picnics are best since the space inside is limited when everyone in the family is involved. Try to have a special form of entertainment for the children (such as a clown or magician) since the parents will want to socialize, and your staff may be overburdened trying to watch the children and entertain parents.

During the year activities like a "Mommies' Lunch" just before Mother's Day or a "Daddy's Breakfast" near Father's Day, can be very enjoyable, especially if the children take part in preparing the food and setting the table for the parents. Keep in mind, of course, the children from single-parent families and decide if this would be too awkward for them. Instead, you might have a Parent Lunch and hold it outdoors if necessary.

Fund raisers are another way to involve parents in the center. This is particularly helpful if there is a piece of equipment the center badly needs. Try to get the teachers involved in the campaign as well. However, be very careful not to offend any parents; for example, many working parents just do not have the time to spend on such activities. You should also check local and state laws about fundraising if you own or operate a private, for-profit center.

DAILY AND MONTHLY UPDATES FOR PARENTS

Keeping parents regularly informed about details of the care and news of their children's programs is an important part of your relationship and communications with them. If you are providing infant and toddler care, the effectiveness of your communication with parents is even more important, since these young children cannot let their parents know about their day. The most effective method is to keep a daily record: provide a clipboard for each child and have the caregiver make note of the important events as well as the eating, sleeping and diapering routines. The parent usually takes the note home at the end of the day in case there is a problem in the evening. If the caregiver in charge of the child has been observant, these notes will be a real source of information.

With the very young child, it is especially important to have the primary caregiver present either in the early morning or late afternoon to see each parent personally. The notes will help, of course, but there are times when a parent needs to talk over an issue with the caregiver. Also, it is important that the caregiver by very careful in transmitting information to the parent. For example, if the infant has rolled over onto his back, it is best to tell the parent that you think the child is *about* to roll over. The parent should ALWAYS see the "firsts!" And whenever the caregiver has to say something negative, it should be said only in mild terms after making a positive statement. For example, a parent may feel very guilty if the caregiver bluntly states that the child had a terrible day. However, if the caregiver says that the child ate well but seemed a little crankly and did the parent notice anything at home, the parent will be concerned, but not feel guilty. The approach is the important issue, and you will have to train anyone working with the younger children to be very positive.

In addition to the staff's personal daily updates about a child's individual care, a single-page, informal, monthly newsletter or just a "Parent Notes" sheet is sufficient. To produce the letter you may need to enlist the help of a staff member who enjoys writing or taking pictures. Several short articles can convey more information than one long one, and the simpler the articles are, the more likely the parents are to read them. Some effective eye catchers are:

- A catchy title for the newsletter itself
- Two or three drawings by the children
- News of the staff
- An "Employee of the Month" (or "Quarter") article
- Mention of how GREAT parent help is—and it is!
- Seasonal graphics or drawings by children
- Colored paper (preferably print on yellow or pink paper)

Most important, parents love funny anecdotes about the children, or some of their hilarious comments and *these do happen often!*

Every teacher has some to tell, but encourage them to write the incident down right away before they forget!

As an added service for busy parents, you may want to attach a reprint of an article about a child-rearing issue. Some excellent ones can be purchased from Hacienda Press (see Appendix F). If you reproduce an article from a publication, be sure to get permission and give your center credit on the reprint for making it available. If it's a really good piece, parents might share it with other working parents, and this is excellent advertising for you.

COMPLAINTS

If you sense that a parent is unhappy about something at the center, it is your job as a manager to attempt to allay their anxieties while you investigate and try to correct the problem. It is important to remember that in a service business the customer is *always* right! There will undoubtedly be times when you will sincerely feel that a parent is wrong; however, your job is to tactfully point out to the parent that you respect his or her opinion, that you'll consider the issue carefully in light of your center's policies and philosophy, and yet *never* state that you feel that he or she is wrong. Most parents will usually meet you halfway on an issue, realizing that you are trying your best to satisfy many different requirements.

Any complaint should be handled swiftly and professionally. If you are unsure of the basis for a complaint, investigate the issue thoroughly and speak to the teacher involved. Emphasize to your teachers that it is the job of the director to handle complaints and that they should not become involved, except at your request. This way you retain control over how complaints are handled and don't have to involve individuals who may complicate the issue and not have the tact or ability to resolve the problem efficiently. The teachers' primary job is to work with the children, whereas your job as a manager is to concentrate on issues that involve the total administration of the center and the teacher/parent/child network.

A typical example is a request that a child who has been ill be kept inside during outdoor play. Now you know that to do so will require having a teacher from that age group stay inside while the other teacher goes outside with 15 children. This is not acceptable because it is extremely unsafe. However, you may be able to have the child join another group inside for that period of time or bring a quiet activity into the office for a short time. Also, you may want to point out to the parent that if the child is well enough to attend the center, then he should be well enough to go outside. As a last resort, have an article handy explaining why fresh air is good for children and may actually help the healing process!

With more serious complaints that could be reported to the licensing authority, you should speak to the parent immediately to hear the parent's point of view. Try to diffuse any anger as quickly as possible by assuring the parent that you will investigate the matter thoroughly, take corrective action if necessary and get back to them within 24 hours. And if you say you will do these things, follow through and be firm and confident in your manner. Do not involve the parent directly in the investigative process; for example, do not speak to the teacher involved while the parent is present.

If the complaint is serious and may have further implications, be sure to keep detailed, accurate notes. Include the date, time and description of the event but be as objective as possible. Conclude your notes with suggestions for follow-up. Also, ask any of the staff who were involved to do the same and file the reports together. Keep the notes in a completely secure and private location.

Accident and Incident Report Forms

Have accident and incident report forms available for your staff to fill out as necessary. The accident report describes injuries—no matter how minor they may seem—including the time, date, location, supervising staff present and first aid procedures that were used. It is also a good idea to write down when the parent was told, by whom and what the reaction of the parent was.

The incident report should include the same type of basic information, but its purpose is somewhat different. In an incident report the staff describes any troubling incidents that take place with a child. When this is done conscientiously, you and your staff may see a pattern linked to a particular event, for example, a child who is troubled or acts out every other Monday morning after a parent visitation. The incident reports become especially important when there is the possibility that a child or family may have to be referred for counseling or when there is a suspected case of child abuse that may need to be reported to the authorities. It is very important to keep the report objective and factual so that there is no doubt as to *what* was observed. In the case of a complaint by the parent, the proper reports may help to substantiate your staff's version of their role in the incidents and later to respond to any potential charges.

EVALUATIONS

During the course of the year, you will want to evaluate the children's progress. This is usually done in preparation for a meeting with the parents or may be necessary if a child is having some difficulty.

The question of formal on-site testing has been debated for many years because it leads to many other issues. For example, the teachers doing the testing should be trained in giving the tests; if they are not, the results may be inaccurate and the parent might mistakenly be told that his child has a problem. Also, the person relaying the information may not be tactful in telling the parents that their child has a problem. It takes practice to learn the best way to approach parents on such an issue. To protect yourself, as well as to insure that the proper testing is done, do not undertake testing at your facility unless you have qualified staff and a virtually foolproof system. There are many new test systems being developed, especially as researchers attempt to quantify the effects of child care. However, if you decide to use a testing system at your facility, make sure that you acquaint yourself with its positive and negative aspects.

Assuming you do not do actual testing at your facility, what type of evaluation should you conduct? Generally, the purpose is to assure the parents that they have a wonderful child who is developing normally. To determine this, your teachers will need to know what the normal levels of child development are for the age they are teaching and positively communicate the details of each child's progress to the parents. The best tool for this is a progress report that, even by its title, implies that progress has been made. In a well-designed report, there should also be a section for the teacher to express any particular concerns. Once the teacher has discussed these concerns with the parents, the director might suggest testing by an outside source. In this way, the teacher remains a positive *facilitator* of progress in the classroom and is not the one to suggest the more serious possibility of remedial help for the child.

Evaluations should be positive and should help parents feel confident about your center's curriculum and staff. Once the progress report has been sent home, an informal, nonthreatening meeting should be scheduled between the parent and the teacher. You should be present at all meetings until you have confidence in the teachers' abilities to adequately represent the philosophy of the school and *not* to say anything for which you or the center could be held liable. Later on, the director should attend the meeting only if difficulties are expected or there may be need for further referral. And remember that although formal evaluations may be done only once a year, your staff should be continually on the lookout for any area of undue concern.

RESOURCES

Before you are confronted with a situation in which a referral must be made, have the resources that can provide assistance ready to give to parents. The most frequent referral in child care is probably for speech testing, and this is generally done through the public schools. Contact your local school board's special education representative first, and make sure that they provide the required testing free of charge and in a timely manner. Parents sometimes find the prospect of working with the public schools threatening, even in regard to a relatively minor problem, so you should obtain *written* permission from the parent before using any names in discussion with the public school or any outside professional. However, try in every way possible to diminish those fears and support their individual efforts. In some cases the parents will prefer private speech therapy, so have ready the name of a therapist in the area who has worked with young children.

Next, find one or two child psychologists who agree with your school's philosophy and who have worked with young children. Be sure to check their method of therapy (i.e., family, behavioral, psychotherapy, etc.) and ask for references. And watch your first referrals to see how effective the therapy is. If possible, have the psychologist come and speak to your staff and parents on a common problem, such as discipline.

In addition, have a list of physicians in the area, support groups for parents new to the community, local services related to children, the local facilities and programs available for children and emergency treatment facilities if a child's physician is not available. Most centers also have the name of a contact at a women's crisis center since chances are high that you will have to find support for a mother or family in crisis at some point.

One referral that you should be hesitant to make is for babysitters or auxiliary unregulated child care, because if there is a problem with the service or an accident occurs as a result of the referral, you could be held liable.

Having the proper resources available for parents can only increase your value to them and make them more appreciative of having found a quality child care facility for their child. They will respect your professional attitude and be supportive of any new programs and especially of your efforts on behalf of the children.

THE REFERRAL PROCESS

Once you have successfully accomplished the delicate task of making referrals, you will have the experience to handle most problems involving the children within your center. To begin with, it is very important that the setting for the meeting help parents and all those involved relax. Also, do some homework beforehand so you understand which areas are sensitive for the parents involved.

As a key person, you should try to alleviate the parents' initial feelings of guilt. The best way to do this is to gently point out that they have not received formal training as parents. Indeed the only training they have received is from their own parents, which may have been superb or may have inherent problems. Next, point out that this means they are bringing into their parenting style four sets of parenting standards that may or may not be in agreement. Chances are, there are some conflicts, and you will usually see a hint of recognition come to their faces. Then, you can gently explain that getting professional help to handle a situation can help to sort out these differences. It may even be advisable to recommend that they do not discuss the situation with their *own* parents in case they find it threatening.

It is sometimes helpful to point out that children can be very clever and play on an adult's weaknesses to achieve their own ends. Thus it is important that parents are consistent and in agreement on the methods they use to handle a particular problem or set of problems.

Finally, stress how important it is, as their counseling progresses, that they give you and your staff guidance on handling the particular problem. Reiterate that you are willing to work with them and the professionals involved to effect a change. However, it is essential that the parents recognize the problem and agree to work as part of the team. If they do not, and the situation is intolerable in the classroom, you may decide to ask that the child be removed for both his own good and the good of the other children.

This last step is the most difficult for a director. However, it is also necessary in some cases, and regrettably, nearly every director has had a situation about which she'll readily admit, "I wish I had acted sooner. The class has changed totally and my teachers can *teach* again!" If this seems to be the case and the parents will not cooperate, remember that there will be cases that you cannot help. At all times, you must place first the well-being of the entire center.

PART FOUR
MAXIMIZING YOUR SUCCESS
· ·

With your new center or improvement plans well under way, it's time to reexamine a few essentials to ensure your profit-making potential. First, see how innovative marketing and advertising will help to make your business more visible to prospective clients and the community at large. Next, consider the specific aspects of your business that always warrant some extra attention and effort—your facility, your staff and your program—so that the result is a first-rate child care center.

Then, examine the principal concerns that have caused trouble for other centers so that they won't cause trouble for you. Finally, studying the mistakes that others have made can often be instructive and give you insight into ways to avoid common pitfalls. These chapters cover:

15. How to market your program and advertise effectively with various media.
16. How to increase your sales by creating, maintaining and promoting a quality child care center that sets yours apart from other centers.
17. How to evaluate and solve problems unique to the child care industry.
18. Understanding the 10 most common mistakes that other center directors have made and the 10 most unfounded fears, so that you'll have more confidence in managing your center.

15

Marketing and Advertising

• •

Implementing a flexible program is the most vital step in making your center a profitable one. Using marketing and advertising strategies that make your center and its flexible care highly visible to clients is essential.

To map out such a strategy, consider these questions:

1. Who exactly are the center's potential clients?
2. Can the exterior of the facility be used as a giant advertisement for the center?
3. What is the most effective way to produce a brochure that is concise, well designed and colorful?
4. What are the best ways to distribute brochures and fliers effectively? Would it be a good idea to give current customers brochures to pass on to prospective clients?
5. Where should ads be placed so that potential customers are most likely to see them?
6. Which business contacts could be potential sources for new customers?
7. What opportunities are available for free advertising?
8. How are the phones answered? Should an answering machine be used during business hours? Or if someone is answering the phones, has that person been trained to give accurate information in a friendly and cheerful manner?
9. As owner/director, am I spending enough time at the center to know it is being promoted effectively? (This is especially important during the first few weeks.)

CUSTOMER BASE

The first step in marketing your program effectively is to assess who and where your customers are. (See also Chapter 1 for market analysis.) With a flexible program your customer base will include parents other than those working a traditional five-day 40-hour week. Therefore, a primary focus of your efforts should be to seek out potential clients with different needs. Listed below are some professions and employer sources to explore.

Contact any potential resources in your community by sending them a brochure with a cover letter or even just a letter introducing yourself and your flexible child care services. Some employers may not want to get involved or pass the information along, so also try to contact the employees directly. For example, give waitresses in a restaurant or office personnel in a doctor's office some of your cards or a brochure.

Professions:

> Ambulance technicians
> Beauticians
> Firefighters
> Obstetricians
> Office temps
> Pediatricians
> Police officers
> Nurses
> Real estate agents
> Receptionists
> Teachers and professors
> Waitresses and waiters
> Writers

Employers:

> Accounting firms
> Answering services
> Banks
> Law firms
> Manufacturers
> Newspapers
> Nursing services and nursing homes

Retail stores
Secretarial services
Temporary agencies

Next put together a list of the following in your community:

Major companies and names of key officers (C.E.O.s, personnel)
Contact groups for parents (newcomers, PTAs, etc.)
Board of realtors with key officers
Physicians, dentists, chiropractors
Town/municipal officials
Any existing support groups for company officers (i.e., Personnel, Purchasing, Management Associations)
Chamber of Commerce
Small business organizations

These organizations may in turn have other resources to help you better understand their members' needs. Pay particular attention to any support organizations that serve the nonworking or cottage industry parent; these two groups of parents will use the flexible program most, so identify them as early as possible. And finally, be sure to look at adjacent communities and their need for child care, as some of these parents may be commuting through your area or be willing to drive further to reach your quality, flexible service. Use the same criteria you did for your local community and identify the resources, professionals and employers.

NAME AND LOGO

The visibility of your center will depend on several factors but most important will be its name and logo. These are crucial elements in creating an identity for the center that in turn enhances a professional image. The center's name and logo should appeal to the type of client it serves. Stay away from cutesy titles unless you feel such a name is absolutely appropriate for the community. If your clientele will be upscale parents and you want to develop a classy center, have a name to match.

Keep in mind the age groups you plan to accommodate now and in the future. Let's say you start with an infant and toddler center, but your long-term business plan anticipates the possibility of developing an after-school program. If you call your facility the "Wee-Ones Child Care Center," not many school-age children will want to attend, and it is difficult to change a name later. This brings up an important point: once the center has a recognized identity established through its name and logo, it should not be changed as this is the most visible sign of your business identity in the community. When you purchase an existing facility, you may be saddled with a name or a logo you don't like; often one can live with the name and not with the logo or vice versa.

The logo should create an immediate and memorable impression. A particular feature of the center might make a good logo/symbol. For example, one school has a gingerbread play house, and a drawing of it became its logo. Another example of how a name can create an image is "Kids Club," which is a before- and after-school care program. For the children, the name definitely makes a statement that means "older than preschool." "Room to Grow" is another name that creates an immediate impression. These names are explicit and relate to the particular age groups they serve or the center's philosophy. For new ideas for names and logos, make a point of looking through the Yellow Pages whenever you travel. Be sure that any name you think of using is not trademarked or previously reserved in your state.

FACILITY EXTERIOR

Consider the physical exterior of your building. Stand across the road or drive down your street and see how it looks from the outside. Is it attractive? Does it look like an institution? Would you want to drop your children off there each day? Are the entrances easily accessible? Can you see the playground and the brightly painted play toys? Is there a way to improve the physical appearance?

For example, one center was housed in an institutional, square building with no character at all; the owner put up window boxes and shutters, painted a little design on the door, put molding around the door frame and created a warm, welcoming exterior. There were always pretty flowers in the flower boxes no matter what the season of the year; during the winter she placed holly in them. The children placed bird feeders outside for decoration and interest.

If you have to use a chain link fence around the property, plant bushes so it won't look quite as sterile. No one wants to think they are leaving their children in an institution for a full 11-hour day. There must be a homelike, cozy atmosphere for parents to really feel good about a center.

Next, consider your sign. A sign on the building itself may be difficult for passersby to see from the road. It is better to have a sign in front of the building, facing oncoming traffic—from both directions. If it is parallel with the street, it will only advertise to people who turn their heads. If possible, it should also be visible day or night.

Some communities have regulations that restrict the type of sign one can use. Check with your local zoning department regarding what type, size and color of signs are allowed. Are you allowed to have decorations and/or a logo on it? How large can the sign be? Does it have to be attached to the building? If it is free-standing, how far from the building are you allowed to place it? Are you restricted within that particular zone?

When you put up your sign, be very careful not to block parents' view of the entrance and/or exit from the building. You don't want your sign to cause an accident—that would be extremely poor publicity.

BROCHURES AND FLIERS

Brochures and fliers are an important way of increasing your exposure, but you can easily spend a great deal of money on them without getting very much for your dollar. Keep them brief, clear and to the point. Remember with advertising you have approximately 20 seconds to catch your clients' attention.

Whether you are opening a new center, expanding your facility, implementing flexibility or promoting a new program, emphasize the main feature of your new venture. What is the "point" that you want your clients to know? Put it into one- or two-word phrases for the headline or highlights of the brochure. If you use too many words, no one is going to read all of them.

The layout of your brochure should be simple and straight-forward. "Bullets"—small dots before a list of phrases or sentences—are graphic attention-getters. Your phone number should be repeated at least three times and should be in large type face. If your location is an important selling feature, put in a small map.

If the brochure is going to be a self-mailer (a piece that is not enclosed in an envelope), use a threefold brochure format, and be sure the stock is heavy enough to hold up in the mail. If you decide to mail the piece first class, make sure to have "First Class" printed near the address label so you don't have to hand stamp every one. Also, it will help to prevent its being mailed by the postal service with third-class mail. It is obviously cheaper to send a brochure third class, but owners generally want the word to get out as quickly as possible once they are ready to advertise.

Our experience has been that your choice of paper color is very important because certain colors seem to sell better than others; yellow, pink and orange sell the best. Red will sell, but it is very difficult to read print on a red background. However, red ink on white paper works well. Ivory is an okay, classy color but does not sell particularly well. Gray is a very "down" color and doesn't sell well at all, and blues and greens are too cool. These color considerations also apply to fliers. Also, using two tones of ink may not be worth the extra price.

If your primary concern is building enrollments, don't worry about glossy brochures with pictures. Although photographs attract parents, four-color printing is so cost-prohibitive that you probably won't be able to afford enough brochures to flood the market, which should be your aim. It is preferable when you are starting out and have a limited budget to produce several brochures with different messages or headlines about your center. This way your logo is seen repeatedly and people come to recognize it.

If you do decide to use pictures on a large brochure, make sure that the pictures are small enough so that your logo is more visible than the picture. Captions under pictures are likely to be the first thing read, so make sure they are descriptive. Keep in mind that your primary goal is exposure for your center, not exposure of the children's faces. Also, remember you must obtain parents' written permission to use a photograph of their child in any advertising or commercial material.

Once you have a brochure, remember that it won't be visible sitting on your desk. Too many times directors have created lovely brochures that only collect dust in their own offices. It's nice if parents take them home; however, if they just sit on a desk at their home, it doesn't help your advertising efforts either. Explain what you are trying to do and ask parents to take them to their workplace. *A satisfied customer is your best advertisement!*

Most important, place your brochures with pediatricians, lawyers, convenience stores, supermarkets, health clubs, libraries, newsstands, hairdressers, real estate offices, newcomers' clubs, churches, synagogues, etc. Give special emphasis to placing bro-chures in locations *where people have to wait and may be bored!* Have a brainstorming session with your staff and make it clear that a group effort will benefit the entire center.

NEWSPAPER, YELLOW PAGES, AND RADIO ADVERTISING

If you decide to advertise either in newspapers or on radio, think carefully about where your advertising dollar is going. Make sure you know your clientele, where they are apt to look for ads and when they are looking for child care. For example, do you think working parents have time to read a newspaper on a daily basis? If not, what days of the week will they be reading a newspaper, and are they apt to read the display ads? Most people go straight to the classified ads when they need child care.

Make your classified ads very simple: Use bold type wherever possible and only two- or three-word descriptive phrases. "Rea-sonable rates, convenient location, quality child care." Parents look first at the price, then location, and way down their list is the program itself. So rather than promoting the program—al-though you want a quality program—promote the aspects of your center that are of the greatest interest to the client.

Early advertising (classified or in general) can be done even if your license has not yet come through. Because you can't really advertise the name of your center if you don't know that your license has been approved, start, say four weeks earlier, with an ad that says "Coming Soon . . ." The next week say "Coming Soon in Hoboken"; and the third week might be "Coming Soon in Hoboken, a new child care center" and the fourth week, when you are licensed, put the details in. This approach definitely gets the community wondering when and where this new child care center is going to be. People start talking and asking questions and that's exactly what you want them to do—ask questions about what's new in child care.

Advertising in the Yellow Pages is a must in nearly every com-munity, since the telephone companies have effectively con-vinced the population that any service or commodity can be found there. If you have a new business, check the advertising dead-lines for the Yellow Pages in each of the local phone books. When the sales representative comes by, ask questions. For example, until recently there was no "child care" category in most Yellow

Pages and all centers were listed under "nursery schools"; however, continued pressure from the owners of child care centers and clients has led to a separate listing in many directories.

Check what services the particular phone company provides for ad design. Usually they will design the whole ad for you using your logo and copy. Be sure to *insist* on proofreading the final version and make any necessary changes promptly. Do NOT clutter the ad with unnecessary information and drawings. In some directories there is an option to use red type, which has a definite advantage since it attracts the eye. Unfortunately, you will generally not be able to request a specific position for the ad, but if you can, ask for the upper right-hand corner of the page since this is where the eye tracks first. (By the way, the same principle holds true if you place a display ad in the newspaper.) With the Yellow Pages, you can run a large ad for the first few years of your business, but as the center becomes better known and its word-of-mouth reputation grows, the ad can become smaller.

Make sure any radio advertising you buy runs during the commute time. When you are trying to attract different types of employees for your flexible care program, the commute time may vary; but people generally listen to the radio in the morning between 7 and 9 A.M. and in the afternoon between 4 and 6 P.M. Depending on the area, commuting hours can run from 6:30 to 8:30 or 9:30 A.M. and 4:30 to 6:30 P.M. Usually the radio station will be able to assist you with your ad and the schedule in which to run it. Advertising during these hours will cost a little more; however, if you want to make a quick go at the market, radio ads can be extremely effective.

Be sure to ask parents who call where they have heard about your center and keep track of which are the most effective forms of advertising.

NETWORKING

Developing a network of business acquaintances is a great way to promote your business. Visit local coffee shops and get to know the local business people, especially those in small businesses. They will help to promote your center—particularly a flexible one—faster than any other media.

For example, local realtors generally know the local business market very well; make sure you provide them with accurate information about your center. Write the local realty offices a polite letter, or, if possible, talk to the Board of Realtors, or at the very least distribute your brochures at a Board of Realtors meeting. They are the first people to be in touch with new people in the community and can be very helpful. Every community in the country has a Board of Realtors, and almost without exception, they love to have brochures and/or fliers as part of their packet. If you have a new or special program—particularly a flexible care program—it might even benefit some of the realtors themselves, because they often work erratic hours.

If there is a large apartment complex nearby, make sure that the management or rental agent knows about your center. It is easier for them to rent to a young family if the family knows that there is child care nearby.

Alert local hospitals about your center because their staff work erratic hours. Many hospitals are being pressed by their employees to start on-site child care, but most are too small to make it feasible. They would love to have a child care center nearby to fill that need. You may be able to work out a voucher system with the hospital. Again, a clever letter of introduction to the nursing staff may bring new clients (see sample letter in Appendix E).

Look around your community for small companies that have split shifts or manufacturing companies that have double shifts. Their employees may need the off-hours of care that you can provide.

Also, be on the lookout for seasonal opportunities to supplement income from full-time care. Several centers in one area were approached by large stores who said to them, "We can't get workers at Christmas time. Could you offer child care in the evenings until 10 o'clock so that we can stay open later and attract new clerks?" These centers responded, "Yes, we'll be open, and we can make sure that your employees have preference for these slots if you will pay us x amount per week." The payment from the stores covered basic staff costs to keep the center open for those hours; anything they received from the parents was profit. If you decide to try something like this, be sure to check state regulations, because in some states it is more difficult to provide evening care. For example, in the South evening care is abundant in nearly every town and city. On the other hand, in the northern states evening care is rare.

Finally, watch for businesses that are having trouble recruiting employees by checking for repeated wants ads in the classifieds or by checking with employment agencies. They will probably be a good resource for new clients; you may even be able to work out a special arrangement with the management. Also, the resource and referral services in your area may know of businesses that may need assistance with child care services.

FREE ADVERTISING

There are several forms of free advertising that work very well to enhance the methods discussed so far. Some of the suggestions require a particular expertise, but someone on your staff or a friend can perhaps assist you.

For example, volunteer to give talks on child care to various civic organizations. Ask to speak with parents in a prenatal class about child care and then offer them a tour of the facility during the next week. When you give a talk, be sure to have information from other sources on the subject of child care and encourage the parents to ask questions. Your local resource and referral service can often provide information, statistics and handout materials. Also, whenever you give a talk, be sure to incorporate your philosophy on flexibility. You will discover how popular flexible care can be; people will talk about it, especially if you are enthusiastic and explain how this new service should really benefit the community.

No matter where you go, always carry a supply of your business cards with you. Whether you're talking to a potential client, another educator or a casual acquaintance, it pays to present yourself as a professional with a service that may be useful to them. This way you can make sure that anyone you contact has your name and number for a follow-up call or referral.

Another form of free advertising is a press release. If possible, send along pictures (obtain written permission from the parents first to use photos of the children) and submit them to *all* area newspapers. It's best to go to the newspaper first and get the proper format as newspapers have different requirements and deadlines. Remember that every publication likes pictures of children—they have great visual appeal.

If you offer a school-age program, be sure to tell the guidance department at local schools. Inform the high schools as well, because there may be some students with babies who really need your flexible scheduling. In many cases financial assistance is available through the town social worker or the state department of education to help these students get back to school and stay off welfare. Also, contact personnel departments in the schools to assist their substitute teachers with child care needs. This is a nice favor to the school systems, and it will help to improve the center's relationships with the public school system.

HANDLING INQUIRIES, TOURS AND SPECIAL REQUESTS

Phone Responses

If increased visibility causes more prospective clients to call, make certain that the phone calls are answered properly. If someone else is answering phones for you, be sure to call yourself from outside the facility and see how the phone is answered. The caller should receive a polite reply with efficient answers to all questions. Any prospective client should be encouraged to make an appointment to come for a visit.

Tours

A tour can be useful to assure parents of the center's quality. Set up a system for having parents tour the center. Most centers do this on an on-going basis, but schedule specific times for tours so that there is as little interruption as possible of the existing classes.

On the initial visit it is usually wise to discourage parents from bringing their child for several reasons:

- The child may not have had the required immunizations.
- The child may distract others in the class since the child does not know the classroom rules.
- The materials in a given room may not be age-appropriate.

For example, a two-year-old could easily choke on materials found in a classroom for older children. Explain to the parents that the purpose of the visit is for them to observe the center objectively and to ask questions without interruption; this may be difficult while trying to keep an eye on their own child.

If you want to keep the disruption of the classrooms to a minimum, you could also have a videotape about the center available for parents to take home and view. During a visit the parents are only able to see one small segment of the day while the video can show several different activities. Don't worry about having the video done professionally—in fact, the more professional the video, the less believable it is to parents. When making the video, a simple microphone can be attached to the home camera and your narration can explain various procedures. Start with the entrance into the facility and a welcome, and then follow with segments from the typical daily activities in order of their occurrence. Also, if you do this regularly and make copies, your regular clients may want to purchase or borrow a copy, which will again increase your popularity and visibility. When shown at home, the video can also put a nervous prospective child or anxious grandparent more at ease.

Have the necessary literature for enrollment packaged and readily available in the office so that a prospective parent feels even more welcome. Extra brochures promoting the features and quality of your program should be prominently displayed near the entrance. If your state allows, pictures of the children doing fun activities are always well received, but be sure to obtain the parents' permission before using the pictures outside of the facility. If you have a few spectacular pictures have them enlarged, place them in clear plastic frames and hang them in the hallways.

Special Requests

No inquiries about your program should be put off and every effort should be made to accommodate the parent's schedule no matter how strange it may seem. For example, if you decided that your preschool program will take place between 9 and 11 A.M. and a parent calls and wants care between 10 A.M. and 2 P.M. you should accommodate that parent initially. Once the child is enrolled and enjoying the program, you can always approach the parent and say, "I know that you work from 10 to 2, but your child is missing a little of the program. Would you mind if he started at 9?" You may decide to charge for the extra hour or you may feel that it's worth the extra benefits and waive the fee. However, if you initially had said that you don't allow children to enter the 9 to 11 program at 10 A.M. because it starts at 9 *sharp*, you would have lost that client. The parent would probably never call your center again and would have left thinking, "They don't want to meet my needs, they want to meet *their* needs and I want my child with me as much as possible." Adjustments in schedules can be made later when the client is in love with your program and the teachers.

You want the community to understand from the start that the center is there to serve its varied needs and to provide a top-quality program. Marketing will be a main concern for the first few weeks of your promotional program, but once you have satisfied parents and happy children, your success will snowball.

FOR CONTINUED SUCCESS

Initially, you may be the only center in your area providing flexible alternatives for child care. However, a year later you may have competition, and then you will need to be more aggressive in your approach. Ascertain if your current marketing is effective by asking yourself this simple question: do 60% of the adult members of the community—including all age groups—know about the center? You want the majority of the adults to think of your center first if they need or know of someone who wants child care.

And of course, once you have clients, you want to keep them by making your center top quality. To emphasize the excellent aspects of your center, purchase brochures describing "How to Distinguish a Good Early Childhood Program" or "How to Choose Child Care" and indicate to parents that they should feel free to ask you any questions pertaining to the pamphlets. These and other informative materials are available from the National Association for the Education of Young Children and other professional organizations listed in Appendix D.

Make sure parents and children are warmly welcomed each day. This means smiles on your teachers' faces, nice bright corridors and halls and an entranceway that says, "We are glad you are here!" Whatever you do, be constantly and critically aware of how one enters the building. Does it look good to you? Would you want to stay there all day?

The interior should be freshly painted, clean and orderly. Are there enough things at the child's eye level to make a child say "I like this place," or are too many materials only visible at an adult's eye level? Is the space designed for children or for adults? There should be something that says to the child, "Would you like to come in this room and stay?" Consider:

- a table with play dough on it
- some pretty pictures and mobiles
- a nice cubbie that they can call their own
- a special piece of equipment that is an eye-catcher to both the parent and the child

- a play house within the room
- pictures of the children doing typical, fun activities

Remember that all the advertising and marketing in the world cannot make up for an unappealing interior. Your center, its rooms and its interior must be inviting to the children and the parents for your center to become a success.

16
QUALITY EQUALS SALES!

• •

Quality is defined in Webster's dictionary as "that feature that distinguishes or identifies someone or something." However, when discussing what is meant by "quality child care," the opinions of parents and professionals vary greatly. The perceptions of people in your community will vary according to their cultural backgrounds, their general knowledge about child care and the strength of the competition. In order to create a center that is perceived by your community as providing the highest quality care, you need to know what factors are most important to them. Possible factors include:

- Physical facility: neat and orderly; all surfaces clean, attractive and well maintained.
- Staff: compassionate, warm and understanding with at least a working knowledge of the appropriate materials and programs to present for optimum development in each age group.
- Group size and ratios: acceptable and manageable standards with low staff-child ratios.
- Management and administrative personnel: organized, friendly and professional, so that parents are convinced their children will be well cared for and that any crisis will be handled efficiently.
- Equipment and materials: appealing, well maintained and applied in a program that is developmentally appropriate for each age group.

There is plenty of room for interpretation and variation in this list, and you should determine what your clients feel is important and what will help you the most in your work with the children.

Unfortunately, all too often the emphasis is on finding adequate funds to meet the facility, program and teacher costs rather than on the quality of the facility and programs. A flexible program as outlined in Chapter 6 should generate sufficient revenues to provide at least a 20-35% profit margin, which in turn will give you the ability to pay your staff well and maintain an excellent facility and program.

PHYSICAL FACILITY

The first impression a parent has of your center is likely to be a lasting one. So it is important to maintain a neat and orderly appearance at the entrance of the building. Avoid clutter throughout the center at all costs. There should be order in the rooms, but also a sense of freedom for the children to be happy. All surfaces should be cleaned regularly, and there should be no pervasive odors in the rooms. Parents should be convinced that the management places a high priority on the health and safety of the children. This attitude will be seen through the upkeep of the toys and equipment as well as the cleanliness. All broken toys should be removed and equipment repaired and nicely kept.

The rooms should be bright and airy with cozy spaces for quiet time. So that the surroundings are not confusing, there should be a sense of purpose and not chaos. The ultimate goal in a quality center is to convince the parent that the child will have a place where he can be happy and safe for up to 11 hours a day while taking part in an age-appropriate program.

The appearance of the office area is also important and again can portray either chaos or organization to the parents. If the area is cluttered and there are papers everywhere, the parent who is a professional has to wonder if you really know, for example, where the necessary numbers are in case of an emergency. They may also wonder if you have accurate, accessible records of all the children's inoculations or critical allergies. And to the business-oriented parent, there will be obvious questions about your ability to run your business on an ongoing basis if the office area is disorganized. Anyone will wonder whether you've paid the necessary bills or if you can even *find* them!

STAFF

You will need one key employee for each age group—infant/toddler, preschool and school age—who thoroughly understands the curriculum, the materials and equipment necessary for that age group. It is preferable to have someone who has formal training as well as experience with a given age group. This teacher would also be your head teacher for that age group and be able to train other staff in developmentally appropriate practices for those children. If the capacity of the center is small, consider hiring one head teacher or curriculum director who can oversee all the age groups. Obviously, the qualifications for this position would need to be more extensive than those for individual head teachers.

Because having staff with professional preparation is the topic most discussed when determining what makes for a "quality program," this issue needs to be closely examined. When interviewing for staff positions, don't let yourself be overly impressed by the number of degrees a person has; instead, try to discern whether the person has the human qualities that make a good child care professional. For example, when hiring staff you should be most concerned whether they are *compassionate, warm and understanding* with children. The quality of the program is determined by your administrative ability and the center's warmth and atmosphere as opposed to the number of degreed teachers.

As a manager, you must be keenly aware of the potential for child abuse by the staff and screen each applicant thoroughly. The vast majority of individuals with early childhood or child development degrees are wonderful, sincere teachers. However, there are some individuals who are abusive and who knowingly earn a degree to give them legitimacy, as a "license to abuse." Unfortunately, prospective employers and parents can be fooled by the degree.

Probation periods of employment are very important, and you should spell this out when hiring an employee. It will be nearly impossible in most areas to obtain much information about a candidate's previous work; often the law requires only that the dates of employment be verified when you call for a reference. However, check discreetly with associates in the area and try to discern whether there is a problematic history. This is a good reason to meet regularly with other professionals in your area and exchange information informally; such informal exchanges can help protect your businesses as well as the children in the community.

Compensation for the staff is a controversial topic, but it is true that the better you treat your employees, the more likely you are to have them stay with you. And when you have consistency in staff, the quality of your program improves enormously. Parents like to know that their children, especially the very young ones, have the same caregiver throughout the year. In one case, the parents left a center because their child had had 15 different caregivers between September and May!

If you implement a flexible program, you should be able to pay well above the market average and include attractive benefits such as vacation pay, sick pay, profit-sharing, personal time and health insurance. Utilizing the available benefits packages with pretax dollars, you should now be able to offer a variety of supplemental insurance options, such as dental, accident and intensive care. A relatively recent addition to the benefits scene is the option of implementing a 125 plan. A 125 plan is the written plan required by the federal government which allows an employee to deduct payments for benefit programs, such as health insurance, from their gross pay before taxes and social security are withheld. Under this plan the employer should save considerably on social security, Medicare and federal and state unemployment payments. The savings could be used for additional benefits.

You should also offer the staff the opportunity to continue their professional development by encouraging them to attend professional workshops and conferences.

GROUP SIZE AND RATIOS

Group sizes and staff : child ratios that promote optimal development are easier to address once you have a cost-effective program. The staff : child ratios have been discussed in previous chapters, but you might consider using the ratios recommended by the accreditation system of the National Association for the Education of Young Children. In some cases, it will be more feasible to meet these standards by using a "floater," as described in Chapter 8, during the peak hours of the day.

In every case it will be necessary to design the facility to accommodate the correct ratios in the best group size for each age range. Again, if you are striving for quality, it is best to keep the total age group size as small as is feasible for you within the following guidelines:

Age Range	Best Group Size
Infants (birth–12 months)	6–8
Toddlers (13–23 months)	6–12
Two-year-olds (24–35 months)	8–12
Three-year-olds	14–20
Four-year-olds	16–20
Kindergarteners	16–20
School-age children	20–24

The above are only guidelines; there has been some controversy about the numbers and their compatibility with different philosophies. For example, in at least one state the Montessori schools lobbied successfully to be exempt from a group size restriction of 20 children per group for preschool children. However, if you are attempting to promote the quality of your facility, consider the group size carefully as well as the overall design of your rooms and the flow of children.

Most regulatory agencies require division of the children into manageable group sizes according to the guidelines. Recently, there has been a trend in some areas to have very large spaces with minimal division between the activity areas; various age groups then rotate among these areas on a prearranged schedule throughout the day. Technically, the centers with this spatial arrangement are complying with the licensing requirements, but the advisability of this spatial arrangement is questionable. When the maximum licensed capacity is reached, the atmosphere can be chaotic.

In one Midwest center the space is large enough for 90 children. Four groups (three-year-olds, four-year-olds, prekindergarten and kindergarten children) rotate through the space throughout the day. The programs are well organized and run smoothly; however, the noise level is high and the degree of distraction between the activity areas is very noticeable. Worse yet, the parents in the community think of the center as a "warehouse" for children and are seeking alternatives. (See Chapter 17 for creative solutions to various types of situations.)

MANAGEMENT AND ADMINISTRATIVE PERSONNEL

Your own administrative ability will determine the overall quality of the facility. Your attitude toward the children and philosophy of delivering child care will be the most important factors, because they set the tone of the center. The staff will follow your example in their attitudes toward the children. Especially during the initial visit, the parents will notice the atmosphere that you have established at the facility and how you expect the children to be treated.

For example, one parent had decided to move her children from a small local program to a large, elaborate program. A few weeks later she came back to the smaller center and asked to return. When asked why, she had difficulty pinning down her exact reason, but finally said, "I was speaking to the director the other day and a small child came up in tears. The director patted the child on the head and told the child everything would be OK and to go back to his teacher. In the same circumstance, you would have picked the child up and comforted him—while finishing our conversation!" In other words, the parent perceived that the smaller center was more caring, put the needs of the children first and was better able to handle difficult situations.

Your attitude toward the children will influence the parents' perception of the quality of your center's care. When you walk into a new environment, nothing makes you feel better than a friendly, warm attitude, so try to help your visitors feel relaxed by seeing happy faces. In a child care setting, a sense of humor can be your most valuable asset. Also, during a tour be sure to point out the positive attributes of your teachers and answer all questions openly. If you show pride in your staff and facility, it will be contagious.

The physical appearance of the management and staff will also be important if parents are to see the center as top quality. If the director and office staff are in old shirts, jeans or sloppy shorts, it will be fairly obvious to any parent that they do not see themselves as professionals. Providing neat smocks for the staff will encourage them to wear nicer clothing.

PROGRAM

It is absolutely essential to provide age-appropriate programs for each age group and a well-trained staff to implement them. The methods for this are outlined in Chapters 7 through 10. To insure the continued quality of the program, you should have an evaluation process in place. As you become more experienced, you may want to include the parents in this process as is required by the NAEYC to receive their accreditation for your center.

In every way possible, exhibit your pride in your staff, the facility and the program and your joy in the wonder of childhood. If you exude enthusiasm, you will find that it is contagious and that the staff and parents will quickly pick up on your positive outlook. Best of all, this wonderful attitude will filter down to the children, and you will have the best advertisement for a quality program—a center full of smiling faces!

17
CREATIVE PROBLEM-SOLVING

• •

O ver the past 10 years we've had the opportunity to assist many child care centers and have heard a myriad of problems; fortunately many had happy outcomes. Sharing some of the experiences of these centers can provide you with new insights into problems you may face now or in the future. These solutions are representative of the many we've encountered, but each shows how critical analysis can lead to a workable solution. But first, a brief explanation of some problem-solving techniques which should be part of your management skills and which can also help you train your staff to become problem-solvers.

THE TECHNIQUES

Start Successfully

First, ask yourself whether you really think that *all* problems have a solution. If you immediately answered "No," you are not thinking creatively yet; all problems do have a solution even if the solution is to do absolutely nothing! In deciding to do nothing, you have considered the situation and made a decision. Isn't it nice to give yourself a pat on the back for doing nothing?

This reasoning has another benefit—it allows you to succeed under any circumstances! Many management books have described this "positive permission" as being crucial to the success of many men and women. It is an inner strength and belief in yourself that gives you the power to succeed.

Remember too the old adage that "Nothing succeeds like success!" Give yourself a chance to succeed initially by taking on relatively simple problems. For example, focus on the physical aspects of your program, since these usually have concrete solutions. Start by making a wish list for your center or by examining the playground; find something you'd like to change or improve. Try to come up with a few theoretical solutions to the problem. While doing this exercise once at a seminar, several directors suddenly realized that their dreams for an extra piece of equipment or rearrangement of the playground actually could become a reality without much difficulty.

Let's say the books in the four-year-olds' library are getting battered and torn and are not receiving the respect they deserve. List the *obvious* causes of the problem:

- The storage for the books isn't adequate or well designed.
- The teacher isn't teaching proper respect for the books.

But, when you look more closely at the problem, you find:

- There are over 70 books in the area.
- Many of the books are not age appropriate.
- The teacher is dismayed about the reading program.
- The area is not conducive to reading.

In such a case, you may have several solutions—some short range, others medium and some longer as follows:

Short Range: Remove badly torn books and any books that are not age appropriate. Decrease the number of books drastically by storing some outside the children's area. Place two bean bag chairs or several smaller cushions in the space. Display stories that children have related to the teacher and then illustrated.

Medium Range: Order book display cases and meet with teacher about the reading program and story-time activities. Place attractive book display shelves in this area of the room to create a quiet haven where reading is emphasized. Change wall displays in area frequently.

Long Range: Install softer indirect lighting. Find storytelling, reading and/or writing workshops for your teacher to attend. Give the teacher a monthly allowance to buy four new books. Build more storage in the room so that the teacher can rotate the books easily and create more respect and interest.

Work Your Way Up

Once you have mastered simpler problems, try some things that are more complicated. For example, you may think your enrollment could be higher if you changed your marketing and advertising. In this instance, you will want to write down the various areas to be considered.

Define your goal explicitly. It's not enough to say that you want to have more children using your center. You need to come up with a real number—exactly how many more children would you like to see using your center? With an *actual* goal in mind, you'll feel a greater sense of achievement when you reach it.

Next, determine how you are going to reach your goal AND within what time frame. A deadline will help you clarify your goals further and intensify your efforts. But estimate your time realistically, again giving yourself a chance to succeed.

To decide what steps to take, look carefully at what you are presently doing. Where do you feel you can improve? And once you have exhausted all of your own ideas, ask colleagues for suggestions.

Let's follow a specific example. Your goal is to increase the enrollment at your center by 45 children (either part time, full time or hourly) within the next 60 days. This seems a reasonable time span since it is October, and you can still expect some enrollments. Analyze what you are currently doing to increase enrollment at your center:

- Forms are ready when parents come to visit.
- Brochure is available, though only at the center.
- Display ads have run in the local papers.
- Nice sign is on the front of the building.

What short term remedies can bring in enrollments quickly? (See Chapter 15 for more details and suggestions.)

1. Increase flexibility!
2. Place brochures throughout the community—get them OFF your desk!
3. Take the sign off the building and place it (or an additional one) near the road so that it can be read from both directions.
4. Create colorful fliers and put with them your business cards throughout the community.

5. Send a cover letter with your brochure to all businesses who may have potential customers.
6. Invite your local realtors for a visit.
7. Place business cards at child-related services and businesses.
8. Paint an outside toy a bright eye-catching color.
9. Hang balloons near your sign.

And for medium- and long-range remedies:

1. Revamp or renew your playground so that it attracts the attention of passersby.
2. Add infant/toddler or before- and after-school programs.
3. Redesign your brochure into a better, more attractive advertisement.
4. Offer employees or parents a bonus or reward for bringing in new clients.

The possibilities are only limited by your imagination or your budget. However, you should be able to reach your goal with your new positive attitude—on time!

Break Down the Big Problems

Occasionally you will encounter an extremely difficult problem, as you would in any business. This problem may take several weeks or months to resolve and will usually require the use of outside expertise. For example, deciding whether or not to expand your facility can be extremely complex. Actually it is probably less of a difficult *problem* and more of a difficult *decision,* since you must already be in the enviable position of having enough demand for your services to warrant considering expansion.

Here the parameters will be different and your approach may be on several fronts at once. For example, if you are renting space you may talk with your landlord about leasing more space or moving elsewhere. If you own your facility, you may want to add on or purchase new space. Or you may consider a combination of the above. Set a realistic time limit and state your goals, considering each aspect of the issue separately. This breakdown of issues will help you clarify your thinking and speed up the decision-making process.

Train Others to Help You

As your management style improves and your business grows, you will eventually want to give "ownership" of some problems to your staff. However, you can't delegate these tasks until you've trained your staff to be effective problem-solvers.

There are several steps involved. First, help them to define a simpler problem and to decide what the important aspects of it are. The degree of difficulty should depend on the employees' natural capabilities. Of course, you will also have to make sure that they have the self-confidence and assertiveness to take any action that is required. In some instances you will need to cultivate these traits over a period of time.

Then, let your staff test their problem-solving abilities with you nearby for guidance. As in any situation when you are building confidence, do not criticize unless it is absolutely necessary to do so. And give praise when it is deserved so that they dare to take on other new challenges.

What to Do If You Get Bogged Down

If you or staff members are having difficulty finding a creative solution to a problem, try changing the atmosphere where you do your thinking. For example, get up from your desk or leave the facility and go think in a new surrounding. You may not even need to take paper or pen with you, but just a mental outline of the problem. Remember to consider only one piece of the problem at a time.

One director always took her problems or some reading material to her own children's doctor's appointments. She realized that her most productive time was at the orthodontist's office, because the large fish tank bubbling in the waiting room triggered her thought processes. And this was true even if the waiting room was full and there was chaos all around! She installed a fish tank that bubbled in her office and found her time was much more productive—and relaxing!

Another director installed a shower in her new center. The shower served a dual purpose: it was not only a good place for her to think, but also a nice convenience for the teachers when they were confronted with a sick child and needed to get cleaned up.

In addition to finding the most effective backdrop for thinking, find the patterns that help you to become more productive. For example, some individuals need plenty of time to think through a problem, working through the solutions slowly and methodi-cally. However, others work best only under pressure and must have close deadlines to produce results. If the latter is the case, create your own deadlines with incentives at the end. Challenge yourself to reach the required deadline repeatedly. The sense of accomplishment will be wonderful, and you will continue to suc-ceed in many areas.

If you thrive in the midst of chaos, you still need the necessary materials to function, so make sure that you have all your tools for thinking nearby. For example, if a problem requires that you look up numbers in a phone book and you can't find the phone book, valuable time will be wasted.

In line with this, delegate the easier information-gathering tasks so that you can concentrate on the overall problem and see the larger, total picture! If you don't have an assistant, perhaps a staff member can do some of the chores during nap time. Or there may be a staff member who would like to earn extra money by tackling a task after hours. Try to reduce your workload in this manner and make time for creativity.

Also, be sure to find a way to allow your mind to relax. Like any other part of your body, your mind won't function as well if it's not properly rested. This may take the form of a quiet walk during lunch time or a relaxing dinner with friends. Better yet, stretch your body by exercising regularly, and you will find that your thinking capacity and sense of well-being improves.

And finally, keep in mind that as part of the problem-solving process, you *will* make mistakes and that this is just fine—with-out mistakes you won't grow professionally and discover new methods and techniques.

CREATIVE SOLUTIONS

Here are some ways that these methods have been creatively ap-plied to solve problems that could have threatened the viability of the centers involved.

The "Too Much" Center

Late one summer, an owner called with a sad story. His center had been open for three months and was losing approximately $8,000 per month. He asked that we meet as soon as possible.

We met with him and his administrator to get the details of the story. In May of that year, the owner had decided to open a child care center as a hobby for his wife should he pass away. He advertised in a large city newspaper for a director, liked one applicant in particular and hired her on the spot.

The owner and his director proceeded to set up the child care center and were doing fine until the licensing agent made the initial visit. To their astonishment, the director did not meet the state's requirements for the director of a center; she had neither the education nor the experience for the job. To be helpful, the licensing agent suggested another qualified individual, who was subsequently interviewed and hired. The initial director continued on as the administrator.

The new director's only experience in child care was operating a federally funded center with large funding resources; as a result she proceeded to order expensive, high-quality equipment and materials. The new director also hired staff immediately so as to have everyone in place when the children enrolled. Over three months, the new director's purchases and staffing decisions amounted to some very high bills.

At the initial meeting with the owner and administrator, we found out that there were three children attending the center and five staff! The owner had spent at least $10,000 on advertising and another $35,000 in equipment for the child care center that was supposed to be caring for 30 children. Now he was convinced that the center would fail!

As we sat discussing the issues, the problems became clear and we asked them whether they *really* wanted to succeed. They thought about it briefly and replied yes. Would they agree to try a radical approach? The reply was yes to that as well. The total cost would be less than $500 but would bring about results in at most six weeks if they strictly adhered to the plan. The owner was surprised and skeptical, but realized he had little choice.

First, we lowered the overhead by laying off some excess staff until more children were enrolled. We also recognized that the present director did not have the ability or training to promote the program, had used poor judgment in hiring staff and had spent an excessive amount on equipping the program—so the next step was to let her go. The present administrator would take her place and also take responsibility for promoting the program. A percentage of net profits would be added onto her salary as an incentive. To satisfy the state requirements until she had the required experience, a new head teacher would be hired who had the necessary education qualifications.

Next, the program was made more flexible with changes in rates and hours to meet the needs of the parents in the community. The owner also wanted to offer a week's free care to attract a customer base. The advertising methods were totally revamped: no more expensive display ads placed in various newspapers but instead fliers, brochures and letters announcing the new program were distributed throughout the community.

The administrator showed all clients around the center personally and took phone calls herself instead of using an answering machine. She was assured that once the enrollment was built up, she would have an assistant, but for now she would have to learn each task thoroughly herself.

A week later we visited the center and helped rearrange the rooms so that the traffic flow was more conducive to a flexible program. Because we decided to add a two-year-old program, we temporarily divided a room using the available equipment and a bolted-down bookshelf. Once staff and facility changes were in place, the center was ready for new customers. The marketing campaign began by the middle of the second week. By the third week, 18 new children had enrolled (over half for part time); hourly slots and the two-year-old program were filling rapidly. During the next week the director was wondering if she would be able to maintain her staff ratios and was gradually hiring back the staff that had been let go. She was also using a new tracking system for enrollments and could easily see when she needed a "floater." She was even thinking of adding another toddler area!

By the end of the sixth week, the center was at break-even, well on its way to success, and looking forward to expansion. And the issue was no longer having "too much" equipment and staff but rather "too many" children.

Get Set and Hope to Go!

Five partners were building a very large dream that was turning into a nightmare. They had started construction of a building for a child care center nearly two years earlier and were supposed to have been up and running for months at the time they called me. Construction and approval delays had devastated their scheduling. Now they had no money to pay the bank the necessary large sums on their construction loans.

Each of the five owners had originally run a family day care home licensed for six children with several children attending on an hourly basis. They had maximized their profits and were enjoying success. When they joined forces and decided to build a center, they had projected an opening date for eight months after construction began. The cost of the project was $1,200,000, and they put up their homes as collateral. It was now 18 months after the projected opening, and they had once again begun taking care of children in their homes—this time to meet their loan payments.

We were first asked to help the owners with scheduling children and staff to maintain the required ratios. The center was going to have a capacity of over 150, and they wanted advice on how to schedule without a computer. (They already knew they could not have a computer since the cost had not been budgeted.) After analyzing their initial plans for the enrollment of children, it became apparent that they would actually be decreasing their flexibility and thus decreasing their potential income.

But the overwhelming problem at the moment was that the opening was still some time away, and the owners were at their financial limits. After visiting the facility it was clear that the contractors were stalling and being untruthful. Our decision was to force the contractors' hand by planning an open house for a specific date within a reasonable time frame and, best of all, widely advertising the date. The contractor was informed of the plans and the open house was announced. This meant hours of work by everyone and a frantic last-minute rush. But the open house was a huge success. For four hours one evening and six hours the following day, we registered students and answered questions about flexibility.

It should be noted that at this point only the first level of the facility had been completed. It filled quickly to its licensed capacity of 75, and the center broke even in the first seven weeks, including the mortgage payments of over $10,000 per month. When they opened the upper level several months later, they doubled their licensed capacity and more than doubled their profit margins. However, if the owners had not taken positive action and kept the contractors to a schedule, it is doubtful that the center would ever have been ready to go!

The Multiple Complex

As an entrepreneur succeeds, he often decides to expand and have several centers within reach of each other. To do this takes considerable organizational skills and a real knack for understanding how to motivate the managers of the various centers.

An entrepreneur who had expanded his business rapidly was having difficulty with the commitment his directors were willing to give to their individual centers. When we first met him, he had six centers and was contemplating a seventh. However, he was having enrollment problems in three of the centers.

After speaking to several of the directors we learned that their boss was not only demanding but also reluctant to disclose important facts about the business to any of them. For example, he was unwilling to share information about the business's finances. As a result they were each convinced that the owner was making a "killing" for doing very little, while they were working long hard hours for little pay.

Once the owner understood the issues, the solutions became clear—at least in the beginning. He immediately explained the finances of the individual centers to the respective directors. He then went one step further and gave each of them something to gain by seeing the center succeed—10% of the net profits instead of just an annual increase in pay. This brought immediate positive responses from the directors and increased profits overall as well.

One side benefit was that the directors also watched for new ways to increase profits and, hearing our presentation on flexibility, insisted that the owner let them try not only flexible scheduling but new marketing methods as well. Since they were more than willing to do the resulting increased work, the owner agreed. Although the administration of the multiple centers became more complex, they also became more profitable!

The Empty Preschools

This is a common scenario that all too often ends sadly—a center closes without having tried several options. Here's one case where such an unfortunate end was averted. In this instance the owner had two small preschool programs within a short distance of each other. One program, licensed for 32 children, was run on a full-time basis for children ages three through five. When the owner contacted us, it was operating at only 48% of capacity although there were 26 children using the center. The second program was licensed for 16 and was in a small house conveniently located near a main thoroughfare. Run on a part-day basis but with only 10 children enrolled, it was operating at a large loss.

Analysis showed their target market to be primarily a blue-collar work force with some commuters to nearby cities. As in most areas, there was a larger need for infant/toddler and before- and after-school care than for preschool child care. The director knew that she was not serving her market but didn't know where to start.

To better meet the communities' needs, the center for 32 children needed a more flexible program with before- and after-school care. Like other facilities in town, the center was then open between 7:30 A.M. and 5:30 P.M. However, this schedule did not accommodate the needs of many parents in the area, some of whom worked on shifts that started at 7 A.M. and others who couldn't arrange for evening at-home care until after 6 P.M. Although the director recognized this, she was reluctant to change her schedule from what the other centers had.

But sometimes the most effective method to attract clients to your center is to do something very different from what everyone else is doing. In this case extending the hours was just what was needed! The director also realized that the space at the center was underutilized and that, once the center was full, she would be able to increase her licensed capacity by renovating some unused space.

The smaller center was a more difficult problem. Given the number of inquiries received on a daily basis at the center, there was an obvious demand for infant/toddler care. So a kitchen at the rear of the building was converted to infant space, and the licensed capacity was increased to 20 children. The facility not only became a lovely and profitable infant/toddler center, but also served as a complementary program to the other larger center a short distance away.

Preschool centers that are unable to fill up with preschoolers can most often expand in the toddler area. Then as the demand grows and the staff and management improve, there can be further expansion into infant care.

Wide Open Spaces

A different problem is exemplified by a newly purchased center whose three previous owners had not been able to fill it or make it cost-effective. The center had two floors—one for 20 children and the other for eight. There was also room to expand on the property, but expansion could not be justified since the existing space was nowhere near filled. The main difficulty was the arrangement of the space and the resulting lack of atmosphere. The new owner couldn't run the high-quality program she wanted in such a facility.

Dark walls and wide-open space made the rooms grim. Because there was no division of the rooms, the atmosphere was chaotic and the children had no privacy for reading or having quiet time to themselves. The activity level was on a constant "high," and this was difficult for even the most active children to handle.

We cut up the space into smaller areas and made the total space more workable. Initially we moved existing shelving units into new positions, but eventually the owners built more permanent dividers. By the time they had finished, there were many cozy areas in which the children could learn and explore, yet overall the space appeared much larger! The children's concentration powers also improved in the smaller, more manageable spaces, which minimized distraction. And prospective parents found the space attractive as well and readily enrolled their children.

They Said It Couldn't Be Done!

In several instances, we've been called in after several experts had told the owners that they just wouldn't be able to make a facility work—and certainly not at a profit. This happens most often in new, as yet unopened, facilities, usually with smaller capacities (under 40 children).

In one case in particular, a new entrepreneur had been told by two consultants to cut her losses and forget it. After we met she decided to try flexibility and some different marketing ideas, and she felt more confident about her original projections for her business.

As with many small centers, she had had to virtually strip the facility, remove doors from closets and even a dividing wall in order to get the maximum licensed capacity possible. The space was difficult to visualize so we graphed every inch to scale and then drew in proposed equipment for each area. At least one manufacturer/distributor provides computer models of basic equipment placement to further help with planning. The owner's original plans had space for 23 children, but by the time the reconstruction was finished there was ample room for 32! The resulting space was wonderful for children, with little nooks and even a nice reading area on the bottom three curving steps of an unused staircase. (The upper portion was blocked off.)

The owner kept the equipment simple and comfortable and planned the traffic flow to accommodate the demands of flexible scheduling. To maximize the use of the facility, she used a flexible program with a goal of 60% full-time children and 40% flexible. Within seven weeks she was at break-even and confident enough to add space within the first 18 months!

The Profitable "Nonprofit" Center

Throughout the country there are many centers run under the auspices of nonprofit organizations—both large and small. One center was under the umbrella of a large, nonprofit organization and was floundering because of low enrollment, poor staff morale and an unattractive facility.

During our first session we established goals and outlined the necessary steps that had to be taken to make the center successful. We had found that the center was operating at 48% capacity (based on actual occupancy of the hours opened, not percentage of the licensed capacity). This was actually high compared to other nonprofit centers, but not nearly as successful as it could be. Fortunately, the center had just received a grant to purchase new equipment and materials. It took under $20,000 and about six weeks to renovate the eight large classroom spaces and make them optimally suitable for flexibility.

In the meantime, they added hourly programs and adjusted the rates accordingly. As usually happens when you add flexibility, the rates for some children went down slightly. If your rates go down, you are certainly more popular with the parents and then you get more of the best form of advertising—word of mouth!

At a staff meeting, we helped the director explain the concept of the flexible program and that it would soon bring many new children into the program. They could expect at least 300 children using the facility each week as opposed to the current maximum of 75! Each staff member was then given a piece of paper and asked to write down anonymously any questions about the changes. In this way the director identified the "hot spots" and could compensate for them where necessary. For example, several teachers were concerned with how they would know which children would be in their classroom each day. The director explained that they would receive an updated list each week and would be told any daily changes either verbally or on notes posted near the employee sign-in area.

The center soon became popular with young parents in the community and the enrollment rose right way. By the end of the first year, the nonprofit center had increased its net profit by $150,000 and was theoretically profitable!

The Pricing Dilemma

The director of one large center decided to run a flexible program from the beginning. The total licensed capacity would be 164 and the location was excellent—in the suburbs of a large city immediately off the main commuter highway.

The owner was a former nursery school teacher and had originally planned to care only for preschool and kindergarten children. However, when we reviewed the designs, it seemed she could easily include a large toddler room and two small infant spaces and thus guarantee full enrollment. As the construction progressed, the director had other terrific ideas such as a screened-in play area for the infants.

A week before the opening, the director mailed us the final packet of materials for the parents. Over 150 prospective clients had already received this information. Unfortunately, we found she had missed the major financial advantage of using a flexible program: she had priced the full-time care at $100 per week and the hourly care at $2.50 per hour! A basic principle had been overlooked—namely, that the fewer hours a client uses the center, the higher the hourly fee. She was in effect not receiving any more payment for the children attending on an hourly basis than for the full-time clients.

The director could not make any price changes for a year. Although the available flexibility did keep the level of the center's usage high during the initial phase, the projected income was 20% to 25% lower than it should have been because of the pricing error.

A Potential Parting of a Partnership

Unfortunately, child care business partnerships often run into serious problems. This is usually because both partners, often teachers, decided that running a child care business would be fun and easy, but never talked through how they would work together.

In one such instance, the partners reached an impasse after the first six months. They were barely speaking to each other, and the business and the children were being negatively affected. When we were called in, it was obvious that immediate intervention was needed. After we listened to them both, it became clear that neither had any concept of her own or her partner's strengths and weaknesses. So first we had them write out a comprehensive list of their own talents and shortcomings—no matter how good or bad. Each also asked a close friend or relative to do the same. The next, more difficult, assignment was to do the same about the other partner.

Then, with both of them present, we compared the lists and matched them up with a list of the necessary tasks for directors. (See Chapter 11.) The gaps became obvious to each partner. But, more importantly, each partner could easily see that there were areas that were naturally easier for one partner or the other to cover. Also, either due to a lack of trust or ignorance of the other's strengths, there were several areas where both partners were trying to do the same job and were crossing each other's paths.

These discussions were kept confidential. There was no need for the staff and parents to know that there had been problems now that they were being resolved. Fortunately, with reorganization and delineation of specific jobs for each partner, the partnership was saved and the center once again flourished.

Too Many Children!

A final example describes a center operating at well below its licensed capacity but seemingly overflowing with too many children. The space had plenty of dividers in the preschool area and the square footage was more than that required by the licensing agency. However, the space still seemed crowded and confusing.

The owners had tried many different ideas, including alternate scheduling for the use of space within the area. At present they were on a rotating system: the 50 children that were in the preschool space (which had a licensed capacity for 60) were divided into five groups of 10, with one teacher for every 10 children and the individual groups "rotated" through the open rooms.

The materials were bright, new and attractive, and the teachers were well schooled in developmentally appropriate activities. However, the level of stress for both the teachers and the children was evident. After observing the activities within the space for some time, we realized that the dividers—mainly low bookcases—were not high enough to decrease the noise levels or afford any visual or auditory division for the activities. Children who had any difficulty in concentrating were easily distracted; even teachers had trouble reading a story if there was a noisy activity in another area of the room.

The solution was to divide the space further with visual and *auditory* barriers, such as higher dividers with carpeting on the sides, and to decrease the group size and increase the concentration level. This alleviated the environmental stress that affected everyone and it no longer seemed that there were too many children.

18
STEERING CLEAR OF THE 10 MOST
COMMON MISTAKES AND WORRIES

• •

From the various experiences described in this book, it is obvious that there are some pitfalls to avoid in the child care business. This chapter summarizes the most common mistakes and fears of child care center owners. Use them as an easy reference for reviewing the factors that can keep your business out of danger, and also allay any unnecessary fears you may be harboring.

THE TOP 10—MISTAKES!

These are the most common mistakes that can lead to the failure of a child care business or necessitate a premature sale:

One—Inflexibility

This book's premise is that you can have a profitable business by making flexible, quality child care available to your community. However, do you really feel that a flexible program will work in your center and that you can implement it effectively? Do you feel that you have the ability to manage the increased load of a flexible program, and if not, are you willing to get the training necessary to do so?

Because the marketplace will be constantly changing, you yourself need to remain flexible. For example, estimates are that by the year 1995 elderly day care will be as much in demand as child day care. Are you ready to add a room or two for elderly care if needed? And do you feel positive about the possibility of intergenerational care?

Are your attitudes sufficiently flexible to realize that successful businesses are in a constant state of flux and that managers must be ready to adapt to changes? Would you be willing to get additional training to refine your management style?

Two—Inadequate Start-up Funds

Some child care businesses fail in the first few months because the owners haven't calculated the need for a start-up cushion in their business plan. Centers using flexibility do reach break-even more quickly; however, even the best entrepreneurs will need to cover the expenses until they reach this point.

Generally, you should have enough funds to meet all basic expenses for the first six months. As you may already know, most businesses take three years to reach break-even; it should not take as long for a well-managed child care center. If, in fact, it takes three years for your center to reach this point, there may be some question about its potential to ever become a long-term success.

If you must have an additional income at this stage, remember to calculate it into the start-up costs. This is a common mistake that can strangle both the business and your own security. And do not plan on going back to your initial financing source for more money once you're in operation. That source will expect to see some degree of success before investing more money.

Three—Incompatible Partnership

As in all businesses, this is probably the most common cause for failure. When a partnership begins to fail, it is very difficult to maintain a positive attitude and still conduct business as usual so that your clients are not aware that there is a problem.

It is often said that a partnership is like a marriage—without the advantages of compassion and understanding! When you enter into the partnership, be sure to evaluate the reasons for the agreement and whether you truly LIKE your partner and her business ethics. Also examine closely what each of you bring to the business and whether the contributions are equal. If not, discuss the issue thoroughly before you sign the final agreements.

If you feel that a disagreement is minor and could be resolved, try to call in a mediating third party as quickly as possible. This person should be neutral and know how to facilitate a positive discussion. And you both should try to be open to change in your relationship.

If the partnership seems doomed to fail, try to dissolve the relationship as quickly and cleanly as possible. Occasionally this can only be done by terminating the business, but usually, if the business is successful, one partner can secure funds to purchase the other partner's interest in the business. Also, you may decide to have a buy/sell agreement right from the beginning that can eliminate many difficulties in dissolving the partnership.

Four—Incorrect Pricing

While you are setting up your business and during the ensuing years, you must be able to accurately ascertain what price to charge for your services. You must also be able to decide how changes in the economy or the strength of your competition affect pricing. Take into account the professions of your clients and their relative incomes and ability to pay. As we discussed in Chapter 15, the rates for full-time use should be between 5% and 15% of the gross family income, depending on the income.

Be sure that the rates remain consistent as your business grows and becomes more popular. For instance, you may decide to capture a segment of the market by undercutting your competition during your first year, but as time passes you may need to adjust your rates. Be sure to give your current clients plenty of notice, and remember that rate increases made on an hourly or weekly basis are perceived by the consumers as being lower than increases added onto a monthly rate. Of course, if the economy takes a drastic downward turn, you may decide to adjust the rates downward as well.

Five—Inability to Manage Staff

If you cannot manage your staff and have a lot of turnover as a result, enrollment will decrease and you'll have difficulty recruiting new employees. It is also damaging to the reputation of the center, and word gets around quickly if you're having employee difficulties. This is particularly true of infant/toddler programs, where consistency is especially important for the children. Also, if the staff is not well trained, the program, no matter how well you've planned it, will not run well.

Keep in mind that you are in a management position and that your employees are not. As you develop your own management style, remember not to base control of your employees on friendship and favoritism but rather on respect and fairness. This invariably makes employees more cooperative and willing to express their concerns.

Finally, if you don't do periodic evaluations, you will find it difficult to be fair. It is amazing to see the effort some employees will make to improve just after the evaluation process is complete. It is also useful to check that your expectations are realistic, especially if you are not happy with the job someone is doing. For example, one director always found fault with the head teacher of her four-year-old program. She came to realize it was because she herself was not well versed in early childhood education. As a result, she was uneasy about this part of her program and demanded more of the teacher than she should have. There will probably be some curriculum areas that you feel comfortable with and others that you will have to leave to someone more knowledgeable.

Six—Inaccurate Professional Advice

Trust your business instincts to determine when your professional advisors have reached the limits of their ability to assist you. For example, if a consultant has not been able to deliver requested materials on time, there may be a problem either in communication or follow-through.

All too often, consultants say that it's difficult to make money in the child care business; this is the kind of advice to question. If you feel that the particular consultant is right and that you will have great difficulty in making ends meet, you have to question why you're in the business to begin with. In the past year for example, we have assisted six businesses that had had other consultants tell them that they could not succeed financially. All six increased their flexibility, changed their age groups and were thriving only months later.

Also, feel free to question any advice that doesn't seem economically feasible. For example, a consultant might tell you that the conversion or construction of a building will cost $185/square foot build out. If you research it, you might find the maximum for build-out costs in most areas of the country is $120/square foot. Unless you charge an excessively high rate per child, there is no way you could recoup your investment at the $185 rate.

Or let's say you've hired a local lawyer who deals primarily with estates and divorces to represent your local interests. This may be fine for reviewing insurance policies, contracts and leases, but for a zoning problem you should probably have an attorney who is knowledgeable about zoning regulations—and preferably child care as well.

Does your accountant understand the nature of the child care business? If, for example, he cannot advise you on making the right investments or help you take the best deductions, find another accountant. One new center actually had five accountants in two years until the right one was found. Don't be afraid to switch if *you* need to!

Seven—Poor Marketing Techniques

Your potential clients find out about your center mainly because of your marketing, and if you don't do it correctly, you cannot succeed! Your goal is to have at least 60% of the community know of the center's existence and its excellent services! Unfortunately this kind of extensive exposure is usually not even budgeted in the start-up expenses, or if it is a line item, it's usually inadequate.

Where would your prospective clients, the parents, be most likely to read or hear about your center? Generally, you have to catch them while they are:

- waiting for a service (doctor, train)
- have extra time (beauty parlor, health club)
- traveling to work (radio, signs)
- actually at work (personnel offices, employee bulletin boards).

Only rarely will a parent read about the center in a newspaper ad, and then it is usually one in the classified section when they are desperate to find child care. Remember that many working parents just don't have time to read the newspaper and would rarely notice a display ad!

Some promotion can be done relatively cheaply, but you should plan to spend some money on advertising, especially in the initial stage. Your main objective is to get out the message that you are *open* and convenient and reasonable. Remember, parents buy child care services primarily because of price and location! But you should also emphasize that your hours are flexible and that you're there to serve *their* needs! Chances are good that you will be the only one in the community offering the flexibility, and that alone will be an added attraction.

Radio ads are expensive but very effective, especially if they are repeated frequently enough, and your center's location and pricing are attractive. But use the right station—if your market analysis has shown that your clients will be primarily in their late twenties, you do not want time on a "light" station listened to by forty-year-olds! And pay that little bit extra to have the ads run during commuter times.

Finally, watch the content of your ads and fliers. For example, don't let the salesperson at the radio station talk you into a cutesy ad. You have to include the information that sells to the child care consumer: price, location and flexibility! And for printed promotions, leave white space in the ad and use primarily pinks and yellows for the paper on brochures or fliers. Keep the contents simple and emphasize only the important points.

Eight—An Unhealthy Atmosphere

One familiar story we've heard many times is, "People walk in the door and they just don't sign up!" The best thing to do in these circumstances is to physically go outside the door and come back in pretending in earnest that you are a prospective parent and use *all* your senses to evaluate your center's general atmosphere.

Start with *smell!* There is nothing that turns parents off more than the smell of urine or mold, and if either of these is evident, it must be eliminated immediately! Not only are the odors disgusting, but they are also a sign of an unhealthy facility.

Next, *look* carefully at the facility and see if it's clean—actually, spotless is best! When you walk into the rooms, are they cluttered? More important, are the toys well taken care of or are they in a jumble in a toy box in the corner? Do you see broken, dangerous toys and equipment in the room? Are there age-appropriate learning materials available for the children to use? Is there evidence that the teacher respects the child's sense of order and encourages both self-help and fun activities? Is there enough to do at the center for each age group?

Use your *hearing* as well. Are the children happy and do you hear laughter? Is there a baby crying incessantly that can't be comforted? Do the teachers use language on the children's level? In the toddler area, is there plenty of verbal interaction between the teach ers and the children to promote good language development. All of the noise that you hear—both good and bad—affects the emotional health and well-being of the center and the children.

Use your sense of *touch*. Is the atmosphere relaxed so that children are encouraged to explore and touch and grow? Do they go outside on most days, and is the playground a fun place with adequate equipment? Will the child be able to develop his sense of touch with a wide variety of tactile materials?

Finally, would you want to spend 11 hours in this place every day?

Nine—Untimely IRS Payments

Nothing can make your business fail faster than not making your payments to the Internal Revenue Service on time. In some cases the unpaid tax that has accrued over the years with interest and penalties has amounted to so much that businesses have had to declare bankruptcy.

Most new business owners find keeping their accounts in order and making on-time payments to the IRS and Unemployment Compensation Department overwhelming in the beginning. This is why it is so important to have a good accountant who will tell you how to calculate what you owe and when to make the payments. The IRS does not consider ignorance of the process an excuse for nonpayment, so be sure you have at least a basic understanding of these taxes and their due dates. There have even been cases where business owners have been found guilty and jailed for mistakes their accountants or partners have made.

And partners are another issue. If you have a partner, you should have a signatory for your checking account, and each partner should have access to the bank statements so that you can readily ascertain whether payments were made on time to the appropriate place. Unfortunately, some center owners have found that the amounts that should have been paid to the IRS and Unemployment were put into an escrow fund by their partners and, even if paid just a little late, were still accruing interest and penalty charges. The only way to avoid this is to be certain about what account the monies are put into before you need them.

Ten—Unrealistic Projections

When you open your child care center, even the most accurate projections for the first year may be just too optimistic. And if your initial budget did not include the start-up costs for your basic expenses, you may be surprised how long it takes you to see a profit.

To avoid the backlash of poor projections, take your figures for the projected gross incomes for the first six months and assume that you're only going to make 80% of that. This will give you an extra 20% cushion and make your estimate more realistic.

Theoretically, you should break even in six to eight weeks and be able to draw a salary shortly after that. However, if at all possible, try to put a percentage of the net profits back into the business immediately to help it succeed even further. This will also make the business more stable over the long run, which will increase the net profits by a larger measure.

THE TOP 10—WORRIES!

These are the 10 most common fears that directors have. With the proper precautions and knowledge, they can readily be eliminated.

One—Inability to Find Staff

Finding qualified staff should not worry you unnecessarily if you have a clear idea of how to manage people and you are prepared to be fair to your employees. Just keep in mind that you will make some mistakes and that this is normal, especially when you first begin hiring. For this reason, get as many applications as you can for each position, and keep the best on file in case you have to let someone go or the enrollment builds quickly.

As suggested before, the most difficult areas to find staff for will be the before- and after-school program and the infant/toddler program. There is very little training available currently in this country for either area, and your best bet will be to send any potentially qualified staff to special workshops and professional conferences. Another alternative is to have the training done at your facility by a consultant whom you hire yourself. This person could help set up your program, train the staff and do the initial supervising. If you sit in on this process, you will be able to oversee any future training procedures and keep future use of a consultant down to a minimum.

Two—Unjustified Lawsuits

Because of the current climate in this country with regard to lawsuits, everyone seems to have worries about potential liabilities.

However, there are several steps that you can take to avoid difficulties.

First, make certain that the policies in your parent handbook are clear and reasonable so that parents realize you are serious about your business. Follow up by establishing a good rapport with the parents—friendly, yet professional. It is difficult to sue someone frivolously if you both respect and like that person!

Next, make certain that any accidents or incidents are written up properly and that excellent notes by all concerned are on file. This will give you the back-up in case there should be a threat by a parent. Of course, you must speak to the parents about all accidents immediately after they happen, no matter how silly they seem at the time. This is one potentially volatile area that you cannot avoid; to extend the time between when the accident happens and when you notify the parents can be both foolish and dangerous.

As an example, in one center a baby fell down a flight of stairs just before the end of the day, but the parents were not told when they picked up the child. There could have been medical complications during the night, and the parents would have had no idea why. The director realized her mistake and had to drive to the parents' house and explain what had happened AND her reason for not telling them right away. How much easier it would have been to talk to the parents initially!

Finally, to diminish your fear of possible legal complications, have a very competent attorney review your insurance and make sure that it is adequate for your purposes. A good attorney will also know ways to limit your liability. And the attorney undoubtedly will realize that when you work with children, there are bound to be accidents, and your best protection is to have a safe facility and a staff where *everyone* takes first aid courses on a regular basis—usually every two to three years. And if you are caring for infants and toddlers or have a child with a serious illness, you should insist that the staff take CPR as well.

Three—Hiring a Child Abuser

Perhaps the most frightening prospect is that you will unknowingly hire a child abuser. Needless to say, a true molester will not walk up to you and admit what his/her problem is; on the contrary, the hard-core molester will be proficient at hiding the problem and will definitely be searching for jobs in child-related fields.

The best protection is your network of other child care directors in the area who may have heard of a problem. We used to think that you could trust your instincts; however, one of the child abuser's main traits is that he/she is wonderful with children, and this can fool you as well as attract children to them.

You might think that job references would be a dead giveaway for these people. But they are not, primarily because previous employers now only have to verify the dates of employment. And furthermore, the child abuser will usually give you names of people who either cannot for legal reasons or will not for personal reasons tell you about the problematic past history.

For example, one individual that we were interviewing passed through all phases of the interview process with flying colors and seemed to be excellent with the children. When we called his references, including a junior college (where he had recently earned a degree in early childhood education), the supervisor of the local parks and recreation department and a high school teacher, all had high praise for his ability with children. (As it turned out, the individuals were friends of his family and the college could not, by law, say anything.) Three weeks after he started employment, we were instinctively beginning to feel uneasy, but our decision was made when a parent referred to an article about the abuser in a neighboring town's newspaper. Although this individual was hired, he was fired after a few weeks and never had a chance to harm the children in any way, because as a matter of policy and also a state requirement, there were two people present with the children at all times.

How can you protect yourself from this potential nightmare? First, make sure your screening process is extensive and lengthy. The individual may well get nervous and not want the job. Also keep on good terms with your local police department and contact them confidentially if you have a question about a potential employee. Many states also can provide a police check on child care employees, but this does little to protect you, as the state rarely even verifies that the check has been completed and that all is well.

And, of course, as you become more firmly established, you can more easily find people who are familiar to either you or your staff. To protect yourself and your staff from false charges, always have at last two people in the facility at all times so that one can verify the actions of the other. Also, encourage an open door policy for parents so that they may come and go at any time.

Hopefully there will one day be a good computer-based checking system between states so that the molesters cannot move around easily. This is an issue you should be an advocate for with the state and federal government.

Four—Getting Poor Advice

This issue was discussed above as a mistake to avoid, but it should definitely not be a source of worry for the new business owner. If you have checked the background of your advisors carefully, made sure they have adequate experience in child care and have helped other small businesses, you should be fine. If you are establishing a private, for-profit child care center, you probably would be ill advised to use a consultant whose primary experience was with a federally funded center, a local Y or even a center sponsored by a corporate park. Each of these entities usually has a certain amount of on-going funding, and often their space is provided at little or no cost to the center. Your more crucial need to make ends meet quickly may not seem a priority to a consultant with this limited financial background, but on the other hand the individual may have excellent skills to guide your educational or program needs.

So, by deciding what advice you need, you can better match your needs with the background of the right advisor.

Five—Fear of Competition

To sell your program you must be able to convince parents that your staff and facility are the absolute best. You need to do this even if you think that it might temporarily be "second" best, because the center down the street has a better equipped playground and has just hired away your best head teacher. Don't blow issues like this out of proportion; your premise should always be, "We have an excellent facility with wonderful, caring staff and a developmentally appropriate program." And next year you may improve your playground—and no one is irreplaceable, even the head teacher!

Remember to accentuate the positive and never speak negatively with a client about the competition. To do so only makes you seem unprofessional and may come back to haunt you at a later time.

If you use a flexible program, your own lack of confidence in promoting and selling it—and not what your competitors are doing—will be about the only factors that can hinder increasing enrollment. Right from the start, know what your goals and objectives are. If you can visualize how many children you would like to have enrolled in three months, six months and a year, you are quantifying your goals and clarifying your thinking. Many successful entrepreneurs have been using this method for years and have found that if you believe in your goal completely, you can achieve it!

Finally, good competition is nothing to be afraid of: a quality competitor only keeps you on your toes. What hurts is the bad competition that lowers professional standards and gives child care a bad image in your community.

Six—Reporting Child Abuse

Perhaps one of the most unpleasant issues you will have to address during your career as a child care manager is that of child abuse. To see or suspect that a child is being abused can absolutely tear at your heartstrings. As you approach the issue of making a report to the authorities about the child abuse, recognize that, unless you are extremely lucky, there is no way to avoid having the parent involved know that you have made the report. If the case involves drug abuse, or violence is suspected, your fears can become even more real.

Out of ignorance or fear, many directors do not report suspected child abuse even though they are mandated to in most states. Unfortunately, the agency to whom you must make the report is often understaffed and apt to be uncooperative at times. And, of course, there are some directors who would rather pretend these things do not happen in their community; but they *do* happen in every community, and chances are you will see cases of abuse during your career.

To overcome your fear of reporting a suspected child abuse case, you must be knowledgeable about the system and methods for reporting and, of course, have an accurate idea of what constitutes abuse. In most states, but not all, the law still comes down in favor of the adult, even when the evidence overwhelmingly shows that the circumstances in the home are detrimental to the child. Hopefully, this will change in all states when child advocacy groups become stronger. In the meantime be careful if you live in a state where this is the case. By reporting abuse before you have enough evidence, you may do the child more harm than good and put yourself and your center in jeopardy physically and legal.

Once your center is underway, get to know the police and social workers in the community. They will be your biggest supporters if you need to report a case, and their support and the backup they can provide will alleviate many of your fears. In fact, if you suspect there is violence involved, be sure to get a restraining order through the courts to protect you and your staff. One center recently failed to do this in a case where there was evidence of two children being beaten with a baseball bat. The children were removed by the authorities and placed in foster care, and that same night two teachers were beaten—with a baseball bat.

If you do make a report, keep in mind that sometimes you may have misjudged the situation; but it is better to err on the child's side than not to report your suspicions and have a child be maimed or die as a consequence.

Seven—Writing a Brochure

There are two basic options for this popular promotional piece. The first contains a brief description of your services, something about the history or development of the program, a short statement about your philosophy and some details about licensing or accreditation. Since this is often a long-term piece of literature for your center, it is best not to put the prices in the copy but to include a cover letter with the current rates and any other information subject to change.

The second type of brochure is more "quick and dirty" and is needed to announce a new program, advertise your summer camp or do a special promotion. For a new center, the "quick and dirty" brochure will be used first for the initial promotional purposes. This should be more eye catching, in bright colors and with very simple and straightforward text.

The main problem with *both* types of brochure is that many managers are shy about putting down in writing the great things they are already doing with the children in the center. If *you* don't believe in your business and promote it, no one else will. This is truly not a time for modesty!

If you are stymied by this task, look for other examples you like and hire someone to help you produce it—but write down your own thoughts first. And, once the brochures are printed, get them out of your office. Set a date by which they should all be gone, and distribute them by then!

Eight—Dealing With a Distraught Employee

The first time that you have to deal with an employee who is extremely upset—whether it is about something at the center or in her personal life—can be terrifying. However, remember that you are now training yourself to become the super problem-solver of the center—for children, parents and teachers. Be confident that you can handle it effectively, and keep peace at the center by having the right skills and resources.

First, you need to become a good listener, who also asks just the right questions. For example, it's better to ask, "Do you think, Miss Smith, that the children get upset when we raise our voices in anger?" than, "You were awful to raise your voice in the classroom!" If this is a skill that you lack, there are many courses offered throughout the country on handling employees; even if they are not related to child care they can still be excellent.

And next, have the right resources at your fingertips. If a distraught employee needs counseling, do you have the number of someone who is appropriate? If the employee's husband has beaten her and you get a late night call, do you know the number of the nearest shelter? If an employee desperately needs to talk and you can see that something has her very upset, can you make the time to listen? And can you get her back on track for work that day or does she need a personal day?

As you will soon find out, every circumstance is different, but that is part of the challenge of caring that will make you a great employer!

Nine—Using a Computer System

For some entrepreneurs, the most frustrating job can be paperwork. Nearly every child care manager I know has expressed exasperation about the quantity and complexity of the bookwork this business brings with it. They know they need a method to stay on top of the paperwork in order for the center to be successful and well run. For example, if a child is injured on his second day at the center and the emergency release card and necessary numbers are buried beneath a pile of paperwork on a desk, there will be an unnecessary delay in getting the child medical attention. Also, if Mrs. Jones has decided to use the center for extra hours this week and would like to pay you, it's not going to help your cash flow to say that you have no idea what she owes because the account book is misplaced.

As centers start to modernize, there are more computer programs being written that handle much of the updating and paperwork on a regular basis. It is also only a matter of time before parents begin using security cards or personal identification numbers for automatic entrance and attendance and billing recording.

However, many managers are afraid of this technology. The total package of hardware and software may not be cheap, but it will save you considerable time in running your business. The most dismaying thing is to see a nice, efficient computer program sitting at a center unused when it could save the manager many hours each week and make record-keeping more accurate and efficient. If you are afraid of computers, take a course at the next conference, and if you have an unused program, either hire someone to show you how to use it or sell it! By the time you get around to trying it, it will be outdated anyhow!

Ten—Setting Firm Rules for the Staff

To be a manager, you must not be afraid to set firm but fair rules. Let the children, staff and parents know—discreetly—who is in charge. In some centers you actually wonder who is in charge: the employees seem to make all the major decisions, and the director is often not physically present. You can't expect anyone to follow your rules if you're not there at least some of the time.

Some directors have had to take a course in assertiveness training in order to learn to manage a staff. This may be particularly true if you have a strong-minded staff with definite ideas on what should and should not be done at the center. All too often I've seen a director who does not have a background in early childhood education or child development, but who does have excellent business training and sense, being put down by the "educated" staff members. When this happens it is unfortunate, but you will have to sort out the ring leader and have a short, to-the-point chat. Your staff manual can be invaluable in such situations especially if there is a section about insubordination and loyalty. Sometimes just making a copy and reading the section with the employee is all that's needed. But don't, under any circumstances, be timid about reasserting the rules as set forth in your employee manual.

In conclusion, if you can avoid the top 10 mistakes and overcome the top 10 worries, you will succeed as a child care manager and have a happy, safe and financially successful center. Your business and your chosen profession will be profitable financially and emotionally. What more could you ask for?

APPENDIX A:
STATE LICENSING AGENCIES

• •

ALABAMA
Department of Human Resources
Division of Family and Children's
  Services
50 Ripley Street
Montgomery, AL 36130
(205) 242-9500

ALASKA
Department of Health and Social
  Services
Division of Family and Youth Ser-
  vices
1002 Glacier Highway
Suite 305
Juneau, AK 99801 (21p)
(907) 790-3221

ARIZONA
Office of Child Care Licensure
100 W. Clarendon
Suite 520
Phoenix, AZ 85013
(602) 255-1272

ARKANSAS
Child Care Licensing
626 Donaghey Plaza South
P.O. Box 1437 Slot 720
Little Rock, AR 72203
(501) 682-6734

CALIFORNIA
Department of Social Services
Community Care Licensing Division
744 P Street, Mail Section 17-17
Sacramento, CA 95814
(916) 657-2346

COLORADO
Office of Child Care
Licensing Administrator
Department of Social Services
1575 Sherman Street, Room 420
Denver, CO 80203-1714
(303) 866-5958

CONNECTICUT
Department of Health Services
Day Care Licensing Unit
150 Washington Street
Hartford, CT 06106
(203) 566-2575

DELAWARE
Office of Child Care Licensing
Delaware Youth and Family
  Center
1825 Faulkland Road
Wilmington, DE 19805-1195
(302) 633-2700

DISTRICT OF COLUMBIA
Department of Consumer and
  Regulatory Affairs

Service Facility Regulations Administration
614 H Street NW, Room 1031
Washington, DC 20001
(202) 727-7226

FLORIDA
Department of Health and Rehabilitative Services
Children and Families Program Office
1317 Winewood Boulevard, Bldg. 7, Room 201
Tallahassee, FL 32399-0700
(904) 488-1800

GEORGIA
Child Care Licensing
Office of Regulatory Services
Georgia Department of Human Resources
878 Peachtree Street, Room 607
Atlanta, GA 30309
(404) 894-5688

HAWAII
Licensing and Registration Unit
Department of Human Services
Family and Adult Services Division
420 Waiakmilo Road, Suite 101
Honolulu, HI 96817-4941
(808) 832-5025

IDAHO
Division of Family and Children Services
450 West State Street, Third Floor
Boise, ID 83720-5450
(208) 334-5700

ILLINOIS
Department of Children and Family Services
406 East Monroe Street, Station 60
Springfield, IL 62701-1498
(217) 785-2688

INDIANA
Social Services Administration
Division of Family and Children
402 West Washington Street, Room W364
Indianapolis, IN 46204
(317) 232-4469

IOWA
Division of Adult, Children and Family Services
Department of Human Services
Hoover State Office Building, Fifth Floor
Des Moines, IA 50319
(515) 281-6074

KANSAS
Kansas Department of Health and Environment
Bureau of Child Care Licensing and Registration Section
900 Southwest Jackson, Suite 1001
Topeka, KS 66612-1290
(913) 296-1270

KENTUCKY
Division for Licensing and Regulation
275 East Main Street
CHR Building, Fourth Floor East
Frankfort, Kentucky 40621
(502) 564-2800

LOUISIANA
Department of Social Services
Bureau of Licensing and Quality Assurance
P.O. Box 3078
Baton Rouge, LA 70821-3767
(504) 342-4131

MAINE
Licensing Unit for Day Care
Bureau of Child and Family Services
221 State Street
State House, Station 11
Augusta, ME 04333
(207) 287-5060

MARYLAND
Child Care Administration Region 2
New Community College of Baltimore
2901 Liberty Heights Avenue
Baltimore, MD 21215
(301) 333-0193

MARYLAND
Department of Child Care Licensing and Regulation
600 East Lombard Street
Baltimore, MD 21201
(301) 333-0193

MASSACHUSETTS
Office of Children
1 Ashburton Place, 11th Floor
Boston, MA 02108
(617) 727-8900

MICHIGAN
Michigan Department of Social
Services
Child Day Care Licensing Division
235 South Grand Avenue, Suite
1212
P.O. Box 30037
Lansing, MI 48909
(517) 373-8300

MINNESOTA
Division of Child Care Licensing
Department of Human Services
444 Lafayette Road
Saint Paul, MN 55155-3842
(612) 296-3971

MISSISSIPPI
Child Care Licensure
Mississippi State Department of
Health
P.O. Box 1700
Jackson, MS 39215
(601) 960-7613

MISSOURI
Missouri Department of Social
Services
Division of Family Services
Attention: Licensing Unit
P.O. Box 88
Jefferson City, MO 65103
(314) 751-2678

MONTANA
Department of Family Services
P.O. Box 8005
Helena, MT 59604
(406) 444-5900

NEBRASKA
Department of Social Services
301 Centennial Mall S., Fifth Floor
P.O. Box 95026
Lincoln, NE 68509-5026
(402) 471-3121

NEVADA
Licensing Bureau
Division of Child and Family Services
711 East Fifth Street
Carson City, NV 89710
(702) 687-5911

NEVADA
Carson City Health Department
Environmental Health
1711 North Roop Street
Carson City, NV 89710
(702) 887-2190

NEVADA
Clark County Social Services
1058 West Owens
Las Vegas, NV 89106
(702) 455-7208

NEVADA-City of Las Vegas
Department of Business Activity
Privileged License Division
400 Stewart Avenue
P.O. Box 1900
Las Vegas, NV 89125
(702) 229-6281/2

NEVADA-Washoe County
Child Care Licensing
P.O. Box 11130
Reno, NV 89520-0027
(702) 328-2300

NEW HAMPSHIRE
Division of Public Health Services
Bureau of Child Care Standards
and Licensing
Health and Welfare Building 6,
Hazen Drive
Concord, NH 03301
(603) 271-4624

NEW JERSEY
Division of Youth and Family Ser-
vices
Bureau of Licensing

Department of Human Services
CN 717
Trenton, NJ 08625-0717
(609) 292-1018

NEW MEXICO
Children, Youth and Families Department
P.O. Drawer 5160
Santa Fe, NM 87502
(505) 827-7683

NEW YORK
Bureau of Early Childhood Services
New York State Department of Social Services
40 North Pearl Street, 11th Floor
Albany, NY 12243
(518) 474-9454

NEW YORK CITY
Bureau of Day Care
New York City Department of Health
65 Worth Street, Fourth Floor
New York, NY 10013
(212) 334-7712

NORTH CAROLINA
Division of Facility Services
Department of Human Resources
P.O. Box 29530
Raleigh, NC 27626-0530
(919) 733-4801

NORTH DAKOTA
Early Childhood Services
Children and Family Services
600 East Boulevard Avenue
Bismarck, ND 58501
(701) 224-4809

OHIO
Child Day Care Licensing Section
65 East State Street, Fifth Floor
Columbus, OH 43215
(614) 466-3822

OKLAHOMA
Department of Human Services
Office of Child Care
P.O. Box 25352
Oklahoma City, OK 73125
(405) 521-3561

OREGON
Children's Services Division
Day Care Licensing
198 Commercial Street Southeast
Salem, OR 97310
(503) 378-3178

PENNSYLVANIA
Department of Public Welfare
Office of Children, Youth and
  Families
Bureau of Child Day Care Services
P.O. Box 2675
Harrisburg, PA 17105
(717) 787-8691

PUERTO RICO
Department of Social Services
Services to Families with Children
P.O. Box 11398
Santurce, PR 00910
(809) 724-0303

RHODE ISLAND
Department of Children, Youth
  and Family
Division of Community Resources
610 Mount Pleasant Avenue
Providence, RI 02908-1935
(401) 457-4536

SOUTH CAROLINA
South Carolina Department of Social Services
Division of Program Quality Assurance
Day Care Licensing Unit
P.O. Box 1520
Columbia, SC 29202-9988
(803) 734-5740

SOUTH DAKOTA
Department of Social Services
Office of Child Protection Services
700 Governors Drive
Pierre, SD 57501-2291
(605) 773-3227

TENNESSEE
Department of Human Services
Day Care Licensing
400 Deaderick Street
Citizens Plaza, 14th Floor

Nashville, TN 37248-9800
(615) 741-7129

TEXAS
Texas Department of Human Services
Child Care Licensing Division
P. O. Box 15995
Austin, TX 78761
(512) 835-2350

UTAH
Department of Human Services
Office of Licensing
120 North 200 West
P.O. Box 45500
Salt Lake City, UT 84103
(801) 538-4242

VERMONT
Department of Social and Rehabilitation Services
Children's Day Care Unit
Division of Licensing and Regulation
103 South Main Street
Waterbury, VT 05671-2401
(802) 241-2158

VIRGINIA
Division of Licensing and Programs
Department of Social Services
Blair Building
8007 Discovery Drive
Richmond, VA 23229-8699
(804) 662-9025

VIRGIN ISLANDS
Human Services
Berbel Plaza South
Saint Thomas, VI 00802
(809) 774-0930

WASHINGTON
State Office of Child Care Policy
P.O. Box 45710
Olympia, WA 98504-5710
(206) 753-0204

WEST VIRGINIA
Department of Human Services
Office of Social Services
State Capitol Complex
Building 6, Room 850 B
Charleston, WV 25305
Attention: Day Care
(304) 558-7980

WISCONSIN
State Department of Health and Social Services
Office of Regulations and Licensing
3601 Memorial Drive
Madison, WI 53704
(608) 266-9314

WYOMING
Department of Family Services
Third Floor, Hathaway Building
Cheyenne, WY 82002
(307) 777-6595

APPENDIX B:
REGIONAL CENSUS BUREAUS*

• •

ATLANTA
Regional Census Center
1375 Peachtree Street, NE
Atlanta, GA 30309-3112
(404) 347-2274

BOSTON
Regional Census Center
441 Stuart Street, Fourth Floor
Boston, MA 02116-5000
(617) 421-1440

CHARLOTTE
Regional Census Center
3410 Saint Vardell Lane
Charlotte, NC 28217-1355
(704) 521-4452

CHICAGO
Regional Census Center
2255 Enterprise Drive,
Suite 5501
Westchester, IL 60153-5800
(312) 409-4619

DALLAS
Regional Census Center
6303 Harry Hines Boulevard
Suite 210
Dallas, TX 75235-5228
(214) 767-7105

DENVER
Regional Census Center
6900 West Jefferson Avenue
Lakewood, CO 80235-2307
(303) 969-7750

DETROIT
Regional Census Center
27300 West 11 Mile Road
Suite 200
Southfield, MI 48034-2244
(313) 354-1990

KANSAS CITY
Regional Census Center
10332 NW Prairie View Road
P.O. Box 901390
Kansas City, MO 64191-1390
(816) 891-7562

LOS ANGELES
Regional Census Center
The Valley Corporate Park Bldg. 1
16300 Roscoe Boulevard
Van Nuys, CA 91406-1215
(818) 892-6674

NEW YORK
Regional Census Center
221 West 41st Street

---

* From U.S. Department of Commerce, Bureau of the Census, Washington, D.C. 20233

New York, NY 10036-7294
(212) 997-1920

PHILADELPHIA
Regional Census Center
441 North 5th Street, Third Floor
Philadelphia, PA 19123-4090
(215) 597-8313

SAN FRANCISCO
Regional Census Center
400 Second Street, Third Floor

San Francisco, CA 94107-1400
(415) 243-8913

SEATTLE
Regional Census Center
101 Stewart Street, Suite 500
Seattle, WA 98101-1098
(206) 728-5314

Census Promotion Office
Census Bureau
Washington, DC 20233
(301) 763-1990

APPENDIX C:
SAFETY

· ·

TOXIC PLANTS (DANGEROUS, POISONOUS) *

Acorn
Anemone
Apricot Pits
Arrowhead
Avocado (Leaves)
Azaleas
Baneberry
Betel Nut Palm
Bittersweet
Black Locust
Boxwood
Buckeye
Buckthorn
Buttercups
Caladium
Calla Lily
Castor Bean
Cherry Pits (wild and
cultivated)
Crocus (Autumn)
Daffodil
Daphne
Delphinium

Devils Ivy
Dieffenbachia (Dumb
  Cane)
Elderberry
Elephant's Ear
English Ivy
Foxglove
Holly Berries
Horse Chestnut
Horsetail-Milkweed
Hyacinth
Hydrangea
Iris
Ivy (Boston, English
  and others)
Jack-in-the-Pulpit
Jequirity Bean or Pea
Jerusalem Cherry
Jessamine
Jimson Weed
(Thorn Apple)
Jonquil
Larkspur

---

*Provided by the New Hampshire Poison Information Center; a service of Leba-
  non, N.H. 03756.

Laurels
Lily-of-the-Valley
Lobelia
Mayapple
Mistletoe
Moonseed
Monkshood
Morning Glory
Mother-in-Law Plant
Mushroom
Narcissus
Nightshade
Oleander
Peace Lily
Periwinkle
Peyote (mescal)
Philodendron
Poison Hemlock

Poison Ivy
Poison Oak
Poppy (except Calif. Poppy)
Pokeweed
Potato-Sprouts
Primrose
Ranunculus
Rhododendron
Rhubarb-Blade
Rosary Pea
Snowberry
Sweet Pea
Tobacco
Tomato-Vines
Tulip
Water Hemlock
Wisteria
Yew

NONTOXIC PLANTS (SAFE, NOT POISONOUS) *

The following plants are considered to be nontoxic. However, any plant may cause an unexpected reaction in certain individuals, including choking. Hang all plants up high or keep from a child's reach. Always check with the NH Poison Center if a plant has been ingested.

Abelia
African Daisy
African Violet
Air Plant
Airplane Plant
Aluminum Plant
Aralia (False or Spider)
Arrowood
Asparagus Fern
Aspidistra (Cast Iron
   Plant)
Aster
Baby's Tears
Bachelor Buttons
Bamboo
Birds Nest Fern

Blood Leaf Plant
Boston Ferns
Bougainvillea
Cactus (Certain Varieties)
California Poppy
Camellia
Christmas Cactus
Coleus Species
Corn Plant
Crab Apples
Creeping Charlie
Creeping Jennie
Dahlia
Dandelion
Donkey Tail
Dracaena
Easter Lily

---

*Provided by New Hampshire Poison Information Center; a service of Dartmouth-Hitchcock Medical Center, Lebanon, NH 03756. This is not an exhaustive list. Contact your local poison center for plants that are not included.

Echeveria
Eucalyptus (Caution)
Eugenia
Fuchsia
Gardenia
Gloxinia
Goldfish Plant
Gooseberry
Grape Ivy
Hen & Chicks
Hibiscus
Hoya
Impatiens
Jade Plant
Kalanchoe
Lilac
Lily (Day, Easter or Tiger)
Lipstick Plant
Marigold
Monkey Plant
Mountain Ash
Mulberry

Norfolk Island Pine
Pansy
Partridgeberry
Peperomia
Petunia
Piggyback Plant
Prayer Plant
Purple Passion
Rose
Sansevieria
Sensitive Plant
Snapdragon
Spider Plant
Swedish Ivy
Teaberry
Venus Flytrap
Violets
Wandering Jew
Wintergreen Berry
Yucca
Zebra Plant

APPENDIX D:
PROFESSIONAL ORGANIZATIONS

I: CHILD CARE

Association of Child Care
  Consultants International
1801 Peachtree Street
Suite 160
Atlanta, Georgia 30309
(404) 352-8137

Child Care America, Inc.
14102 Warwick Boulevard
Newport News, Virginia 23602
(804) 886-0862

Child Care Law Center
625 Market Street
Suite 815
San Francisco, California 94105
(415) 495-5498

National Association for the Education of Young Children
1834 Connecticut Avenue NW
Washington, DC 20009
(800) 424-2460

National Association of Child Care
  Resource and Referral Agencies
2116 Campus Drive SE
Rochester, Minnesota 55904
(507) 287-2020

National Child Care Association
1029 Railroad Street
Conyers, Georgia 30207
(800) 543-7161

II: OTHER PROFESSIONAL ORGANIZATIONS

American Academy of Pediatrics
141 NW Point Boulevard
Elk Grove Village, Illinois 60007
(708) 228-5005

American Bar Association
750 North Lake Shore Drive
Chicago, Illinois 60611
(312) 988-5000

American Institute of Architects
1735 New York Avenue NW
Washington, DC 20006
(202) 626-7300

American Medical Association
515 North State Street
Chicago, Illinois 60610
(312) 464-5000

Federal Reserve Bank
20th and C Streets NW
Washington, DC 20551
(202) 452-3000

NAIOP-Association for Commer-
    cial Real Estate
1215 Jefferson Davis Highway
Suite 100
Arlington, Virginia 22202
(703) 979-3400

National Association of Realtors
777 14th Street NW

Washington, DC 20005
(202) 383-1000

Service Corps of Retired Execu-
    tives
1825 Connecticut Avenue NW
Washington, DC 20009
(202) 205-6762

Small Business Administration
409 Third Street
Washington, DC 20416
(800) 827-5722

. . . .

I

SAMPLE OPERATING POLICY

Flexible Scheduling

Parents are allowed flexibility in scheduling. You may schedule your children part time or full time at your convenience. Parents need to enroll their children for specific days/times in advance and are responsible for payment for those days/times. The exception to this is the "occasional child." In this instance the parent can call Creative Child Care Services to see if there are any slots available on a weekly/daily basis. All children must be registered in advance and must comply with the Department of Health Services regulations with regard to physical exams and inoculations.

Tuition

Program fees for children attending the center for specific days/times will be charged on a weekly basis. Fees will be paid at the beginning of each week, and any adjustments for additional hours used will be made the following Monday. For children using the center on an "occasional" basis, fees are due when services are rendered. Nursery school tuitions are paid on a monthly basis on the first of each month. There will be a 10% discount on the tuition (based on the lower fee) for a second child.

Enrollment Fee

For planning purposes, each child will enroll separately in the summer and school year programs. Enrollments are accepted every year during the month of March for the following summer and/or school year. For each segment, a $10.00 enrollment fee will be charged.

For the nursery school program, there will be an enrollment fee of $25.00.

Registration Fee

In order to complete the registration process, a two (2) week registration fee of the anticipated weekly tuition will be required for each child. For any "occasional children" enrolled, this fee will be $25.00. All registration fees will be applied to the last two weeks of final use of the program.

For those children enrolled in the nursery school program, there will be a registration fee of one month's advance tuition, which will be applied toward the fees for the month of June.

Absenteeism and Vacation

Each child registered on a yearly basis will be allowed (1) week vacation without tuition charge as long as the center is notified (2) weeks in advance. Additionally, there will be a 10% reduction in fees for absenteeism for all children, if the center is called before 8:00 A.M. on the date of the absenteeism. (This reduction will be credited to the following week's tuition.) As the staff must be compensated, snow days will be counted as absenteeism days, however the center WILL be open on snow days. If the child will NOT be attending the center and notification is given by the parent before 8:00 A.M., there will be a 10% reduction in the fee for that snow day.

Holidays

The center will be closed on the following holidays:
> Thanksgiving and the day after
> Christmas
> New Year's Day
> Memorial Day
> Fourth of July
> Labor Day

Since the full-time employees are paid for the above holidays, the parents are responsible for payment of those holidays as well.

In addition, the center will be closed for one week in the summer and one day in the fall for church functions, and there will be no fees charged for this time period. The center will notify everyone well in advance and will assist in finding alternative arrangements if necessary.

Termination of Service by Parent

Parents may terminate this service by giving two weeks' notice in writing. Earlier notice, if known, would be appreciated.

Termination of Service by Center

The center reserves the right to reevaluate any child's continued participation in the program who has special needs that cannot best be met by the center or that may be detrimental to the health or progress of the other children. The center may, under these circumstances, request withdrawal of the child from the program. The center will be happy to recommend suitable alternatives that may better suit the child's needs.

Unless the child is an immediate danger to himself or others, two weeks' notice will be given should the center request withdrawal of the child from the program.

Illness

The center reserves the right to temporarily deny any child admittance to the school for reasons of obvious illness, or to request early departure should symptoms become apparent during the course of the day. This is to ensure the continued good health of everyone at the center.

If your child is well enough to attend the center, but is still in need of medication, parents must leave a signed administration of medication form with the Director's office before the center can administer any medication.

Emergency

If the center cannot reach you in the event of a medical emergency, and it is determined necessary by the EMTs that an ambulance and/or hospitalization is required, the local EMTs will transport the child to the hospital. Parents are responsible for any charges incurred in the above.

||

SAMPLE PROMOTIONAL LETTER

Creative Child Care Services
112 Fairmont Drive, New London, CT
203-862-2559

Dear Parent:
Wouldn't it be easier to concentrate on your job if you knew your child was getting the best of care?

Are you tired of getting to work late or having to leave early because of your child care arrangements?

Would your child benefit from association with other children from homes like yours?

Maybe you should look into Creative Child Care Services!

Creative Child Care Services was established by people who, like you, suffered the endless inconvenience, anxiety and concern that attend giving over the care of one's child to someone else.

We're working hard to be sure you'll want to make Creative Child Care Services your one and only stop for developmental child care. Here's how we're doing it:

Its convenience to you is unparalleled. The center is open 13 hours every weekday and, located just one mile off I-95, couldn't be easier to get to. Creative Child Care Services is minutes from every major corporation in the area.

The hours are FLEXIBLE and fair. Our program schedules are designed to fulfill your child care needs. You can use the center on an hourly, part-time or full-time basis. AND we try our best to find available slots for the exact hours that you need—you pay only for the time you need, not for excess hours!

We've made it absolutely safe. Its features include state-of-the-art fire and health protection, security from intruders, meticulous staff selection and age-appropriate play and learning equipment.

Its program environment is ingenious. The center boasts child-sized everything, from sinks and toilets to areas for dramatic play and make-believe. There's even a real kitchen where children can help prepare meals and snacks in total safety.

And, its tuition is affordable. Creative Child Care Services offers programs for children ages one month through 10 years old. Full service programs start at only $90 per week and there are special hourly and part time programs designed to fit your needs and save you money.

Call us today at 862-2559 to arrange for a visit and complimentary lunch for yourself and your child. By the way, there's absolutely no obligation.

Sincerely,
Kathy Smith
Director

(Adapted from Marge and Joe Heffel, Kids Stop, Inc.)

Appendix F:
REFERENCE BOOKS AND PUBLICATIONS
• •

The following is meant to be a guideline and any omissions are entirely unintentional. It is recommended that any person entering the child care business check the possible resources as the industry and the reference materials are growing rapidly.

MANAGEMENT
The Complete Book of Forms for Managing the Early Childhood Program
by Kathleen Pullan Watkins, Ed.D. and Lucius Durant Jr., M.Ed.
Center for Applied Research in Education, Inc.
Rte 9W
Englewood Cliffs, NJ 07632
1990

Complete Early Childhood Behavior Management Guide
by Kathleen Pullan Watkins and Lucius Durant Jr., The Center for Applied Research, Rte 9W
Englewood Cliffs, NJ 07632
1992

A Guide to Effective Administration in Child Care
by Dora Fowler

Associates in Human Development
P.O. Box 256
Palatine, Illinois 60078
1988

Nursery School & Day Care Center Management Guide
by Clare Cherry, Barbara Harkness and Kay Kuzma
Fearon Teachers Aids
P.O. Box 28
Carthage, IL 62321

Policies and Procedures for Early Childhood Directors
by Early Childhood Directors Association
Resources for Child Caring
450 North Syndicate, Suite 5
Minneapolis, Minnesota 55104
1990

PRESCHOOL
Before the Basics
by Bev Bos
Turn the Page Press
203 Baldwin Street
Roseville, California 95678
1987

*Channels to Children: Early
  Childhood Activity Guide for
  Holidays and Seasons*
by Carol Beckman, Roberta
  Simmons and Nancy Thomas
Channels to Children
P.O. Box 25834
Colorado Springs, Colorado 80936
1982

The Everything Book
by Valerie Indenbaum and Marcia
  Shapiro
Gryphon House
3706 Otis Street
Mt. Rainier, Maryland 20822
1983

I Am, I Can
by Dr. Grace Mitchell and Harriet
  Chmela
Teleshare Publishing Co., Inc.
Marshfield, Massachusetts 02050
1987

Them-a-saurus
by Jean Warren
Warren Publishing House
11625-G Airport Road
Everett, Washington 98204
1990

Workjobs
by Mary Baratta Lorton
Addison Wesley Publishing
  Company, Inc.
Jacob Way
Reading, Massachusetts 01867
1972

INFANT/TODDLER
Infant Caregiving
by Alice Honig and J. Ronald Lally

Syracuse University Press
1600 Jamesville Avenue
Syracuse, New York 13210
1981

*Responding to Infants, The Infant
  Activity Manual*
by Inez D. Moyer
T.S. Dennison & Company, Inc.
9601 Newton Avenue South
Minneapolis, Minnesota 55431
1983

*Smart Toys for Babies from Birth
  to Two*
by Kent Garland Burtt and Karen
  Kalkstein
Harper Colophon Books
Harper/Collins
10 E 53rd St.
New York, New York 10022
1981

*Things to Do With Toddlers and
  Twos*
*More Things To Do With Toddlers
  and Twos*
by Karen Miller
Teleshare Publishing Co., Inc.
Marshfield, Massachusetts 02050
1984

SCHOOL AGE
*Activities for Before and After
  School*
by Mardi Gart and David Pratt
Incentive Publications
3835 Cleghorn Ave.
Nashville, Tennessee 37215
1991

Kids America
by Steven Caney
Workman Publishing Company
708 Broadway
New York, New York 10003

*Ready to Use Activities for Before
  and After School Programs*
by Stassevitch, Stemmler, Shotwell
  and Wirth

Center for Applied Research in
  Education
Rte 9W
Englewood Cliffs, NJ 07632

PUBLICATIONS
Child Care Information Exchange
P.O. Box 2890
Redmond, Washington 98073

Child Care Review
P.O. Box 578
Metairie, Louisiana 70004

Early Childhood News
Peter Li, Inc.
2451 E. River Road
Dayton, Ohio 45439

Pre-K Today
P.O. Box 54814
Boulder, Colorado 80322-4814

Young Children
NAEYC
1834 Connecticut Avenue, NW
Washington, DC 20009-5786

Tables and charts are indicated by *"t"* following a page number

• •